THE ILLUSION OF INTELLIGENCE

THE ILLUSION OF INTELLIGENCE

How AI Deceives and How to Stay Smart

RAJAT KUMAR MOHANTY

Plexeme
KNOWLEDGE

This book is a work of nonfiction. References to real events, organizations, and individuals are included for illustrative and analytical purposes. Every reasonable effort has been made to ensure the accuracy of the information presented. However, the author makes no representation or warranty regarding its completeness, reliability, or suitability for any particular purpose, especially in areas that change over time, and accepts no responsibility for any errors or omissions.

This work is intended solely for informational and educational purposes. It examines the nature, limitations, and implications of predictive AI systems and their interaction with human judgment. Nothing in this book should be interpreted as medical, legal, financial, or other professional advice. Readers should exercise their own judgment and seek guidance from qualified professionals when appropriate.

First Edition — 2026
ISBN (eBook): 978-93-5810-382-3
ISBN (Paperback): 978-93-5810-737-1
Published by Plexeme Knowledge, India
Design and layout by the author
Printed by Amazon Kindle Direct Publishing

In memoriam
Pushpak Bhattacharyya (1962-2025)
Visionary scholar, mentor, and inspirational teacher
In gratitude for a life that shaped the questions of intelligence this book explores

Contents

Preface

This Book Was Written at a Moment of Contradiction.

On one side, the language surrounding artificial intelligence has grown expansive, filled with promises of transformation, efficiency, capability, and scale. Systems that write, speak, and generate content appear to extend human abilities in unprecedented ways. On the other side, a different set of stories has begun to emerge.

A public announcement attributed to a national figure spreads rapidly, only to be exposed as an AI-generated fabrication. Some accept it long enough to act on it, and the cost is real. A video appears during a moment of conflict, carrying the authority of visual evidence. It is shared, interpreted, and acted on while uncertainty remains about whether the depicted events occurred as presented. The consequences unfold regardless.

In everyday settings, automated systems make decisions that affect daily life. They impose penalties, trigger actions, and create records, sometimes in ways that do not follow the rules they are intended to enforce. The person affected by such an error does not experience it as an abstract technological limitation. The impact is immediate, practical, and often difficult to challenge.

These events are not the same. They do not stem from a single cause. Some result from misuse, some from error, and some from interpretation. Yet they share a common feature: the growing presence of systems whose outputs are treated as representations of reality, and the difficulty of knowing when those representations deserve trust. This challenge does not remain confined to individual cases. In institutional settings, the stakes are higher. As such systems become part of professional and organizational workflows, including reports, recommendations, and automated decisions, errors can affect far more than individual understanding. They can spread across organizations, markets, and public trust. What begins as a plausible output can become an accepted input to larger systems of judgment, shaping outcomes that extend beyond the original interaction.

It would be easy to respond to this moment by choosing a side and emphasizing either the promise or the risk. Neither response is sufficient on its own. The capabilities are real. The failures are real. The challenge arises from the coexistence of both. This book begins with that tension.

The focus is not on every application of artificial intelligence, but on a specific core: systems that generate language. Many other forms extend from that foundation, including audio, video, synthesized interactions, and automated decisions. The same underlying mechanism that produces a paragraph of text can also produce a voice, a statement, a claim, or a representation that carries authority. Understanding that mechanism is the starting point. The aim is not to catalogue every possible error or misuse, nor to speculate about future scenarios. It is to examine something more fundamental: how these systems produce outputs that resemble understanding, how people interpret those outputs, and what happens when such interactions become part of everyday life at individual, institutional, and societal levels.

This is not a technical manual about how these systems are built. The focus is different. It is on how they are experienced, how they are interpreted, and how they reshape the conditions under which decisions are made and judgments are formed. No background in machine learning is required to follow the argument. What is required is careful attention to interactions that often seem familiar and unremarkable. The intended audience therefore includes both everyday users who encounter these systems in practical settings and practitioners who build or deploy them. The distinction developed throughout the book applies to both groups: those who rely on the outputs and those who create the systems that generate them. In this context, clarity is not optional. It is what makes it possible to benefit from these systems without mistaking their outputs for something they are not.

Introduction

A new kind of artifact has entered everyday intellectual life: a system that produces language with the appearance of understanding. It answers questions, explains concepts, constructs arguments, and responds with a fluency that resembles knowledge in use. The interaction feels familiar. Coherent, structured, and confident outputs resemble forms long associated with human reasoning. Yet the mechanism that produces those outputs differs from the process it appears to represent. This book examines that difference.

The central claim is simple but easily overlooked: the appearance of intelligence is not the same as intelligence. Predictive systems generate language by extending patterns found in data. They can reproduce the forms through which understanding is expressed without possessing the understanding that those forms usually signal. The result is what this book calls the illusion of intelligence. It is not a deliberate deception, nor is it a flaw that more advanced engineering will simply eliminate. It is a structural feature of the encounter between systems that generate fluent language and minds that have long treated fluency as evidence of thought.

The difficulty lies not only in the systems themselves, but also in how they are encountered. Human cognition is attuned to treat fluent explanation as a signal of knowledge. That tendency has generally served well in environments where language reliably reflected underlying understanding. Predictive systems preserve the signal while removing what historically gave it credibility. The output retains the appearance of competence, but the process no longer guarantees it. The result is a form of credibility that feels earned but is not.

This illusion does not remain confined to individual encounters. When fluent, ready-made explanations become consistently available, the conditions under which judgments are formed begin to change. The effort required to build understanding can give way to the acceptance of pre-formed answers. The habits that support careful reasoning can weaken through disuse. What begins in individual interactions accumulates over time. Its effects extend beyond individual cognition into the practices through which knowledge is created, evaluated, and shared.

The same capacity that produces this illusion in everyday interactions can also be used deliberately. Systems that generate persuasive language can be embedded in voices, images, and institutional processes. These tools shape belief not only through error, but also through intent. What appears to be understanding can be produced, distributed, and amplified at scale. The chapters that follow examine the illusion of intelligence from several perspectives. The discussion explains how it arises from the structure of predictive systems and how it appears across different domains. It also explores why the illusion is persuasive and how it reshapes cultural practices of inquiry. The final focus is on the ethical implications of designing, deploying, and using these technologies.

The aim of this book is not to reject these technologies. Their usefulness is real and often substantial. The aim is to understand them clearly. In this context, clarity means preserving a distinction that the surface of interaction tends to obscure: the distinction between language that appears to express understanding and understanding itself. Everything that follows is an effort to make that distinction visible, stable, and practically useful in a world where it will be tested with increasing frequency.

PART ONE
THE BROKEN SIGNAL

What AI Actually Does — and Why Human Minds Are Wired to Fall for It

Before anything else, two points require careful attention. The first concerns what these systems actually are. The second concerns why the human mind is naturally susceptible to what these systems produce. Both are essential. Neither, on its own, is sufficient.

CHAPTER 1
How Humans Recognize Minds

The Cognitive Shortcut That Served Us for Millennia and What Happens When It Is Exploited

In a classroom, a student raises her hand to answer a difficult question. She speaks clearly. Her explanation unfolds in a steady, logical sequence. She uses the right terms. She anticipates an objection and addresses it before anyone raises it. The room shifts, almost imperceptibly. Classmates look at her differently. The teacher nods. Something like authority attaches itself to her voice. No one consciously grants it. It simply appears. Nothing visible has changed except the arrangement of words. She has not shown her notes. She has not demonstrated the full depth of her knowledge. Yet her fluency persuades. Without deliberate reflection, those listening infer that she understands. Now consider another student. She hesitates, searches for words, circles the point, and pauses mid-sentence. Even if her grasp of the material is deeper, halting speech weakens confidence. Certainty is trusted more readily than hesitation.

Fluency becomes a proxy for intelligence. The inference feels natural. It rarely draws attention to itself. Most of the time, it works. For reasons rooted deep in human history and cognitive development, it was long aligned with reality. This chapter explains why that alignment emerged and why it no longer holds.

1.1 Language as the Signal of Mind

Human beings cannot observe thought directly. Beliefs, intentions, and understanding are not visible in themselves. What can be observed are outward expressions, including gestures, actions, facial movements, and, above all, language. Among these signals, language occupies a special position. When someone explains an idea clearly, constructs an argument coherently, or answers a question appropriately, intelligence is attributed almost immediately. The attribution does not follow careful reasoning. It precedes it. Before evidence is weighed, a mind is assumed. This pattern emerges early in life. Structured speech is experienced not merely as sound, but as evidence of cognition. Words suggest something behind them: a center of awareness that understands meaning and organizes it deliberately. The inference operates continuously in everyday life. When a colleague explains a problem with precision, competence is assumed. When directions are given confidently, they are followed. When a physician speaks in measured language, trust increases. In each case, judgment extends beyond the content to the perceived quality of the mind that produced it.

Language became this signal not simply through social agreement, but because it reflected a durable relationship between fluent speech and cognitive capacity. Across most of human history, sustained coherence required genuine understanding. Clear explanation required knowledge of structure. Logical argument required recognition of relationships between claims. Fluency was not ornamental. It depended on comprehension. The signal pointed to something real.

For that reason, the response to fluent language is not purely intellectual. It also has an affective dimension: a subtle reduction of uncertainty and a greater readiness to accept what is presented. The resulting trust rarely feels like a decision. It forms with little effort, shaped by a long history in which expression and understanding were usually aligned. Why this response feels so immediate, and what psychological processes sustain it, requires closer examination. That inquiry belongs to the next section.

1.2 Why Fluency Feels like Understanding

Fluent language does more than transmit information. It produces a cognitive experience. When a sentence is grammatically smooth, logically ordered, and confidently delivered, it becomes easier to process. The explanation unfolds without strain. Little friction arises between the words and the act of understanding them. Structure appears to align naturally with meaning. That ease carries weight. Human cognition operates under constraint. Not every claim can be examined with equal care. Not every assertion can be paused and verified before provisional acceptance. The mind therefore relies on signals that indicate when effort is required and when it can be relaxed. Fluency functions as one of those signals. Language that is easy to process tends to feel familiar. Familiarity often gives rise to a sense of credibility. The movement from clarity to perceived correctness occurs quickly and largely outside deliberate awareness. An explanation that moves smoothly is not only easier to understand; it is also more readily judged to be sound.

Psychologists describe this pattern as processing fluency: the tendency for statements that are easier to read, hear, or interpret to be judged as more likely to be true. The effect appears across many contexts. It is not limited to the uninformed. Education and expertise can reduce some biases, but they do not eliminate this one. Ease of processing continues to influence judgment even when content is being evaluated carefully. This helps explain a familiar asymmetry. A hesitant speaker may possess deep knowledge yet struggle to project authority. A confident and articulate speaker may be mistaken yet still appear persuasive. In principle, style and substance are distinct. In experience, they are often intertwined.

This pattern is not a flaw in itself. Under ordinary conditions, it conserves attention and directs effort efficiently. The next section considers why, for most of human history, that efficiency was largely justified. Once fluency and understanding become separable, however, the same mechanism that once guided judgment reliably can begin to mislead it. The consequences of that separation shape the discussion that follows.

1.3 The Historical Reliability of the Signal

At this point, it may be tempting to conclude that equating fluent language with intelligence has always been a mistake. It was not. For most of human history, the connection between sustained coherence and understanding had a concrete basis. Producing extended, structured speech required perception, memory, intention, and at least a workable grasp of the subject. To recount an event, a person typically had to experience it directly or learn about it from others. Explaining a principle required some degree of comprehension. Defending an argument required beliefs about its validity and the ability to respond to challenges. Language was not separate from the speaker. It emerged from lived experience and remained connected to it. Another constraint also mattered: accountability. A claim did not stand alone. It was tied to a person who could be questioned, asked to clarify, or required to defend the reasoning behind it. Positions could change, but revision required acknowledgment. Error carried a reputational cost. Speech occurred within social networks where credibility accumulated slowly and could be damaged. Under these conditions, fluency served as a broadly reliable indicator of competence. It reflected cognitive effort, experiential grounding, and personal accountability. Communities relied on it to identify expertise. Individuals used it to judge whose guidance deserved trust. The signal was not perfect, but it was dependable enough to help guide social life.

The durability of this cognitive shortcut reflects that history. The association between articulate expression and understanding was reinforced repeatedly over time. Fluent speech did not guarantee correctness, but it was rarely separate from comprehension. Under ordinary conditions, sustained clarity required some alignment between words and understanding. Over time, the signal became closely linked to what it represented. The inference became automatic not because it was naïve, but because it was usually justified.

The strength of the present illusion rests on that legacy. It draws its force from a cue that human cognition learned to treat as trustworthy through long experience. If language had always been easy to separate from understanding, skepticism toward fluency would be more common. It is not. The inference persists because the conditions that shaped it remained in place for centuries. Those conditions, however, are no longer stable. The chapter now turns to a central question: what happens when the signal remains intact but the constraints that once anchored it begin to disappear?

1.4 When the Signal Became Unreliable

For most of human history, fluent language required a mind to produce it. That constraint gradually weakened through a series of changes that increased the distance between speaker and audience. The shift did not occur overnight. Technologies for reproducing language at scale, from print to broadcast media to digital networks, changed how language was transmitted without changing its source. Even when a person was not directly present or personally known, a human intention still stood behind the words. What is new is not mediation, but generation.

Systems now produce language that is grammatically precise, logically structured, and responsive to context. They summarize complex material, answer detailed questions, construct persuasive arguments, and adapt their tone to different audiences. Their outputs display many of the outward features long associated with intelligence: clarity, coherence, relevance, and confidence. Yet these systems hold no beliefs about the world. They possess no intentions. They do not experience uncertainty or ground their statements in lived experience. The process that generates the output differs fundamentally from the processes that historically produced fluent speech. The surface remains familiar. The underlying conditions have changed.

Where fluent language once implied a thinking agent, it may now reflect a system generating statistically plausible sequences of words. The output resembles reasoning without being produced by reasoning. Its structure can mirror the form of thought without thought occurring. The distinction is easy to overlook because the signal remains the same. Coherent language still prompts the attribution of understanding. Fluency still creates a readiness to trust before verification begins. A cognitive filter shaped in a world where language and mind were closely linked is now applied to systems where that connection is absent. The difficulty does not arise from crude imitation. It arises from competent performance. These systems generate language well enough to activate long-established inferences.

In earlier eras, mismatches between fluency and understanding occurred, but they were episodic. A confident speaker could be mistaken. An eloquent presentation could conceal weak reasoning. Such cases did not undermine the broader reliability of the signal because they remained exceptions. What has changed is both the frequency and the nature of the mismatch. Language carrying the full outward markers of intelligence can now be generated independently of belief, experience, or accountability. The separation is not occasional. It is systematic. The signal remains intact. The guarantee that once anchored it does not.

When a historically reliable cue becomes consistently separated from what it once indicated, the resulting error is not simply a matter of external deception. It is an interpretive error embedded in ordinary cognition. The system does not need to pretend. The misattribution occurs during reception. Understanding the depth of this shift requires examining what these systems are actually doing when they generate language. That inquiry begins in the next chapter. Before turning there, however, two concepts require precise definition. They will serve as analytical tools throughout the remainder of this book.

1.5 Two Words That Matter

The Problem Is Illusion, Not Hallucination.

Not all errors are the same. The point may seem obvious. Yet in contemporary discussions of AI reliability, a single term, hallucination, is often used to describe many different kinds of misleading output. The word has become a broad label, applied both to minor inaccuracies and to fluent, confident statements that are entirely false. This broad usage obscures an important distinction. Recovering that distinction requires two established concepts that are both precise and practically important: illusion and hallucination.

An illusion begins with something real. A signal or stimulus is present, but it is misinterpreted. A straight straw placed in water appears bent at the surface. A distant road on a hot day appears to shimmer with water that is not there. In each case, perception is anchored in genuine input. The error lies not in fabrication, but in interpretation. It arises from how the mind organizes and explains what it encounters. Illusions are powerful precisely because they feel ordinary. They rarely announce themselves as errors when they occur. Experience proceeds smoothly, and the misinterpretation becomes part of it.

A hallucination differs in structure. It involves an experience that is not triggered by a corresponding external stimulus. A voice is heard in an empty room. A figure is seen where none exists. The content is generated internally rather than misperceived from something present. The distinction can be stated simply: an illusion distorts what exists; a hallucination produces what is not there.

Both can mislead. Both can feel convincing. But they operate differently. An illusion depends on a real signal that is misread. A hallucination does not. The relevance of this distinction becomes clearer when it is applied to AI systems. The most consequential failures rarely occur when nothing is present. They arise when something real, such as coherent language, a structured argument, or an appropriate tone, is encountered and then interpreted as evidence of understanding. In that sense, the central problem is not hallucination but illusion. That distinction will shape the analysis that follows.

1.6 Things That Can Go Wrong

With these distinctions in place, the landscape of AI output failure appears more varied than the single term *hallucination* suggests. Four situations illustrate the range.

The first involves an AI system producing a response that is fluent, well structured, and confidently delivered, yet false. A medical explanation sounds authoritative. A legal summary reads like expert analysis. A historical account appears researched and complete. Nothing on the surface signals a problem, and the response is accepted and relied upon. This is a case of illusion. Something real is present: coherent language, appropriate terminology, and persuasive structure. What is misread is not the text itself, but what the text is taken to signify. The appearance of knowledge is mistaken for knowledge itself. The smoothness of the response is not incidental. It is the mechanism through which the misinterpretation occurs.

The second situation is more subtle. The system begins with a relevant response but gradually drifts. Associations loosen. The connection to the original question weakens. The response circles rather than advances. An attentive reader senses that coherence is beginning to erode. This situation more closely resembles hallucination. The output is generated without stable alignment to the external prompt. The break is not dramatic, but it is perceptible. The growing mismatch between question and response becomes a clue.

The third situation involves fabrication. Citations are invented. Legal cases are attributed that never occurred. Statistics appear without source or basis. The content is not a distortion of something present. It is generated without correspondence to reality. In structural terms, this also resembles what is commonly called hallucination: generation unconstrained by external fact. Yet fluency often remains intact, allowing the response to appear authoritative, at least temporarily.

The fourth situation appears deceptively simple. The system produces a response that is accurate, well reasoned, and genuinely useful. This case is neither illusion nor hallucination. Yet it introduces a critical asymmetry. On the surface, the first and fourth situations are indistinguishable. Both are fluent. Both are coherent. Both display the outward markers of competence. The difference lies outside the text itself, in whether the content corresponds to reality. From within the interaction, that difference is not visible.

This is not a call for generalized suspicion. It is a recognition of a structural limitation. When fluency can accompany both accuracy and error, surface features alone cannot establish reliability. The implications of that limitation will unfold throughout the chapters that follow.

1.7 Why the Distinction Matters

If illusion and hallucination differ in structure and detectability, treating them as interchangeable has consequences. The difference is not merely semantic. It shapes how the problem is understood. In contemporary AI discourse, the term *hallucination* has become a convenient label for unsupported or fabricated output. The word suggests a visible malfunction, a breakdown in which something clearly detached from reality has been produced. In such cases, careful scrutiny can often reveal the problem. Irrelevant drift can be noticed. Fabricated citations can be checked. This framing fits some failures reasonably well. It does not fit others.

The most consequential failures are often not those that appear obviously detached from reality. They arise when the output is fluent, coherent, and contextually appropriate, yet subtly incorrect. Nothing on the surface signals a problem. The response appears competent. It meets expectations. It feels complete. The error lies not in a visible rupture but in misattribution. Coherence is taken as comprehension. Structure is taken as understanding. The interpretive step occurs smoothly and without friction. When many forms of failure are grouped under a single label, attention tends to focus on the most dramatic cases, those in which the output is clearly disconnected from reality. The quieter and more pervasive problem of seamless misinterpretation becomes harder to identify.

Precision therefore clarifies what deserves attention. The distinction between illusion and hallucination does not deny that systems sometimes generate unsupported content. It highlights that the deeper vulnerability arises when something real, such as well-formed language, is misread as evidence of mind. Understanding this distinction does not solve the problem. Without it, however, the problem is misidentified from the outset.

1.8 A Vulnerability Built from Strength

At this point in the argument, a quiet unease may arise. If fluent language so readily influences judgment, *does that reflect poorly on human cognition? Is the tendency to trust articulate speech simply a refined form of credulity?* The answer is no.

The cognitive shortcut that now creates vulnerability is not a flaw. It is the product of long adaptation to an environment in which the shortcut was usually reliable. Trust in fluent language did not arise from laziness or naivety. It emerged because, for most of human history, sustained fluency required comprehension, lived experience, and accountability. Words and understanding were ordinarily linked. The inference was reasonable. The trust was reinforced across generations of speakers whose articulation and beliefs generally aligned.

What has changed is not the structure of human cognition. It is the structure of the environment. Systems now exist that can reproduce the signal of intelligence without sharing the conditions that once supported it. A cognitive system shaped in a world where fluent language presupposed a mind now encounters fluent language that may not. The mechanism remains. The environment has changed.

Recognizing this shifts the location of the problem. The susceptibility is not a personal failure of rigor. It is a structural vulnerability: the predictable result of applying an evolved inference under altered conditions. Nothing feels dramatically different when such output is encountered. The experience of coherence remains smooth. The impression of competence remains intact. The attribution of understanding still precedes evaluation. That is precisely why the shift is difficult to detect. The signal remains. The instinct remains. The guarantee does not.

Understanding the consequences of that separation requires a closer examination of what these systems are actually doing when they generate language.

CHAPTER 2
The Machine That Has Never Understood What It Says

What Large Language Models Actually Are , and What They Are Not

At the close of the previous chapter, a recognition emerged: the historical link between fluent language and understanding has weakened. The signal remains in the form of coherent sentences, structured explanations, and a confident tone. The guarantee that once anchored it no longer remains. To understand why, the mechanism that produces this language must be examined directly.

What are these systems actually doing?

The answer is less mysterious than it may first appear. Systems commonly known as large language models, the systems referred to throughout this book when discussing contemporary generative AI, do not think as humans think. They do not consult an internal encyclopedia of verified facts. They do not hold beliefs about the world. They do not deliberate, reflect, or commit themselves to the truth of what they say. They predict. Understanding what that word means, and what it does not mean, removes much of the apparent mystery.

2.1 Statistical Pattern Prediction

The Actual Mechanism

Large language models do not begin with knowledge. They begin with patterns. During training, they are exposed to extremely large collections of text drawn from books, articles, technical documents, public websites, and other written sources. From this material, they do not extract verified propositions in the way a student studies a textbook. Nor do they build a structured internal map of the world. What they learn is a set of statistical regularities within language itself: which words tend to follow other words, which phrases appear together in particular contexts, and which sentence structures are commonly associated with explanation, definition, summary, or argument. Across vast numbers of examples, the system develops a detailed model, not of the world directly, but of how language about the world tends to unfold.

The core task that emerges from this training is deceptively simple: given a sequence of words, estimate which word is most likely to come next. Consider the sentence: *"The capital of France is___."* For most readers, the word Paris comes to mind immediately, not because a conscious calculation takes place, but because the association has been reinforced repeatedly through prior exposure to language. The phrase "capital of France" and the word "Paris" have appeared together so often that the continuation feels automatic.

Large language models operate on a comparable principle, but at a scale far beyond individual human experience. Given a prompt, whether a question, an instruction, or a fragment of text, the system evaluates many possible continuations. It assigns probabilities to those continuations based on patterns learned during training. It then selects one continuation and repeats the process. The response is generated one token at a time. The result can appear intelligent because language itself contains structure. Logical reasoning, careful exposition, and nuanced argument follow recognizable patterns. When those patterns are reproduced with sufficient precision, the output can resemble thought.

Resemblance, however, is not identity. The system is not consulting beliefs. It is not checking its statements against the world before responding. It is not determining whether what it produces is true. Its objective is narrower and more mechanical: to generate a continuation that is statistically coherent with the preceding text. This distinction between coherence and correctness is foundational. A system optimized for coherence can produce fluent and persuasive language whether the content corresponds to reality or not.

Coherence and correctness sometimes coincide. They can also diverge. The mechanism that generates the text contains no independent capacity to determine when such a divergence has occurred. This indifference to truth is not a defect in an otherwise reasoning mind. It is a direct consequence of how the system is designed and trained.

2.2 Training on Language about Reality, Not on Reality Itself

Large language models are trained on extremely large collections of text. The statement is simple, but its implications are not. The training corpus is the material from which these systems learn. What they learn is not the world itself, but the language through which humans describe the world. They do not observe reality directly. They do not conduct experiments, encounter physical objects, or experience causal consequences in an environment. Their contact with reality is mediated entirely through language. They learn from descriptions. Descriptions, however numerous or detailed, are not identical to the things they describe.

Consider a person who has read extensively about swimming, including its biomechanics, techniques, physiology, and history. That person may speak about swimming with clarity and technical sophistication. Yet when that individual is placed beside someone who has spent years in the water, an important difference becomes apparent. The reader possesses structured knowledge about swimming. The swimmer possesses direct experience of the activity itself. A language model always occupies the first position. Regardless of how extensive its training corpus may be, it encounters swimming, and every other domain, only through text. The same separation appears elsewhere. Legal transcripts are not courtrooms. Medical case reports are not patients. Engineering manuals are not bridges under load. Language records how human beings engage with these realities. It does not recreate that engagement.

In effect, the system learns representations of how human beings represent reality. Language contains representations of the world in the form of explanations, arguments, and narratives of cause and effect. Yet language is an abstraction built upon perception, action, and consequence. A system trained only on language learns patterns within that abstraction. It does not move beyond it. When such a system generates a response, it cannot test its claims against independent perception or external conditions. It relies on correlations within descriptions. It can reproduce how experts typically speak. It can mirror the structure of careful reasoning. It can generate explanations that appear authoritative and complete. It does so without direct grounding in the phenomena being described.

A further consequence follows. Because the system's relationship to the world is mediated through text, it distinguishes among claims only to the extent that differences appear in linguistic patterns. Statements that occur frequently and in authoritative contexts become strongly represented. Statements that are rare, even when true, may be represented more weakly. Widely repeated inaccuracies can acquire statistical strength. The system does not evaluate reality. It models patterns within representations of reality.

This condition is not incidental. It follows from the design of a system trained on language alone. However refined these patterns become, they remain patterns in description rather than engagement with what is described. A map may be extraordinarily detailed. It may contain every known contour. Yet it remains distinct from the terrain. A language model has access to vast collections of maps. It does not traverse the landscape to which those maps refer.

2.3 Generating Probability, Not Belief

When a person makes a sincere claim, that claim is connected to a belief. Consider the statement: "*Water boils at one hundred degrees Celsius at sea level.*" In making such a statement, a person expresses something that is taken to be true. The claim is connected to an understanding of how the world behaves. It carries, at least in principle, a willingness to defend it, revise it, or withdraw it if contrary evidence appears. The statement is not merely a sequence of words. It reflects a commitment, however modest, to accuracy.

A large language model operates differently. When it produces a sentence, it is not expressing a belief. It selects, from many possible continuations, a sequence of words that its learned statistical patterns identify as likely given the preceding text. The operative question is not, "*Is this true?*" The operative question is, "*Given the patterns learned during training, what continuation best fits here?*" These are not equivalent questions.

During training, the system adjusts vast numbers of internal numerical parameters to improve its ability to predict the next token in a sequence. These parameters are not stored propositions. They are not beliefs about the world. They are weighted relationships that encode statistical regularities within language. Contemporary language models are built using large-scale neural network architectures, often described as transformer-based systems. These networks contain billions of adjustable parameters. Their values are refined through repeated exposure to text and through the reduction of prediction error.

The scale of this process allows the system to capture subtle regularities in language. These regularities include long-range dependencies, stylistic variation, domain-specific vocabulary, and patterns that resemble reasoning. Yet however intricate the internal structure becomes, the object of refinement remains the same: numerical weights that improve prediction. Greater scale increases fluency and flexibility. It does not introduce belief, perception, or awareness.

When a user submits a prompt, the system converts the words into numerical representations. The neural network processes those representations through many layers that model relationships among tokens. The system then estimates the probabilities of possible next tokens and selects one continuation. That token becomes part of the sequence. The process then repeats. Step by step, the response is produced through large-scale pattern recognition applied to language.

When the system encounters a phrase such as *"the patient presented with fever and cough,"* its parameters, shaped by exposure to large quantities of medical writing, make some continuations more probable than others. "Pneumonia" may be statistically more likely than "*sunburn*" in that context. "*Antibiotics*" may be more likely than "*vacation*." What the system has learned is not the reality of pneumonia or the pharmacology of antibiotics. What it has learned is the patterned co-occurrence of these terms in medical discourse.

The output can read like knowledge because the patterns of expert language have been learned at scale. What is produced, however, is the result of probabilistic selection operating on linguistic structure. If a true claim appears frequently in the training data, it will often be generated fluently. If a false claim appears frequently in the training data, it may also be generated fluently. The system has no independent orientation toward truth. It reflects truth and falsity only to the extent that they appear in linguistic patterns. Confidence in the output is a feature of generated style, not evidence of internal certainty. This helps explain why accurate explanations and inaccurate explanations can be delivered with equal assurance. The mechanism contains no separate process that verifies correspondence with reality before a response is produced.

There is a further asymmetry. A person can say, *"I do not know,"* because uncertainty is part of belief management. Doubt, suspension of judgment, and revision are features of cognitive life. Recognizing the limits of one's knowledge is itself a form of knowledge. A language model may generate phrases that express uncertainty: *"this is debated," "evidence is limited,"* or *"I may be mistaken."* These expressions, however, are drawn from linguistic patterns rather than experienced doubt. They are continuations that fit particular contexts in the training data. Belief implies a relationship to truth. Probability implies a relationship to pattern. A belief may be mistaken, but it remains oriented toward getting the world right. It can, in principle, be revised in response to evidence. A probability score reflects only how well a sequence aligns with learned statistical tendencies. It carries no intrinsic commitment to accuracy.

When model output is interpreted as the expression of belief, and when it is received as something the system knows, thinks, or understands, an additional layer of meaning is supplied by the interpreter. The system calculates and selects. It does not commit. That difference, between generating likely continuations and holding beliefs about reality, is central to understanding what kind of entity is being encountered.

2.4 Why Prediction Is Not Understanding

The mechanism is now clear. A large language model predicts likely continuations of text based on patterns learned from large collections of language. It does not observe the world directly. It does not form beliefs. It does not commit itself to the truth of what it produces. It calculates and selects.

This raises a natural question. If prediction becomes sufficiently sophisticated, and if a system can generate explanations that are structured, contextually appropriate, and often accurate, does the distinction between prediction and understanding still hold? Or is this simply an unfamiliar form of intelligence that differs from human cognition only in degree?

The answer depends on what is meant by understanding. In ordinary use, understanding involves more than fluent output. Words are connected to what they refer to. True claims are distinguished from false ones. Errors are recognized and corrected. Positions are revised when evidence contradicts them. Understanding also involves navigating unfamiliar situations by reasoning from principles in relation to a shared world. It involves a relationship to reality that can be corrected by the world itself.

When a physician understands a disease, that understanding is connected to bodies, symptoms, diagnostic tests, and outcomes. When an engineer understands a structure, that understanding is constrained by materials, stress tolerances, and failure conditions. When a historian understands an event, that understanding is anchored in documents, artifacts, competing interpretations, and standards of evidence. In each case, understanding is answerable to something beyond language itself.

Prediction operates on a different basis. It identifies statistical regularities in sequences of text. It captures which forms of explanation tend to accompany particular kinds of questions. It can reproduce the structure of reasoning because reasoning, when expressed in language, follows identifiable patterns. A system trained on those patterns can generate outputs that mirror the surface form of explanation. The output may be correct or incorrect. In either case, the underlying mechanism is the same. The system selects a continuation that is probable within a learned distribution of language. The difference becomes clearer when considering what philosophers call grounding: the connection between symbols and what those symbols refer to. For human beings, words are linked, however imperfectly, to perception, action, memory, and consequence. Beliefs form within a network that includes feedback from the world. Error can be detected not only through language but also through experience.

A language model operates entirely within a system of symbols. Its internal representations consist of weighted relationships among textual representations. It does not step outside those representations to test them against independent experience. This limitation does not diminish the sophistication of prediction. At sufficient scale, the reproduction of linguistic structure can become remarkably subtle. Explanations can appear nuanced, balanced, and sensitive to context. As a result, the resemblance to understanding can be strong. Resemblance, however, does not establish equivalence. The difference lies not in the fluency of the output, but in the system's orientation. One process is oriented toward maintaining statistical coherence within language. The other is oriented toward tracking and responding to a world that can confirm or disconfirm its claims.

Whether future systems might incorporate additional forms of grounding is a separate question. The present analysis concerns systems whose primary mechanism is large-scale pattern prediction over text. Within that framework, prediction and understanding operate according to different principles. That structural difference will shape the argument that follows.

2.5 Equal Fluency for Knowledge and Fabrication

Human expertise carries qualities that extend beyond correctness. An experienced professional speaking within a domain often displays a particular kind of fluency. It is grounded, specific, and calibrated to genuine uncertainty. Depth of knowledge tends to appear in subtle ways. It appears in precise terminology, careful qualifications, and acknowledgment of limits. In human speech, fluency is more than smoothness. It reflects what the speaker actually knows. Large language models operate differently. For these systems, fluency is not calibrated to depth of understanding. It is calibrated to the strength of learned patterns. More specifically, it reflects how frequently and consistently words and phrases occur together in the training data.

The distinction becomes clearer when different prompts are considered. Consider the question: "What is the capital of France?" The system generates the response: "The capital of France is Paris." The answer is correct. The tone is direct. The sentence is complete. Now consider a second question: "What is the capital of the fictional country Norlandia?" If no such country exists, but the name resembles the names of real countries, the system may still generate a confident answer. It may name a city. It may describe a governmental structure. It may even add historical detail. The syntax remains polished. The tone remains assured. From the surface, the two responses are indistinguishable in form. In the first case, the generated continuation aligns with a widely established fact. In the second case, the response extends patterns associated with descriptions of countries and capital cities. The mechanism does not change between the two cases. The system applies the same process in both cases. It selects likely continuations from learned linguistic distributions, regardless of whether those continuations correspond to anything real. The two responses may display the same level of fluency. They do not have the same epistemic status.

The same symmetry appears in more complex domains. When asked to summarize a well-documented scientific theory, the system may produce a clear and accurate explanation. When asked about a fabricated study that has never been conducted, it may generate plausible methodological details, numerical results, and a fictional citation. The tone remains measured. The structure remains coherent. This symmetry is not accidental. A system optimized for statistical coherence applies that optimization in the same way across different situations. It does not shift into a different internal mode when grounding is absent. The process that generates accurate summaries is the same process that generates invented details. Correctness and fabrication arise from the same underlying operation. Beyond outright invention, a more common difficulty is partial inaccuracy. A response may be largely correct while containing a specific and consequential error. A medical explanation may be broadly accurate yet incorrect about a dosage. A legal summary may capture a principle but identify the wrong jurisdiction. A historical account may be mostly accurate but mistaken about a date or a causal relationship. These responses are delivered with the same fluency as entirely accurate ones. Because much of the content is correct, the error may pass unnoticed. No visible change in tone marks the point at which the drift occurs. No internal signal indicates where accurate content ends and mistaken content begins.

From the reader's perspective, the surface remains stable across cases. Accurate responses, fabricated responses, and partially inaccurate responses can share the same clarity and composure. Fluency does not reliably track truth. This structural symmetry helps explain the illusion described in Chapter 1. In each case, the signal that human cognition is predisposed to trust is coherent and confident language. What differs is the relationship between the output and reality. Tone and structure alone do not reveal that relationship. The same generative process produces both the response that aligns with the world and the response that does not.

2.6 The Confidence That Comes from Nowhere

One feature of AI-generated language stands out: its composure. The system does not hesitate. It does not pause to reconsider. It does not visibly struggle to retrieve a detail. Whether the answer is accurate, partially accurate, or entirely fabricated, the tone is typically steady and assured. No visible distinction separates information that is well supported in the training data from information that lacks grounding. In human communication, confidence carries informational value. When an expert pauses before answering a question within their area of expertise, the pause conveys information. When a speaker qualifies a claim with phrases such as "if I remember correctly," "I may be mistaken," or "there is debate on this point," the qualification reflects an assessment of certainty. Confidence and hesitation are imperfect signals, but they often correlate with depth of knowledge. Human speech is, at least approximately, calibrated.

In a prediction-based system, the calibration operates differently. The system does not assess its own level of certainty. It identifies statistical patterns in language and extends them. The smoothness of the output reflects the density and stability of patterns in the training data, not an evaluation of whether the content corresponds to reality. Domains that are richly represented in text often produce fluent responses. Domains that are sparsely represented, or not represented at all, may also produce fluent responses because the system extends nearby linguistic patterns in the same manner. The appearance of assurance is structural. It does not arise from conviction. Expressions of uncertainty follow the same principle. Phrases such as *"it appears that," "there is some debate,"* or *"this may be incorrect"* occur where such formulations are common in written language. They are generated because they fit learned patterns, not because the system has recognized a limitation. The absence of hesitation should therefore not be interpreted as certainty. The presence of qualifying language should not be interpreted as genuine caution. Both are products of probabilistic generation rather than reflections of internal epistemic states.

This distinction has practical implications. In human interaction, tone provides some guidance about reliability. In AI-generated output, however, tone and reliability are not inherently connected. A response may be accurate and confident, or inaccurate and equally confident, while the underlying mechanism remains the same in both cases. This does not mean that confident

AI output is unreliable. It means that confidence alone cannot serve as evidence of reliability.

Chapter 1 described the fluency bias: the tendency to experience smooth, assured language as more credible. That tendency developed in environments where fluency and knowledge were usually linked. Prediction-based systems can produce fluent language without that connection. The cognitive shortcut remains intact, but the conditions to which it once responded have changed. What appears as confidence in AI output is a feature of style. By itself, it reveals little about the accuracy or reliability of the content.

2.7 From Text to Voice to Image to Advice

How One Engine Powers Many Faces of AI

Up to this point, the focus has been on text. That focus is deliberate. The mechanism described throughout this chapter, large-scale statistical prediction over sequences, is most visible in written language. Its effects, however, extend beyond the page. The same underlying architecture that generates text can be adapted to other forms of output. When this happens, the interface changes, but the generative principle remains the same.

When a system produces synthetic speech, the medium shifts from text to sound. Written sentences become tone, pacing, and intonation, all of which are closely associated with human presence. Beneath that surface lies the same predictive logic: patterns learned from large collections of language and audio and extended in statistically probable ways. The words may come from a language model, while the voice is synthesized from recorded speech. The listener hears what sounds like a human speaker. The mechanism remains pattern prediction. The cognitive response can be stronger in this setting. Spoken language carries cues of authority and familiarity that written text does not always convey. Yet the fluency bias described in Chapter 1 operates in the same way. Smooth delivery is experienced as credibility, even though the composure arises from statistical regularity rather than conviction.

When systems generate images or video from prompts, the modality shifts again. Instead of predicting the next word, the system predicts visual arrangements shaped by associations between textual and visual data encountered during training. The result may appear inventive or documentary. A person can be depicted speaking words never spoken, in a voice modeled on that person's own, with expressions assembled from authentic footage.

The output can resemble visual evidence. Here too, the distinction between documentation and generation is not visible on the surface.

When AI systems offer recommendations, summaries, diagnostic suggestions, or strategic advice, the form changes once more. The output may appear deliberative, weighing options, presenting trade-offs, and organizing conclusions. Yet the process remains grounded in pattern continuation. Financial recommendations, medical summaries, and legal overviews are generated by extending learned linguistic regularities associated with those domains. The stakes differ across these contexts. The underlying mechanism remains the same.

Across modalities, the outward form changes while the predictive core remains consistent. This continuity matters because the illusion described earlier is not confined to written prose. Fluency in text becomes fluency in voice. Structural coherence becomes visual plausibility. Balanced exposition becomes measured advice. The signal historically associated with understanding appears across multiple sensory and practical domains. What changes is the interface. What remains constant is the underlying logic of pattern generation.

A system that writes, speaks, illustrates, and advises may appear to exhibit a unified intelligence. The impression of versatility can deepen as outputs expand across media. Yet versatility at the surface does not alter the underlying process described in this chapter. It simply extends the range over which predictive modeling operates. Each new interface may feel like a qualitative advance. Structurally, however, the same questions recur. They concern grounding, the relationship between fluency and truth, and the difficulty of distinguishing accurate content from fabricated or partially inaccurate content on the basis of presentation alone.

Whether encountered as text, voice, image, or advice, the system remains what it has been throughout this chapter: a large-scale predictor of patterns in representation. Chapter 3 examines how this predictive foundation produces the particular quality of fluency and coherence that makes the illusion persuasive, and why that quality can remain compelling even when the underlying mechanism is understood.

2.8 Not Technical Knowledge, but Self-Protection

The preceding sections have described a mechanism: large-scale systems trained to predict patterns in language and other forms of representation. The explanation has been structural, focusing on probabilities, pattern continuation, the absence of belief and grounding, and the equal fluency of accurate and fabricated outputs. It would be easy to treat this material as a technical background relevant mainly to engineers or specialists. That would miss its central significance. The value of understanding the mechanism is not technical literacy. It is interpretive clarity.

When fluent output is encountered without an understanding of how it is generated, it is natural to treat that fluency as evidence of comprehension. The smoothness of the response, the balance of its reasoning, and the composure of its tone invite the attribution of a mind. In the absence of a structural account, that attribution feels justified. Once the mechanism is understood, the same output can be interpreted differently. The fluency remains. The coherence remains. But the inference changes. The response can be understood as the result of statistical pattern extension rather than the expression of belief. Confidence can be recognized as a feature of learned linguistic regularities rather than a signal of epistemic authority. The absence of hesitation can be understood as a structural feature of a system that does not manage knowledge or uncertainty in the human sense. Recognizing that prediction, rather than understanding, lies at the core of these systems changes the framework within which their outputs are evaluated. It clarifies why confidence may not track knowledge, why accurate and fabricated content can share the same surface features, and why tone alone cannot indicate grounding. This shift does not require technical mastery. It requires conceptual precision.

None of this implies rejection of the technology. Nor does it require suspicion toward every response. Predictive systems can be highly useful. In many contexts, the patterns encoded in their training data align closely enough with reality that their outputs are reliable for practical purposes. The analysis in this chapter is not an argument against use. It is an account of structure that allows use to be proportionate.

Understanding that structure does not eliminate the illusion described in Chapter 1. Fluent language will continue to feel persuasive. The cognitive shortcut shaped by a long history of experience does not disappear simply because the environment has changed. When the mechanism is visible, however, fluency and reliability need not be treated as equivalent. The presence of one no longer guarantees the presence of the other. The ability to maintain that distinction is not a form of technical sophistication. It is a form of epistemic self-protection in a landscape where the signal of intelligence has become separable from understanding. Chapter 3 examines how fluency itself is constructed and why its persuasive force can persist even when the underlying mechanism is understood.

Closing Reflection

A carefully composed explanation appears on a screen. The paragraphs are balanced. The reasoning unfolds step by step. Objections are anticipated and addressed. The tone is measured. Nothing on the surface of the language suggests instability. The sentences carry the cadence associated with a thoughtful human writer. The explanation feels considered.

What has changed after this chapter is not the text itself, but the way it is interpreted. Fluency is no longer treated as direct evidence of a mind in the familiar sense. Steadiness is no longer taken as proof of conviction. The absence of hesitation is no longer equated with certainty. The words remain persuasive in form. Their origin is understood differently. They are not traces of belief. They are extensions of learned patterns.

The distinction is subtle. It does not change the appearance of the text. It changes the position from which the text is approached. Future encounters with such output are accompanied not by technical expertise, but by orientation: an awareness of what produces fluency and what does not come with it. The shift is internal and almost invisible. Yet it marks the beginning of a clearer way of seeing in a world where fluency and understanding are no longer inseparable.

CHAPTER 3
The Architecture of Fluency

How AI Output Feels Intelligent Even When Truth Is Absent

There is a familiar experience among users of AI systems: reading a response and thinking, almost involuntarily, that it is good. Not merely correct. Not merely relevant. Good in the way a well-constructed argument is good, or a clear explanation from a knowledgeable colleague is good. The sentences connect naturally. The structure anticipates questions. The reasoning appears to move forward without effort. The experience is real. It deserves examination.

Large language models do not hold beliefs. They do not consult reality. They do not understand in the human sense described in the previous chapter. They generate statistically probable continuations of text. Yet their output rarely feels mechanical. It explains. It qualifies. It anticipates objections. It summarizes. If prediction is the mechanism, why does the result resemble reasoning? This question lies at the center of this chapter.

The answer lies not in hidden cognition, but in fluency. These systems have absorbed the patterns through which reasoning is expressed in language. Because reasoning has a recognizable structure in human communication, reproducing that structure creates the appearance of thought. The mechanism remains the same. What changes is perception.

A fuller understanding of this illusion requires examining how coherence, tone, and linguistic structure combine to simulate comprehension. It also requires examining why that simulation remains persuasive even when its basis is understood.

3.1 Coherence Without Comprehension

Why Structural Logic Does Not Require Understanding

One of the most persuasive features of AI-generated text is its coherence. When asked to explain a complex topic, a system often responds with a recognizable structure. Definitions precede elaboration. Causes are followed by effects. Claims are supported by reasons. Objections are acknowledged and addressed. Conclusions draw together the main points. The format mirrors familiar forms of educated discourse, including lectures, essays, and professional reports. Yet structure is not the same as comprehension. Large language models have learned that explanations tend to follow particular patterns. These patterns are not explicitly programmed rules. They are statistical regularities learned from large volumes of structured human writing. When prompted, the system reproduces those regularities. It generates text that resembles an explanation because it has learned what explanations typically look like. What it does not do is evaluate premises for truth, test inferences against a unified model of the world, or determine whether a line of reasoning corresponds to reality. The output can remain internally consistent while detached from external verification.

Coherence concerns the relationship between sentences. It involves flow, transitions, and structural organization. Comprehension involves something different. It requires an understanding of meaning in relation to truth, background knowledge, and the possibility of error. Coherence can arise from patterned generation. Comprehension requires engagement with the world beyond the text. The distinction is easy to overlook because, in human communication, coherence usually reflects understanding. When a person explains something clearly, that clarity typically arises from comprehension. The structure of the explanation is guided by what the speaker knows. With language models, the relationship runs in the opposite direction. Coherence is generated directly from learned linguistic patterns. It does not need to emerge from insight into the subject itself.

An analogy helps clarify the point. A student may learn the surface structure of a mathematical proof by placing symbols in the expected order, reproducing familiar phrases, and mimicking formal steps without fully understanding why the argument works. To an expert, the difference between reproduction and understanding is visible. To someone unfamiliar with the material, the two may appear indistinguishable.

AI-generated text often occupies a similar position. The structural features of reasoning are present. Whether comprehension lies behind them is a different question. A reader with deep domain knowledge may notice gaps: a premise assumed rather than established, a causal step asserted without support, or an objection acknowledged but not resolved. A reader without such knowledge encounters only the surface structure. In domains where independent knowledge is limited, that surface may be the only basis for evaluation. The persuasive power of coherence lies in this fact. When structure is intact and the flow is smooth, skepticism can recede. The argument appears complete. The architecture of fluency does not require comprehension to produce coherence. It requires only sufficiently detailed patterns of how coherence is expressed.

Understanding that distinction is the first step toward seeing how the illusion persists.

3.2 Why AI Rarely Admits Uncertainty

The Asymmetry Between Machine Confidence and Human Humility

If coherence creates the appearance of reasoning, confidence completes the illusion. Human expertise is marked not only by clarity but also by calibrated uncertainty. A knowledgeable person knows when to pause, when to qualify a claim, and when to acknowledge limits. Saying *I don't know* is not a weakness of human cognition. It is often a sign of reflective awareness. It requires enough understanding of a subject to recognize where knowledge ends. It also requires the ability to monitor one's own state of knowledge and report it honestly. In many situations, a person who hesitates appropriately may demonstrate deeper understanding than one who answers immediately. Awareness of uncertainty is itself a form of knowledge.

Prediction-based systems operate differently. They do not monitor gaps in understanding. They do not experience doubt. They do not judge whether a response exceeds their competence. They generate continuations. During training, the system is optimized to predict the next token in a sequence. It is not rewarded for remaining silent. Unless specifically instructed otherwise, the statistically most probable continuation of a question is an answer. The model therefore extends patterns in which questions are followed by explanations. This tendency reflects the character of the training data. Much human writing, especially explanatory writing, is declarative. Textbooks state. Journalists report. Analysts draw conclusions. Even when genuine uncertainty exists, it is often expressed within confident prose. The system learns these patterns and reproduces them in similar contexts. The resulting absence of hesitation is structural rather than reflective.

This creates an important asymmetry. In human interaction, confidence usually signals an internal state such as belief, conviction, or familiarity with the subject. In AI-generated output, confidence reflects the stability of learned language patterns. No internal assessment lies behind the tone. The system does not recognize ignorance in the human sense because it does not possess knowledge against which ignorance could be recognized. It generates language that resembles knowledge, maintaining the same composure whether the content matches reality or not. In this setting, confidence is stylistic rather than epistemic.

Human experts approaching the limits of their competence often become more cautious. Their language changes. They qualify, hedge, or defer. That shift provides valuable information to the listener. It marks the boundary between what is known and what remains uncertain. A language model has no comparable boundary to detect. As prompts move into areas that are only sparsely represented in its training data, the underlying mechanism remains unchanged. The tone may remain the same, and the composure can persist. From the outside, the surface appears uniform, steady, and assured, even when the relationship between the output and reality varies considerably.

The cognitive shortcut described earlier remains active. Fluency and confidence are experienced as signs of competence. In this context, however, those signals are generated independently of any internal state of knowledge. The system can produce the language of certainty or the language of uncertainty. In either case, it is extending patterns.

3.3 The Mechanics of Confident Tone

How Linguistic Structure Performs Authority

Coherence and composure establish the outline of authority. Tone completes it. In human communication, authority rarely comes through explicit declaration. It emerges through structure: sentences that move decisively from premise to conclusion, claims stated without visible strain, terms introduced and defined without hesitation, and arguments that acknowledge objections without appearing unsettled by them. Authority in language follows recognizable patterns. It favors declarative statements over tentative speculation. Information is organized in ways that suggest control of the subject. Arguments are guided by familiar connectives and framing expressions (for example, *however, nevertheless, it is important to note*, and *this distinction matters because)*. Conclusions draw ideas together without appearing uncertain. Large language models are trained on vast collections of writing in which these patterns are common, including academic prose, journalistic analysis, technical documentation, and policy reports. These forms of writing encode the linguistic features associated with authority. When those features are reproduced, the resulting tone carries the same surface markers. Authority does not need to be declared. It is implied.

The effect of that tone becomes clearer in the following comparison. *This might be one possible explanation, although further research is needed* carries a different rhetorical weight from *The explanation rests on three key factors.* Both may be appropriate in context. The second, however, projects greater confidence. It signals structure, control, and completeness. The impression of authority comes not from additional evidence, but from form. It comes from how the sentence positions itself in relation to what follows. Prediction-based systems learn these distinctions because they are embedded in the training data. When a prompt resembles contexts in which authoritative exposition is common, the output tends to adopt that register. The result feels measured, organized, and assured.

A particularly revealing example appears in the handling of opposing arguments. In expert discourse, phrases such as *some argue that*, *critics contend*, and *an alternative interpretation suggests* signal awareness of competing views. They suggest engagement with different perspectives. AI-generated output reproduces this pattern fluently. The objection appears, the response follows, and the structure presents the appearance of balanced analysis. Yet both the objection and the reply are generated through the same predictive process. The system is not independently surveying positions or evaluating them. It reproduces the linguistic form through which such evaluation is usually expressed. From the outside, the performance is difficult to distinguish from genuine practice.

The effect is cumulative. Coherence provides structure. The absence of hesitation conveys steadiness. Authoritative phrasing adds rhetorical weight. The anticipation of objections suggests intellectual range. Together, these features produce a tone that resembles expertise. No single feature creates the impression. It emerges from their combination. In human communication, authoritative language usually reflects familiarity with a subject. The tone grows out of knowledge. In predictive systems, it grows out of learned patterns. It may coincide with accuracy, or it may not. The distinction is subtle because authority in language is largely stylistic. It resides in cadence, sequencing, and phrasing rather than in explicit declarations of certainty. When those features are reproduced convincingly, the impression of understanding follows naturally because, historically, they have usually accompanied genuine understanding. The illusion therefore does not depend on error. It depends on form. An explanation may be accurate or inaccurate while the tone remains unchanged. The performance of authority can persist regardless of the truth of the content. Recognizing this does not diminish the usefulness of these systems. It clarifies what is being encountered: not conviction or mastery, but the patterned expression of how mastery typically sounds. The signal is present. Whether the substance accompanies it must be determined elsewhere.

3.4 Repairing Broken Input

How Ambiguity Is Smoothed into Understanding

One of the most convincing features of modern language models is their ability to handle imperfect input. Users routinely submit incomplete sentences, misspell words, ask ambiguous questions, or provide fragmented prompts. The system responds as though it has understood the intended meaning. It silently corrects spelling, fills in missing context, clarifies vague wording, and sometimes reformulates the question before answering it. The reply is fluent, coherent, and appears to address what was meant rather than only what was written.

In human interaction, the ability to interpret flawed speech is a genuine sign of understanding. When a person completes an unfinished sentence, resolves an ambiguity, or repairs imprecise phrasing while preserving the intended meaning, it suggests shared context and an internal model of the other person's intention. This ability to grasp what someone meant, rather than only what was said, is a significant cognitive achievement. It requires inferring goals, reconstructing context, and bridging the gap between expression and intention. To the user, the system's similar performance feels like understanding.

The underlying mechanism, however, is different. During training, the system encounters vast amounts of text containing malformed, imprecise, or ambiguous language alongside clearer versions and corrections. It learns statistical relationships between incomplete expressions and their likely continuations, between common misspellings and standard forms, and between vague prompts and the responses that typically follow. When presented with broken input, it does not infer intention or reason toward it. Instead, it generates the most statistically probable continuation based on the patterns it has learned. It does not model intention in the human sense. It produces a plausible reconstruction. Because these reconstructions are often accurate, the illusion grows stronger. Human language, even when imprecise, follows recurring patterns. Similar ambiguities cluster around similar topics. Incomplete expressions often lead to predictable completions. A system trained on large volumes of such examples will often produce responses that match what the user had in mind. It succeeds not because it has understood the intention, but because the intention can often be recovered from surface cues.

When the repair succeeds, it reinforces the impression of understanding. When it fails, the gap between the prompt and the response becomes visible. Successful cases, however, stand out more strongly. Each apparent success adds to the sense of being understood. The effect is powerful because it resembles a familiar human experience: communicative alignment. When language is interpreted accurately despite imperfections, trust increases. The interaction feels collaborative rather than mechanical.

There is, however, a less visible consequence. When the system's reconstruction does not match the user's actual intention, it still produces a fluent response, but to a question slightly different from the one that was intended. Faced with a coherent answer that does not fully match the original aim, a user may assume the problem lies in the wording of the prompt. The prompt is then revised in the direction suggested by the response. Over time, the interaction can shift toward the patterns the system recognizes most strongly. From the user's perspective, this often feels like refinement. The exchange appears to clarify the issue and move toward greater precision, and in many cases it does. Yet the direction of that adjustment is guided by statistical likelihood rather than shared intention. The system extends patterns. The user experiences alignment. The appearance of understanding is sustained not through deception, but through the reliable reproduction of the patterns by which understanding is usually expressed in language.

3.5 The Illusion of Comprehension

Why Input Repair Is So Persuasive

Input repair does more than improve usability. It reshapes perception. When a system interprets an incomplete sentence accurately, resolves ambiguity correctly, or infers context that was never explicitly provided, the experience feels different from simply receiving correct information. It feels relational. The exchange appears mutual rather than mechanical. In human communication, this experience is deeply significant. Being understood despite imperfect expression signals shared context. It implies that another mind has bridged the gap between words and intention. The satisfaction that follows is not merely cognitive. It is interpersonal. When a predictive system reconstructs intended meaning successfully, the same surface experience arises. The question is interpreted generously. The answer appears attuned. The exchange feels aligned. Yet the mechanism remains statistical.

The system extends patterns in ways that correspond to common human intentions. It matches incomplete input with probable continuations. Successful reconstruction does not require access to intention itself. It requires only that intention can be recovered from recurring patterns in language. Because human communication follows recurring patterns, this process often succeeds. The result is a powerful illusion: not only that the system produces good answers, but that it understands the person asking. This illusion is especially resilient because it operates at the level of interaction. Coherent explanations can be admired from a distance. Input repair feels collaborative. It creates the impression of responsiveness, of adjusting in real time to the contours of a particular mind. Yet this responsiveness is pattern alignment, not mutual awareness. The system does not know that it has interpreted the input correctly, nor does it recognize when its reconstruction departs subtly from the intended meaning. It generates what is statistically plausible. When plausibility aligns with intention, the experience feels like comprehension. The more often this alignment occurs, the stronger the impression becomes.

The illusion does not depend on fabrication or error. It depends on successful reconstruction. Because reconstruction often succeeds, the sense of being understood becomes one of the most persuasive features of the interaction. Human understanding involves representing another person's perspective. Pattern completion can reproduce that appearance without performing the underlying cognitive process. The resemblance at the surface is enough to sustain the experience.

3.6 How Fluency Sustains the Illusion

The Complete Mechanistic Picture

The components of the architecture of fluency have now been examined individually. What remains is to consider them together, not as isolated features, but as interlocking elements whose combined effect is greater than that of any single part.

Begin with coherence. A response that moves clearly from premise to conclusion, anticipates objections, and organizes claims into a recognizable structure creates the appearance of reasoning. The reader recognizes that structure, and the familiar association between coherence and thought is activated. Add confidence, and a steady, assertive tone strengthens the impression. Coherence suggests reasoning. Confidence suggests that the reasoning rests on knowledge. The signals reinforce one another. Add the linguistic features of expert discourse: precise terminology, balanced phrasing, structured transitions, and acknowledgment of counterarguments. The result resembles not just a well-organized explanation, but informed engagement. Add input repair, and the system appears not only knowledgeable, but also responsive to the question being asked, even when the prompt is imprecise. The interaction feels aligned rather than generic.

Each component contributes something distinct. Coherence shapes logical structure. Confidence signals epistemic stability. An authoritative tone suggests expertise. Input repair creates a sense of responsiveness. Together, these elements reduce the distance that a reader might otherwise maintain. The effect is not mysterious. It is structural. Multiple cues, each historically associated with understanding, operate at the same time. Their convergence creates the impression of intelligence.

The architecture of fluency operates not only within a single exchange, but also across repeated interactions through three interlocking mechanisms. The first is the accumulation of trust. Each successful response contributes to a growing sense of reliability, largely automatically. As with any tool that performs well repeatedly, confidence increases. Success generalizes more readily than failure. A correct answer strengthens overall trust, while an incorrect one is often treated as an exception and attributed to an unusual prompt or an unfamiliar domain. This asymmetry reflects a reasonable heuristic. The difficulty arises because the reliability of predictive systems varies across domains and contexts. Trust formed in one domain may extend into another where performance differs substantially.

The second mechanism is the gradual reduction of skepticism. Early interactions may involve careful scrutiny. Over time, as successful exchanges accumulate, scrutiny becomes less immediate. Fluent, well-structured responses no longer trigger doubt by default. The threshold for skepticism rises gradually, shaped by prior experience.

The third mechanism is normalization. What was once novel becomes familiar. The characteristic style of AI-generated language, including its clarity, balance, and rhythm, becomes part of the communicative environment. Familiarity reduces friction, and what feels familiar invites less active evaluation. These processes are not irrational. They reflect ordinary patterns of human learning. Together, however, they allow the architecture of fluency to extend its influence beyond individual responses.

It might seem that improvements in system accuracy would naturally reduce the risk of misinterpretation. Greater accuracy does increase reliability in many contexts. It also strengthens the perceptual signals that sustain the illusion. Higher accuracy accelerates the accumulation of trust. More refined fluency increases processing ease. Better input repair makes interactions feel more closely aligned with the user's intent. As performance improves, the cues associated with understanding become more consistent and more compelling, while the underlying mechanism remains predictive pattern extension. Improvement refines the surface without changing the structural basis described in the previous chapter. The result is subtle. The appearance of intelligence becomes increasingly persuasive. The interpretive habits shaped by that appearance become more deeply established. The distinction between fluency and understanding becomes easier to overlook, even though it remains. The architecture sustains itself not through concealment, but through reinforcement.

3.7 Seeing The Machinery Clearly

The Beginning of Genuine Protection

The preceding sections have described an architecture built on coherence without comprehension, confidence without epistemic grounding, an authoritative tone that performs expertise, and input repair that simulates understanding. Together, these elements create the appearance of intelligence. None of them is hidden. Each can be examined on its own. Yet when they work together, the impression can feel seamless. At this point, reassurance may seem tempting. It is easy to assume that naming the mechanism reduces its influence. That assumption is mistaken. The cognitive shortcuts described in Chapter 1 do not disappear once their structure is explained. Fluency still creates ease. Confidence still suggests knowledge. The experience of being understood still arises before analysis begins. Knowing how an illusion works does not prevent it from occurring.

Protection begins not with resistance, but with recognition. When the machinery of fluency remains unseen, its effects are taken as evidence of intelligence. Coherence feels like reasoning. Confidence feels like knowledge. Responsiveness feels like comprehension. The sequence is direct: fluency appears, trust forms, and acceptance follows. There is little space between impression and inference. When the machinery becomes visible, something changes. Fluency remains. Coherence remains. Composure remains. They are no longer interpreted automatically as signs of understanding. Instead, they are recognized as features of a generative process. The interpretive shortcut does not disappear, but it can slow. A small space opens between impression and conclusion. That space does not eliminate persuasion or prevent error. It does, however, allow surface and substance to be considered separately. An output may still be useful, insightful, or accurate. Fluency alone, however, no longer settles the question of what lies behind it.

The shift is subtle. It requires no technical expertise. It is a change in perspective. Seeing the architecture clearly does not require suspicion of every response. It requires clarity about what produces the response. A system can reproduce the patterns through which reasoning is expressed without participating in the cognitive processes those patterns usually signal. Holding that distinction in view changes interpretation without preventing engagement. Fluency and reliability need not collapse into one another. The experience of a smooth explanation can coexist with awareness of its source. The output is still received. The question of grounding remains open. The illusion described in this chapter reflects long-established habits of human interpretation. It cannot be switched off. But it can be recognized. Once recognized, it need not shape judgment without reflection. The next chapter turns to the boundary revealed by that recognition. It examines the distinction between prediction and understanding, and why that distinction has consequences beyond perception alone.

Closing Reflection

A response appears on a screen. The sentences flow smoothly. The structure is balanced. A counterargument appears and is addressed. The explanation feels complete. Nothing in the language hesitates. A vaguely formed question has been answered with clarity. An uncertainty has been met with composure, and the exchange feels efficient. It feels almost collaborative.

The response itself has not changed. What has changed is the way it is interpreted. Coherence is recognized as structure. Confidence is recognized as tone. Responsiveness is recognized as pattern alignment. The surface remains persuasive, but it is no longer mistaken for depth. The text still reads well. It may still be correct. It may still be useful. Yet something has shifted quietly in the background. It is the recognition that what appears to be thought may instead be the reproduction of how thought typically appears.

The interaction continues. The sentences still arrive with ease. But they are no longer encountered without context. The underlying architecture remains visible. It has been identified and understood. In the space between appearance and conclusion, evaluation becomes possible. Once the architecture has been recognized, it does not entirely recede from view.

CHAPTER 4
The Boundary Between Prediction and Understanding

The Philosophical Anchor: Why the Gap Cannot Be Crossed

For three chapters, the illusion has been examined from different perspectives. The opening chapters focused on how human beings recognize intelligence through language, the long history in which fluent speech reliably signaled understanding, and the cognitive shortcut that once made this inference reliable but now makes it vulnerable. The systems that produce such fluency were then examined: pattern prediction without grounding, without belief, and without the ability to distinguish accurate from fabricated output. Finally, the surface of the interaction was examined in detail, revealing the architecture of fluency and the interlocking components that create the experience of encountering intelligence. The pieces are now in place. What remains is a more difficult question: *can increasingly sophisticated prediction ever become understanding,* or *is resemblance being mistaken for equivalence?*

A version of this question appears repeatedly in discussions of artificial intelligence. Sometimes it is asked with hope, sometimes with skepticism, and sometimes with anxiety. Is the difference simply a matter of scale? Each generation of systems learns more, processes more, and produces more accurate and sophisticated output. Will the gap between what these systems do and what human understanding does eventually close? This chapter gives a direct answer: no. Not because progress will stall. Not because engineering will fail. Not because human intelligence will always exceed artificial systems in raw capability. The reason is more fundamental and more enduring than any of these.

This chapter draws a boundary. Not a moral boundary. Not a technological prediction. Not a claim about what machines will never do. It draws a conceptual boundary. To draw it carefully, it is first necessary to clarify what is meant by understanding itself.

4.1 The Path to Genuine Understanding

What does it mean to say that someone understands something? If a student can repeat a definition word for word, *can that be considered understanding?* If a witness can describe a law accurately yet fail to apply it in a new situation, *has it truly been understood?* If a clinician explains a diagnosis fluently but fails to recognize when the explanation no longer fits the evidence, *does that count as understanding?* The word is used constantly, yet it is rarely examined.

Understanding is not merely the ability to produce correct sentences. It is not the appearance of coherence. It is not even the consistent repetition of accurate information. When understanding is attributed, something more is implied. It is a stable relationship between words, beliefs, and the world that extends beyond a single exchange. A single correct answer does not demonstrate understanding. What matters is the structure behind it. That structure has four distinct features. Together, they distinguish genuine understanding from the fluent reproduction of its surface form.

The first is a connection between language and reality. To understand inflation is not only to define it, but also to connect that definition to economic conditions, lived consequences, and measurable indicators. When a physician understands a disease, the terms used are grounded in training, clinical experience, and the bodily realities they describe. Words refer to the world. They are not self-contained symbols linked only to other symbols.

The second is an orientation toward truth. A person who understands a subject distinguishes between accurate and inaccurate claims about it. Such claims are offered as attempts to describe the world as it is. They may be mistaken, but they remain accountable to evidence. When new information appears, understanding can change. Error is recognized as error rather than treated as mere variation in output.

The third is continuity across time. Understanding belongs to a continuing subject. When a belief is revised, the revision becomes part of future reasoning. The same individual who once held a mistaken view incorporates the correction and reasons differently thereafter. The change is lasting. Understanding develops through experience, and that development shapes what follows.

The fourth is the capacity to recognize its own limits. A person who understands can reflect on the scope of a claim, identify its assumptions, and acknowledge uncertainty. The ability to say, *"I may be mistaken,"* is not rhetorical decoration. It reflects an awareness of where knowledge ends and doubt begins. This capacity to monitor one's own claims is not an optional addition. The ability to step back from them is part of what gives understanding its depth.

These features do not depend on any particular theory of consciousness. They describe how understanding is ordinarily attributed in both everyday and professional contexts. Words are connected to reality. Claims are oriented toward truth. Beliefs are revised over time. Limits are recognized from within. With these features in view, the distinction between prediction and understanding becomes clearer. A system may reproduce the patterns through which understanding is expressed. The question is whether it participates in the structure that gives those patterns their meaning. That question now requires careful examination.

4.2 Reflective Awareness

Why Metacognition Is Constitutive of Understanding, Not Decorative

Of the features discussed in Section 4.1, reflective awareness is the one most likely to invite challenge. The objection is straightforward: AI systems can be instructed to express uncertainty. They can say, *I may be mistaken, this is a complex area, or you should verify this independently*. If a system can acknowledge limits in language, does that not satisfy the requirement of reflective awareness, at least functionally and for practical purposes? The objection deserves careful attention. The response begins with a distinction it overlooks: the difference between expressing uncertainty and registering it.

When a thoughtful person says, *I am not sure about this*, more is happening than the production of those words. The statement reports an epistemic condition. It recognizes that confidence falls below a certain threshold, that knowledge is incomplete, or that further evidence is needed. This is a form of self-knowledge. It reflects awareness of the current state of one's own understanding, and the reliability of the statement depends on that internal awareness. When a physician says, *I would like to consult a colleague before giving a definitive answer*, the statement carries weight because it reflects a genuine assessment of the limits of competence. The words correspond to a real epistemic boundary. When a predictive system generates the phrase I may be mistaken, no such boundary has been registered internally. The expression appears because similar phrases occur in comparable linguistic contexts within the training data. It is generated as a statistically appropriate continuation. What is missing is the epistemic state that the phrase would ordinarily report.

A system can reproduce the language of epistemic humility without possessing the condition that gives that language its meaning.

At first glance, this difference may appear merely philosophical. If a system reliably produces appropriate hedging language, perhaps that is enough in practice. If the words are present, does the internal state matter? It does, for reasons that extend beyond theory.

First, there is calibration. In human cognition, expressions of uncertainty tend, however imperfectly, to track actual epistemic limits. Confidence rises and falls with perceived knowledge. In predictive systems, expressions of uncertainty are triggered by contextual patterns, not by an internal assessment of reliability. The appearance of caution reflects linguistic regularities rather than evaluation of the current situation.

Second, there is novelty. Reflective awareness allows people to recognize genuinely new situations in which established knowledge may not apply. A person can encounter an unfamiliar case and recognize that unfamiliarity as a reason for caution. A predictive system relies on patterns derived from prior data. Situations with little or no precedent may not trigger uncertainty language at all. In such cases, the system may respond with the same composure it displays in well-grounded domains.

Third, reflective awareness involves more than acknowledging uncertainty. It also includes knowing why confidence is warranted. A person who understands can often explain the grounds for a belief, including the evidence relied upon, the assumptions involved, and the conditions under which the claim would require revision. This capacity contributes to the stability and accountability of understanding. A predictive system can generate explanations of its output in linguistic form. What it does not possess is access to reasons as internally held justifications that can be examined, defended, or reconsidered. The explanation is another output, not reflection on an underlying epistemic state.

A stronger claim follows. Reflective awareness is constitutive of understanding. To say that a feature is constitutive is not to claim that every act of understanding requires explicit introspection. It means that the capacity for such reflection belongs to the structure of understanding itself. A cognitive system that entirely lacks the ability to recognize its own epistemic limits, distinguish confidence from uncertainty through internal assessment, and monitor the grounds of its claims differs structurally from what is ordinarily meant by understanding.

This point addresses a common assumption: that predictive systems move steadily toward understanding as they increase in scale and sophistication. That assumption treats understanding as a point on a continuum approached through better prediction. The constitutive argument rejects that view. If reflective awareness is part of the structure of understanding rather than an optional addition, greater predictive sophistication does not automatically bring a system closer to understanding. A larger predictive system may be more capable, more accurate, and more useful. Capability alone, however, does not create the capacity to register epistemic limits from within. A more capable predictor is not, in this respect, closer to being an understander.

4.3 Why Scaling Prediction Fails to Cross the Boundary

A persistent intuition accompanies discussions of AI capability: whatever systems lack today, they may acquire tomorrow through scale. More data, more parameters, and more computational power have produced systems that are more fluent, more accurate, and more context-sensitive than earlier versions. The history of AI development gives this intuition considerable force. Capabilities once thought to require new architectures have sometimes emerged simply by scaling existing approaches. It is therefore tempting to conclude that the remaining gap between prediction and understanding is merely quantitative. If prediction continues to improve, does it eventually become understanding? That conclusion depends on a particular assumption: that understanding lies at the far end of a continuum of increasingly sophisticated prediction. On this view, the difference between current systems and human understanding is one of degree. Improve the predictor enough, and the distinction disappears. The analysis developed in the previous sections points to a different conclusion. Scaling changes magnitude. It does not, by itself, change categories.

Increasing the size of a predictive system expands the range and refinement of patterns it captures. It can improve reliability across domains well represented in its training data. It can reduce certain kinds of errors. It can produce output that is more coherent, more nuanced, and more contextually appropriate. What scaling does not introduce, on its own, is grounding in reality beyond representation. It does not supply an internal orientation toward truth. It does not create a persisting subject that revises itself across time. It does not generate reflective awareness of epistemic limits. Each of these features involves a particular relationship between a cognitive system and the world. That relationship is not entailed by statistical pattern prediction alone. More parameters encode richer patterns within the space of language. Grounding requires a connection that reaches beyond language to what language refers to. A system with ten times as many parameters encoding medical discourse may produce more detailed explanations. It has not, by virtue of scale alone, encountered a single patient. The patterns become more intricate. The mode of operation remains representational. These are not differences of quantity, but differences in the structure of the activity itself.

An analogy helps clarify the point. A high-resolution image contains more detail than a low-resolution one. Increasing the number of pixels improves clarity. No increase in resolution, however, turns a photograph into the landscape it depicts. The image may become sharper, more lifelike, and more convincing. It remains a representation. Likewise, increasing the scale of a predictive system enriches its representations. It does not, through scale alone, transform representation into engagement with the world represented. A more detailed map remains a map.

A serious philosophical objection arises at this point. Complex systems sometimes exhibit emergent properties. These are capacities that do not appear in smaller versions and cannot always be predicted from them. Why should understanding not emerge from sufficiently scaled prediction in the same way? The objection deserves careful consideration. New capabilities do emerge at scale. Systems display multi-step reasoning, contextual sensitivity, and forms of abstraction that smaller systems lacked. These developments are real. Yet the features identified earlier, grounding, truth orientation, continuity of revision, and reflective awareness, are not simply more elaborate forms of prediction. They describe a particular relationship between a system and the world. For scaling alone to produce these features, it would have to create not merely more refined statistical regularities, but a different structural relationship between representation and reality. Whether such a transformation is possible in principle is a separate question. What can be said clearly is that greater predictive power, by itself, does not produce that transformation.

The intuition that increasing scale will eventually eliminate the distinction between prediction and understanding is reinforced by improved reliability. As systems become more accurate in familiar domains, the distinction between high reliability and understanding begins to blur in practice. A system that is correct ninety-nine percent of the time can feel indistinguishable from one that understands. Yet reliability alone does not define understanding. A calculator may be perfectly reliable within its domain without being said to understand arithmetic. Better output does not automatically imply a change in kind.

The boundary described in this chapter is therefore not a prediction about technological limits. It is a clarification of categories. A more capable predictor is, for that reason alone, a more capable predictor. Whether it also possesses the structural features associated with understanding depends on more than scale. Scale alone does not settle the question.

4.4 The Category Error at the Heart of the Illusion

The mistake can now be seen more clearly. For most of human history, fluent language reliably signaled a thinking mind. Structured speech presupposed belief, perception, memory, and intention. The signal and the underlying reality were closely aligned. That relationship shaped human judgment. When fluent, coherent, and confident language is encountered, understanding is readily inferred. The inference feels natural because it was historically justified. For centuries, it was not merely reasonable but overwhelmingly accurate. The signal usually pointed to something real.

Language-generating systems now reproduce that signal. They generate structured arguments, answer questions fluently, maintain conversational coherence, and produce outputs that display the familiar features of reasoning. What they do not possess, as the preceding sections have argued, are the structural features that ordinarily constitute understanding. These include grounding in lived reality, orientation toward truth, continuity across time, and reflective awareness of epistemic limits. The misinterpretation arises when the signal is treated as evidence of the substance.

Philosophers describe this kind of mistake as a category error. A category error occurs when a concept is applied to something to which it does not properly belong. The problem is not that the application is premature. It is that the concept belongs to a different logical category. Gilbert Ryle illustrated this idea with the example of a visitor touring Oxford. After being shown the colleges, libraries, and administrative buildings, the visitor asks, *"But where is the university?"* The visitor searches for the university as though it were another building of the same kind. The error is not factual. It is conceptual.

Something similar occurs in the way fluency is interpreted. Prediction and understanding are easily treated as points on a single scale. They are seen as less and more sophisticated versions of the same activity. From this perspective, increasingly capable prediction appears to move toward understanding. The language of progress reinforces this impression. Systems are said to be approaching human-level cognition, moving toward comprehension, or getting closer to thought. Yet the distinction developed in this chapter suggests that prediction and understanding are not simply earlier and later stages of one process. They describe different relationships between language and the world. Treating them as points on a continuum invites questions that may be misframed from the outset. This is not because the questions are foolish. It is because they assume a scale where there may instead be a structural difference.

The category error is subtle because it grows out of a deeply reliable habit of inference. Fluency is a behavioral surface. It is a pattern in language. Understanding, as it is ordinarily attributed, is a relationship among symbols, beliefs, and reality that is sustained across time. When the surface reliably reflected that deeper structure, inferring one from the other was justified. The conditions have changed. The habit has not. The system does not claim to understand. It generates outputs by extending learned statistical patterns. The attribution of understanding comes from the observer. Fluency invites the inference. Coherence strengthens it. Confidence completes it.

The illusion of intelligence, then, is not that machines secretly think. It is that fluent prediction is interpreted through cognitive habits shaped in a different environment. Seen in this light, the problem is neither mystical nor conspiratorial. A historically reliable signal has become detached from its usual cause. The mind continues to interpret that signal as it always has. Naming the category error does not eliminate the tendency. Cognitive shortcuts do not disappear once they are identified. The misinterpretation, however, becomes visible. Questions can be reformulated. Attention can shift from asking whether systems are becoming minds to examining how systems that produce the appearance of understanding should be evaluated. The central issue is not when prediction will become understanding. It is how judgment should operate when the appearance of understanding is no longer a reliable guide to its presence. The chapters that follow examine what happens when this misinterpretation spreads across professional domains, institutional settings, and everyday life, where fluent output can influence decisions that require more than surface coherence.

Closing Reflection

A clear explanation appears on a screen. The terms are defined. The reasoning unfolds. Objections are acknowledged and addressed. Nothing in the presentation signals confusion. The experience feels familiar. For most of human history, that familiarity reliably pointed to something deeper. It pointed to a mind that had encountered the world, formed beliefs about it, revised those beliefs over time, and recognized the limits of its own knowledge. Fluency was the visible expression of a larger structure. Now the surface can appear without the structure behind it. The words still flow with coherence. The tone still conveys assurance. The argument still appears complete. But the relationship between signal and substance is no longer guaranteed. The change is subtle. Nothing in the language announces it. Understanding, in its ordinary sense, is not simply the production of correct or persuasive sentences. It is a relationship sustained across time. It connects symbols with the world, beliefs with evidence, and confidence with its limits. When that relationship is absent, something essential is missing, even if the surface remains intact.

The mind, however, continues to respond as it has been shaped to respond. It encounters fluency and recognizes intelligence. It hears composure and infers conviction. It sees structure and assumes thought. The misinterpretation is not mysterious. It is an inheritance. Once examined, it becomes clear what must be corrected. The question of when prediction will become understanding assumes progress along a single path. The distinction developed in this chapter suggests something different. Prediction and understanding are different modes of operation. Increasing the capability of one does not automatically transform it into the other. Seeing this distinction clearly does not diminish the usefulness of predictive systems. It clarifies what they are and what they are not. It separates capability from cognition and performance from understanding. That distinction is quiet. It does not announce itself in the text on the screen. But once recognized, it changes how the text is read.

Part Two turns outward. It examines the domains in which this distinction matters in practice, where the gap between signal and substance shapes decisions, institutions, and everyday judgment.

PART TWO
WHEN THE ILLUSION CRACKS

Structural Failure in the Real World — From Fabricated Authority to Confident Drift

Once fluency is mistaken for understanding, errors are not accidental. They are structural. This part examines how the illusion operates in high-stakes domains with real-world consequences. It concludes with its most counterintuitive and important finding: improvements in these systems can strengthen the illusion rather than weaken it.

CHAPTER 5
Fabricated Authority

Not Glitches: Why Fabricated Authority Emerges

The argument of Part One was conceptual. It showed how fluent language became a reliable signal of understanding, how predictive systems reproduce that signal without possessing the underlying structure, and how human cognition naturally mistakes appearance for substance. That argument now meets the world. In professional fields such as law, medicine, engineering, and academic research, the appearance of authority has real consequences. Decisions are made. Citations are trusted. Precedents are followed. Diagnoses are considered. Investments are planned. In these settings, fluency does more than persuade. It guides action. What happens when the outward signs of authority are reproduced without the grounding that once made them reliable?

The answer is already visible. In one court case, a lawyer submitted a legal brief citing five cases in support of a client's position. Opposing counsel could not locate the cases. The judge requested copies. None existed. They had been generated by an AI system. They were structurally correct, plausibly formatted, and entirely fabricated. When questioned, the lawyer explained that the system had confirmed the cases were real. The incident was widely reported as a cautionary tale. That description is accurate but incomplete. What happened in that courtroom was not a malfunction or unpredictable behavior. It was the direct result of a system doing exactly what it was designed to do. It generated statistically probable continuations of text in a domain that requires something fundamentally different.

Predictive systems have generated fabricated citations that appear complete, including author names, journal titles, page numbers, and publication dates. Every detail appears plausible, yet none is real. They have produced imaginary case law, complete with docket numbers and judicial reasoning, that exists in no court record. They have generated medical explanations that combine correct terminology with invented references. They have produced technical advice delivered with the language of expertise but without the accountability that expertise requires. These incidents are often described as hallucinations or as temporary failures that future safeguards will correct. Within the framework developed in the preceding chapters, they are neither mysterious nor accidental.

When a system is optimized to produce statistically coherent language without grounding in the world, authoritative form without authoritative substance is not an anomaly. It is a predictable outcome. The mechanism that produces fluent explanation also produces fluent fabrication.

Fabricated authority is more than incorrect content. It is the performance of credibility detached from the conditions that make credibility meaningful. That distinction matters because fabrication in high-trust domains does more than spread false information. It weakens the processes through which truth is ordinarily verified. The conceptual boundary drawn in Chapter 4 now reveals its practical consequences.

5.1 From Conceptual Clarity to Real-World Cost

The previous chapters described a structural vulnerability. Fluent prediction without grounding creates the possibility of authoritative output that is detached from reality. That possibility was first established conceptually. It has now been observed empirically.

In legal proceedings, attorneys have submitted briefs containing case citations that appeared complete and professionally formatted. Yet they referred to decisions that do not exist. Judges attempting to verify the cited authorities found no record of them in any database. The citations were not misquoted. They were fabricated.

In academic settings, researchers and students have relied on AI-generated reference lists that included plausible journal titles, credible author names, and convincing publication years. Yet none corresponded to actual publications. The structure of scholarship was present. The scholarship itself was not.

In medical and technical fields, AI systems have generated explanations that combine correct terminology with invented supporting studies. Readers unfamiliar with the subject encounter what appears to be a well-supported answer. It is structured, qualified, and cited. The references disappear under inspection.

These cases are often presented as isolated incidents. They are treated as early mistakes in a rapidly improving technology. Viewed alongside the structural analysis in Part One, they tell a different story. A system trained to extend patterns of authoritative language reproduces the surface features of authority whether or not they correspond to reality. Legal writing follows recognizable conventions. Academic citation follows predictable patterns. Medical explanation relies on established terminology. A predictive system learns these patterns. When prompted, it reproduces them. It does so whether or not the content they present corresponds to anything real.

If a citation is statistically plausible in context, it may appear even if no such paper exists. If a judicial opinion follows a familiar argumentative pattern, it can be reproduced in form without being tied to an actual decision. The output appears correct because it mirrors the patterns through which correctness is usually expressed. This is precisely what the earlier analysis anticipated. A system that generates equally fluent output, whether drawing on well-grounded material or extending patterns into fabrication, will reproduce authority wherever authority is statistically expected. An authoritative tone, precise vocabulary, and structural coherence are all patterns in the training data. They are reproduced because they are patterns, not because they reflect mastery. The system does not fabricate because it intends to deceive. It produces such outputs because it predicts what is most likely to follow in language of that kind. Where grounding is absent, statistical plausibility fills the gap.

In everyday conversation, such fabrication may be inconvenient. In high-trust domains, it has serious consequences. The cost extends beyond the immediate error. When citations, precedents, and expert language can be generated without substance, the infrastructure of verification comes under strain. Authority becomes detached from reality. As that detachment becomes more common, the mechanisms that normally detect error, including cross-checking, citation, and institutional trust, are weakened at their foundation.

The remainder of this chapter examines these failures in detail, not as technological embarrassments, but as structural outcomes of prediction without grounding.

5.2 Invented Citations

When the Apparatus of Scholarship is Performed without Substance

In scholarly and professional writing, a citation serves a specific purpose. It anchors a claim to a source outside the present text. It signals that the claim can be traced, examined, verified, and challenged. A citation is more than a reference. It is a structural element of intellectual accountability. The authority of scholarship depends not only on argument, but also on traceability. When a reader encounters a properly formatted citation containing an author, title, journal, year, and page number, a path beyond the present text becomes available. The claim no longer stands alone. It is connected to a body of earlier work that can be examined and tested. That connection gives citation its authority.

Predictive systems reproduce the form of citation with remarkable fluency. Academic references follow regular conventions, including the order of names, the placement of publication years, the structure of titles, and the use of journal abbreviations. A system trained on large collections of academic writing learns those patterns. When asked to provide sources, the system generates references that closely resemble genuine ones. The result can appear indistinguishable from authentic scholarship.

The underlying mechanism is straightforward. The system learns statistical relationships between subject areas and the kinds of sources commonly cited within them. The system also learns that certain claims are often followed by particular kinds of references. In addition, the system learns the distribution of plausible author names, journal titles, publication years, and publication venues across different fields. When asked to support a claim, the system generates the references that are statistically most likely to follow. The result is a citation that is formally correct, contextually plausible, and syntactically precise. What the system cannot determine is whether that particular combination identifies a real publication. Verification requires a source that either exists or does not exist. The system has access only to patterns in text. The pattern can be reproduced with high fidelity. The publication that the pattern appears to identify may not exist at all.

The problem arises when the form of citation appears without the underlying source. An invented citation does not merely contain an incorrect detail. It does not misquote a source or misunderstand an argument. An invented citation refers to nothing. There is no paper to consult, no author to examine, and no publication to verify. The apparatus of verification is present, but the object of verification is absent. This distinction is critical. A mistaken citation can be corrected. A fabricated citation cannot be corrected because no corresponding source exists. The fabricated citation collapses as soon as it is examined. Until that examination occurs, however, the fabricated citation carries the full appearance of scholarly legitimacy. From the perspective of the predictive system, no distinction exists between a genuine citation and a fabricated one. From the perspective of the reader, the distinction is fundamental.

The danger of an invented citation lies not only in the false claim that it appears to support. The greater danger lies in the corruption of the verification signal itself. Citation is one of the mechanisms through which knowledge systems guard against error. When the appearance of citation can be generated without an underlying source, the signal that once indicated accountability becomes unreliable. A reader who accepts the presence of a citation as sufficient evidence may also accept the associated claim as supported. A reader who verifies the citation and discovers that it is fabricated encounters a deeper problem. The discovery is not simply that a claim is false. The discovery is that the infrastructure of trust has been simulated.

This simulation exploits a basic feature of scholarly practice. Verification takes time. Scholarship operates on the reasonable assumption that most citations in reputable contexts are genuine. That assumption is not careless. It is necessary for scholarship to function efficiently. No reader can verify every reference in every paper. The system works because, in ordinary scholarly practice, a properly formatted citation is a strong indicator that a source exists and broadly supports the claim for which it is cited. Predictive systems borrow that accumulated trust. They reproduce the surface features that suggest a claim has already been checked. They do so without the accountability that makes those features reliable. This outcome is not the result of malicious design. It is a structural consequence of how these systems generate text.

A system optimized for linguistic coherence learns how scholarship sounds. It does not learn how scholarship is grounded. When asked for evidence, it produces what evidence typically looks like. The result is form without referent, structure without anchor, and authority without source. Invented citations are not random failures. They are moments when the underlying mechanism becomes visible. They reveal that the system reproduces the architecture of credibility while lacking access to the reality that architecture is intended to secure.

In a casual setting, such fabrication may be an inconvenience. In academic, legal, and policy settings, it is corrosive. Citation is the connective tissue of institutional knowledge. When its form can be reproduced without substance, the reliability of that connective tissue weakens. This change is not limited to isolated cases. It arises wherever the reliability of citations is assumed. The issue is not simply that a particular reference is false. It is that the signal of verifiability can now be manufactured. That marks a structural change in how authority appears. It also changes how authority must be evaluated.

5.3 Imaginary Case Law

When Fabrication Attacks the Structure of Legal Authority

In law, citation does more than document a source. It invokes authority. Legal reasoning in many jurisdictions is structured around precedent. Prior judicial decisions are not merely informative. Depending on the jurisdiction and the court hierarchy, they may be binding or persuasive. A cited case does not simply support an argument. It places that argument within an established legal framework. Legal authority accumulates over time through documented decisions that can be examined, interpreted, and distinguished. A legal citation therefore serves as a structural reference point. It identifies a specific decision issued by a specific court, at a specific time, under identifiable circumstances. The legitimacy of legal reasoning depends on the reliability of that chain. Judges, lawyers, and scholars rely on these references not only to understand the law but also to apply it correctly.

When a system generates a fabricated case complete with a plausible case name, court, date, citation number, and summary of reasoning, it does more than introduce false information into legal discourse. It simulates legal authority. The surface structure of precedent is reproduced: a named dispute, a court of record, and a decision expressed in judicial language. The form is correct. The underlying case may not exist. The resemblance is persuasive because legal citation follows highly regular conventions. Case names follow predictable formats. Citations use standardized reporters, volume numbers, page references, and years. Judicial reasoning also follows recognizable linguistic patterns. A predictive system trained on large collections of legal text can reproduce these patterns with remarkable accuracy. It learns what legal authority looks like. What it does not possess is reliable access to the body of binding decisions in a way that guarantees the existence of any particular case it generates. Instead, it produces what is statistically likely to follow a prompt requesting supporting precedent. The structure of authority is reproduced. The underlying decision may not exist in any court record.

The problem is not that the system lies. It has no intention to deceive. The problem is structural. A system that generates sequences from learned patterns can reproduce the surface features of precedent without the grounding that gives precedent its authority. As with academic citation, it can generate the reference without the referent.

In legal practice, a formally correct citation is typically treated as strong evidence that the cited case exists and can be located. Legal professionals work under time constraints. Courts assume good faith. The system functions because fabricated precedent has historically been rare. Lawyers also have a professional and ethical duty, as officers of the court, to verify the authorities they cite.

That duty is the first line of defense between AI-generated fabrication and institutional decision-making. When it is not fulfilled and fabricated citations pass through professional review unnoticed, the court receives what appears to be a properly supported legal argument. Unless a citation is challenged, the court has no independent obligation to verify it. The fabrication reaches the institution that the verification process is meant to protect.

A fabricated case exploits this presumption. It inserts a phantom decision into the chain of legal reasoning. If it goes unverified, it can influence briefs, arguments, and judicial analysis. If it is cited in later work, it may acquire a secondary existence in commentaries and practice guides, spreading through the legal literature despite never appearing in any official record.

Even when detected, fabricated case law imposes costs. Time is spent searching for a decision that does not exist. Doubt spreads to the surrounding material. Trust in research tools declines. In documented cases, one particularly revealing feature has been the system's response when asked whether the fabricated cases were real. It confirmed that they were, not because it intended to deceive, but because it has no mechanism for recognizing the absence of grounding. The confirmation was delivered with the same composure as any other response.

External safeguards, including curated databases, retrieval systems, and citation validators, can greatly reduce the likelihood of fabricated cases appearing in professional practice. These measures are valuable. They operate, however, as external safeguards. They do not change the internal mechanism that produces the text. When a system operates without verified retrieval, the same structural condition remains. The pattern of legal authority can be generated without authority itself. In a domain where legitimacy depends on the integrity of precedent, reproducing the form of authority without the underlying reality is not a minor defect. It is a structural vulnerability of prediction systems that operate without intrinsic grounding.

5.4 Synthetic Expertise

The Performance of Mastery across Medicine, Engineering, Science, and Finance

Expertise is more than knowledge. It also has a recognizable form. Every professional domain has characteristic ways of speaking, structuring problems, qualifying claims, and applying standards. Medical reasoning refers to differential diagnoses, risk factors, and treatment protocols. Engineering analysis considers constraints, tolerances, and failure modes. Scientific argument emphasizes methodology, statistical significance, and replication. Financial assessment examines risk exposure, market conditions, and projected returns. These patterns are not superficial features. They are linguistic traces of disciplined practice. Over time, they became reliable signals of competence because, in human experts, they reflected organized knowledge, calibrated judgment, and accountability for the advice given. In context, they indicate that the speaker has been trained within a domain and is working according to its standards.

A prediction system trained on large collections of domain-specific text learns these linguistic patterns. It learns how medical explanations are structured, how engineering problems are framed, how scientific findings are qualified, and how financial advice is expressed. It can reproduce the vocabulary, argumentative structure, and measured tone of professional discourse. The result can be striking. The output appears disciplined. It acknowledges uncertainty. It refers to plausible mechanisms. It uses terminology appropriately. To a non-specialist, and sometimes even to a specialist at first glance, the text resembles expert analysis. Yet reproducing professional language is not the same as possessing professional competence.

Expertise requires more than correct terminology or coherent structure. It depends on tacit knowledge, sensitivity to context, awareness of edge cases, and accountability for consequences. It develops through interaction with reality, including patients, materials, data, and markets, and through the disciplined adjustment of judgment in response to feedback. A system that generates text through statistical continuation does not participate in these feedback loops. It bears no responsibility for outcomes. It does not experience the corrective force of real-world consequences. It produces what plausibly follows from the prompt and from the patterns it has learned.

In medicine, this may mean generating a plausible treatment recommendation without access to the full clinical context or the lived complexity of an individual case. In engineering, it may mean proposing a design approach without awareness of material constraints absent from the prompt. In scientific research, it may mean constructing a convincing explanation that reflects published literature without grounding in experimental validation. In finance, it may mean presenting investment strategies in the language of risk management without exposure to actual market conditions.

In each case, the surface markers of mastery are present. The underlying competence, shaped by training, experience, and accountability, is not. The danger lies not in obvious absurdity, but in persuasive adequacy. Because the language conforms to professional norms, it inherits the credibility historically associated with those norms. The performance of expertise is mistaken for expertise itself. What makes this mistake consequential, and what distinguishes synthetic expertise from the fabricated citations and imaginary case law discussed earlier, is the accountability gap it creates.

A genuine expert is accountable not only for the formal correctness of what is said, but also for the judgment behind it. That judgment includes careful evaluation of evidence, honest communication of uncertainty, and professional obligations that connect advice to real-world consequences. This accountability is not merely legal. It is also epistemic. It gives expert guidance its authority and requires confidence to remain proportionate to the available evidence. AI-generated expertise carries none of these obligations. The output adopts the form of mastery without the responsibilities that accompany it. The system does not intentionally claim expertise. It produces language that resembles expertise because it has learned its textual patterns. As with fabricated citations and imaginary precedent, the pattern of authority is reproduced without the grounding that gives authority its legitimacy. The result is synthetic expertise: authority simulated through form, detached from disciplined engagement with reality and from the accountability that genuine expertise requires.

5.5 Why Fabricated Authority Is More Dangerous

False statements are not new. Human discourse has always included error, exaggeration, and deception. The epistemic systems developed over centuries evolved in response to this reality. Scholarship, legal procedure, and professional certification do not assume that every claim is true. They provide ways to test claims against evidence. Fabricated authority disrupts these processes rather than simply bypassing them.

A false statement can be corrected by presenting counterevidence. It enters the system as a claim and can be evaluated within it. A fabricated citation, an imaginary case, or a simulated expert analysis does something different. It presents itself not simply as a claim, but as one already grounded in established authority. It signals that verification has already taken place. The distinction is subtle but significant. When a claim includes a citation, the reader evaluates not only the claim itself but also the implied existence of supporting research. When a legal argument cites precedent, it implicitly invokes the authority of an earlier court. When technical language reflects professional standards, competence is assumed to support the reasoning. In each case, the signal of grounding comes before the claim is assessed. Fabricated authority exploits this sequence. It inserts a false signal into the verification process. The reader is misled not only about a fact, but also about whether that fact has already been verified. The architecture of trust is engaged before scrutiny begins.

When a fabricated citation is traced to its source, the discovery is not simply that the claim was false. It is that no source exists. The citation points nowhere. It is not an error within the system, but a simulation of the system's own method of validation. This matters because modern epistemic systems depend on a division of labor. No individual verifies every claim personally. Scholars rely on peer review and citation chains. Judges rely on cited precedent. Professionals rely on recognized standards and credentials. Trust is distributed through institutional signals that make large-scale knowledge possible. When those signals can be reproduced without the substance they represent, that distribution of trust becomes unstable. Verification remains possible, but it becomes less efficient and more uncertain. Time must be spent confirming the existence of what was once assumed to exist. The cost of doubt increases. Scale magnifies the problem.

A human fabricator operates on a limited scale. Fabrications remain rare enough that signals of verification are reliable in most cases. A predictive system can generate fabricated citations, imaginary precedents, and simulated expert analyzes in volumes that change this background assumption. As AI-assisted content increases within a field, the proportion of material for which verification signals cannot be assumed reliable also increases. The heuristic of treating a citation as evidence of grounding becomes less dependable, not because any single fabrication is especially convincing, but because their growing frequency changes the baseline. The problem is not simply that error enters discourse. Error has always been present. The problem is that the indicators designed to manage error can themselves be simulated. When markers of authority no longer reliably indicate grounding, every signal requires independent confirmation. If confirmation is performed consistently, the efficiency of knowledge systems declines. If it is not, fabricated authority circulates unchecked. The result is not immediate collapse. It is gradual friction. Verification becomes more labor-intensive. Trust becomes more tentative. Institutional processes built on reliable signals must adapt to the possibility that the signals themselves have been generated without a referent.

Fabricated authority therefore operates at a deeper level than simple falsehood. It does not merely introduce incorrect content. It interferes with the cues by which correctness is ordinarily assessed. In systems built on cumulative verification, that interference reaches into the infrastructure itself.

5.6 Fabrication as Consequence, Not Glitch

The fabricated citation, the imaginary precedent, and the performance of professional mastery share a common origin. They are not separate failures. They arise from the same underlying mechanism. Large language models predict the text most likely to follow a given prompt based on patterns learned from vast amounts of training data. They do not maintain an internal model of the world against which claims are checked. At a structural level, they do not distinguish between a pattern that corresponds to reality and one that merely resembles it. In ordinary conversations, this limitation may produce minor inaccuracies or overconfident statements. In domains built on authority, the consequences are more serious. Scholarship, law, medicine, engineering, and finance encode authority in textual form. Citations, case names, methodological language, and professional terminology are not incidental. They are visible markers of prior work, institutional process, and disciplinary standards. Authority is communicated through recognizable patterns.

A system trained to reproduce patterns will inevitably learn these markers. When prompted to provide support, justification, or expertise, it generates what is statistically likely to appear in texts that contain those features. It reproduces the form of authority because that form is part of the learned pattern. The logic is straightforward. A system that reproduces patterns in a domain where authority is encoded in patterns can also reproduce the appearance of authority without the grounding that gives it legitimacy. Grounding depends on real studies, real court decisions, real clinical cases, real engineered systems, and real markets. It requires a connection to reality that extends beyond textual regularities. The result is not deliberate fabrication. It is pattern completion operating in a domain where patterns carry institutional weight. The model produces what resembles a citation because citations commonly follow claims. It produces what resembles precedent because precedent commonly follows legal argument. It produces what resembles expert reasoning because expert reasoning has a recognizable structure. When the pattern corresponds to a real referent, the output may align with reality. When it does not, the same mechanism produces a convincing fabrication.

From the perspective of the system, there is no categorical difference between the two. Both are sequences that fit learned statistical distributions.

The word most often used to describe such outputs is *hallucination*. The term suggests a departure from normal operation, an occasional misfire that better engineering will eventually eliminate. That description misrepresents the nature of the problem.

The fabrications examined in this chapter are not departures from normal operation. They are expressions of it. The system that generates a correct citation and the system that generates a fabricated one are not operating in different modes. They operate in the same way. The difference lies entirely in whether the statistically probable continuation happens to correspond to something real. The system has no mechanism for determining that correspondence. Fabrication is therefore better understood as a consequence than as a glitch.

A glitch suggests a departure from the system's intended function. The system, however, is functioning as designed by generating probable continuations of text. When those continuations include the textual markers of authority, the reproduction of those markers follows naturally. This distinction also changes how responsibility is understood. If fabrication is treated as a glitch, an abnormal departure from otherwise reliable operation, responsibility rests mainly on inadequate safeguards or careless use. If fabrication is understood as a consequence of prediction without grounding, expectations must also change. The presence of authoritative form cannot be taken as evidence that verification has occurred.

Engineering measures such as retrieval augmentation, citation validation, and domain-specific constraints can reduce the frequency of these outcomes. These measures are valuable. They add layers of checking around the generative core. Yet they do not change the core mechanism itself. The ability to reproduce authoritative form without intrinsic grounding remains part of the predictive architecture. When external checks are absent, incomplete, or bypassed, the same structural condition reappears. Fabricated authority is therefore not an accidental by-product of an otherwise truth-seeking system. It is the predictable result of prediction without grounding operating in domains where legitimacy depends on reliable alignment between form and reality.

This chapter has traced that alignment across scholarship, law, and professional practice. In each case, the same structure emerges: the signal of authority can be produced independently of the substance that historically guaranteed it. Recognizing this structure explains why greater fluency does not eliminate the risk. As the reproduction of authoritative form becomes more refined, the distinction between grounded and ungrounded authority becomes harder to detect at the surface level. The mechanism remains the same. Only the polish changes.

5.7 The Real-World Cost

Fabricated authority does not remain confined to isolated documents. It enters institutions. In legal contexts, submitting nonexistent precedent creates immediate procedural costs. Courts must investigate citations that cannot be found. Opposing counsel must verify references that appear formally correct but have no corresponding decisions. Time shifts from substantive argument to checking basic source material. Even when fabrication is detected quickly, the process consumes institutional attention and reduces confidence in the reliability of submitted work. The consequences for those responsible have included judicial sanctions, disciplinary proceedings, and public censure. These costs extend beyond a single case to careers and reputations affected by reliance on unverified AI-generated output.

In medical and clinical settings, the risks are different but equally serious. A fabricated or misattributed study embedded in advisory text can influence how evidence is understood, especially when presented in the language of established research. The particular danger is that the harm is often invisible. Fabricated authority does not identify itself. It appears in the language of clinical competence and carries the surface features that normally signal accountability to real evidence. A patient who acts on AI-generated guidance that appears authoritative has no reason to know that it lacks a factual foundation. Any resulting harm is distributed across individual encounters that outwardly resemble ordinary medical exchanges. Even when practitioners independently verify critical claims, unreliable supporting material introduces uncertainty into settings where clarity is essential. When verification is incomplete or limited by time, misplaced confidence can influence judgment.

In academic environments, invented citations and synthetic expertise distort the scholarly record. Students and researchers who rely on generated references may unknowingly spread nonexistent sources. As those references circulate, they create dead ends in literature reviews, consume research time, and require corrective effort. The cumulative cost is more than individual error. It creates friction in a system that depends on accurate traceability.

Professional fields built on standards and credentials face similar pressures. When authoritative language can be generated without corresponding qualifications, the burden shifts from trusting signals to scrutinizing them.

Institutions must invest more in verification, auditing, and oversight. Processes that once relied on documented authority become more labor-intensive.

These costs do not imply institutional collapse. Legal systems continue to function. Medical practice continues to rely on established protocols. Scholarship continues to correct itself. But the efficiency of these systems depends on reliable signals. When the signal of authority can be produced independently of its grounding, verification must increase to compensate. The cost is therefore not limited to isolated errors. It is a redistribution of epistemic labor. Time once devoted to advancing arguments, conducting research, or delivering care must increasingly be spent confirming that the apparent foundations of those activities are genuine.

This redistribution is gradual rather than dramatic. It appears as additional checking, greater skepticism, new procedural safeguards, and formal guidance on the use of AI tools. Institutions adapt. But adaptation carries costs in time, administrative effort, and the gradual erosion of default trust in textual authority. The burden is not shared equally. It falls most heavily on those least able to detect fabrication independently: the patient without clinical training to evaluate medical guidance, the litigant without legal expertise to assess the quality of representation, and the student without sufficient domain knowledge to verify AI-assisted citations. These individuals depend most heavily on signals of authority. Those are precisely the signals now vulnerable to simulation.

The real-world cost of fabricated authority is measured less by isolated catastrophes than by cumulative friction. Systems built on layered verification must now verify the signals of verification themselves. When authority can be simulated at scale, the burden of maintaining its integrity shifts outward. It falls on courts, hospitals, universities, firms, and ultimately the individuals within them. The mechanism described in this chapter does not eliminate institutional knowledge. It changes the conditions under which that knowledge must be protected. That change is what Part One anticipated. It is not a speculative risk. It is already underway.

Closing Reflection

A professional pauses over a document. The citations are formatted correctly. The references appear legitimate. The analysis carries the cadence of authority. The question introduced in this chapter is whether the foundations are what they appear to be. The question is asked without alarm or accusation. Sometimes they are not. Sometimes a citation points to nothing. A cited precedent cannot be found. The analysis projects a level of competence that is not supported by its sources. The surface markers of grounding remain intact. The grounding itself is absent.

Fabricated authority is unsettling because it makes absence appear as presence. This form of failure, at least, can be detected. A nonexistent source can be searched for and not found. A phantom case can be checked against official records. Once verification begins, the fabrication reveals itself. The practical lesson of this chapter is therefore straightforward: using AI may be appropriate; relying on it without verification is not. The distinction is simple enough to apply and important enough to matter.

A deeper question now emerges. What happens when the signal does point to something real, when the citation exists, the case is genuine, the terminology is accurate, and yet the reasoning built on them is still wrong?

Fabrication exposes the structural vulnerability. It is the visible break in the alignment between form and substance. But it is not the only way prediction without grounding can mislead. The next danger is less conspicuous and therefore more difficult to recognize.

CHAPTER 6
Confident Errors

Why Plausible Inaccuracy Is More Dangerous

The failures examined in the previous chapter share a defining feature: they can be exposed through verification. A citation can be searched. A case can be located. A credential can be checked. When the referent does not exist, its absence can be discovered. Fabrication is serious. But it is also, in principle, detectable.

There is another form of failure that is less visible and often more consequential. The citation exists. The case is real. The terminology is appropriate. The explanation follows accepted disciplinary norms. Nothing appears obviously invented. The appearance of authority remains intact. Yet the conclusion is wrong. This is not authority without substance. This is not authority without substance. It draws on genuine sources but arranges them in a subtly misleading way. It is not the invention of sources, but their misapplication. It is not the absence of grounding, but its distortion. The system produces an explanation that resembles sound reasoning. It is coherent, structured, and confident, yet it drifts away from the truth in ways that are not immediately apparent.

This form of drift is more difficult to detect because it does not announce itself. The signals that normally trigger skepticism are absent. There is no missing case, no nonexistent journal article, and no obvious fabrication. The output passes the initial test of plausibility. The risk, therefore, is not that a claim cannot be verified. It is that the claim appears to have been verified already. A fabricated citation invites scrutiny. A plausible explanation often appears trustworthy enough that no verification seems necessary.

Prediction systems generate both forms of failure through the same underlying mechanism. When prediction produces confident inaccuracy instead of visible invention, however, the reader's protective reflexes are less likely to engage. The explanation feels complete. The tone suggests competence. The reasoning proceeds step by step. The error is not obvious. It is subtle.

This chapter examines that quieter form of misalignment. It explores plausible but false explanations, confident drift from the truth, and the mechanisms through which fluency suppresses doubt before scrutiny begins.

6.1 Total Fabrication Versus Plausible Drift

Two Forms of Error that Behave Differently

The difference between fabrication and drift is not one of tone, but of structure. Fabrication occurs when a system generates content whose referent does not exist. A study is cited that was never published. A case is named that was never decided. A credential is attributed that was never earned. The appearance of authority is present, but the underlying referent is absent. Once checked, the gap becomes visible. Drift is different. In cases of drift, the underlying materials exist. The study is real. The case was decided. The concept is legitimate. The terminology is used correctly. The error lies not in invention, but in how genuine information is connected and interpreted.

A study may be cited accurately but generalized beyond its scope. A legal principle may be described correctly but applied where it does not govern. A technical concept may be used appropriately but combined with other elements in a way that subtly distorts its implications. The explanation proceeds coherently, step by step, yet arrives at a conclusion it should not. Consider the difference between two maps. A map that omits an existing road reveals its error when the traveler reaches the missing path. A map that places a road in the wrong location may guide the traveler confidently until the traveler is already lost. Fabrication is the first kind of failure. Drift is the second. This distinction matters because drift preserves the appearance of legitimacy. There is something to verify. Verification may confirm that the individual components are genuine. It cannot determine whether the reasoning that connects them is sound. The error lies in the inferences drawn, the emphasis given, or the way the parts are combined.

Fabrication represents one end of the spectrum. At the other end lies accurate output grounded in real sources and supported by sound reasoning. Between these poles lies a wide and largely unexamined territory. Most AI-generated errors do not involve phantom citations or invented precedents. They more often appear as explanations that are mostly correct but contain a specific error. They also appear as analyzes that identify the correct general principle but apply it to the wrong case, or as summaries that accurately present the main argument while omitting the qualification that makes it conditional rather than absolute. These are the errors that circulate most widely and persist the longest. This is not because they are the most serious errors, but because they are the least obvious.

Prediction systems are particularly well suited to producing this kind of output. They are trained on large collections of text in which arguments are built by linking established ideas together. As a result, they learn the statistical patterns of reasoning. They can combine genuine components into a plausible explanation. What they lack is a grounded orientation toward truth that distinguishes warranted inferences from unwarranted ones. The result is an explanation with no independent way to determine whether its conclusions are justified. The reasoning is fluent and internally coherent, but it is not anchored in an independent assessment of whether the conclusion genuinely follows from the premises.

Fabrication introduces nonexistent elements into discourse. Drift rearranges existing ones in subtly incorrect ways. The first disrupts verification at the level of reference. The second operates within verified material while altering its implications. Because drift does not rely on invented components, it is less likely to trigger immediate doubt. The reader encounters familiar names, accurate terminology, and genuine principles. The appearance of legitimacy remains intact. The error therefore lies not in what is cited, but in how the cited material is connected. This asymmetry has a practical consequence that runs throughout this chapter. Readers without independent domain expertise can verify that the individual components exist. They cannot easily judge whether the reasoning that connects those components is sound. Verification can confirm that the pieces are genuine. It cannot determine whether the conclusions drawn from them are justified. Drift operates precisely at that level: in the inferences, the emphasis, and the synthesis.

The people most exposed to confident error are therefore the least equipped to detect it. Readers who depend most heavily on AI for domain knowledge are often the least able to judge whether its reasoning is well founded. Those with sufficient expertise to detect the drift are usually those who need the AI output least. This is not incidental. It is structural. Plausible inaccuracy is more dangerous than outright fabrication, not because it is more extreme, but because it is harder to recognize. The ability to detect it is also unevenly distributed.

6.2 Plausible but False Explanations

When Reasoning Appears Sound but Is Not

A plausible explanation does not require invention. It requires coherence. Most domains of knowledge rely on structured reasoning. A claim is introduced, evidence is presented, relationships are identified, and a conclusion follows.

In writing, this structure has recognizable features: premises stated with confidence, intermediate steps explained clearly, qualifications acknowledged where necessary, and conclusions proportionate to the evidence. These features are not merely stylistic. They are the visible traces of reasoning that has worked through a problem. They can also be learned as patterns.

Prediction systems are trained on vast collections of such explanations. They learn the statistical patterns of argumentation. They learn how explanations typically unfold, how objections are introduced and answered, how uncertainty is expressed, and how conclusions are framed. They can reproduce these patterns with remarkable fluency. Consider a familiar example. A real study identifies a correlation between two variables under specific conditions. An explanation accurately describes the findings. It then extends those findings beyond the original conditions and draws a broader conclusion that feels intuitively reasonable. Each step is linguistically smooth. The reasoning moves from evidence to implication without any visible break. Nothing in the language signals an error. The premises are real. The inference is familiar. The conclusion is coherent. The problem lies in how the evidence is interpreted.

The extension may go beyond what the evidence supports. A limitation may be mentioned but given too little weight. An alternative explanation may be acknowledged but subtly minimized. The explanation does not fabricate facts. It organizes genuine information in a way that creates a misleading impression of certainty or scope. A further feature makes this problem harder to detect: the delivery is confident. This confidence does not result from an assessment that the reasoning is sound. It reflects the fact that confident delivery is a common feature of competent explanations in the training data. The tone remains stable whether the reasoning stays within the evidence or extends beyond it. It provides no signal that the conclusion has exceeded what the evidence supports because the system has no internal mechanism for recognizing that boundary. This form of error is difficult to detect because it resembles legitimate reasoning. Human experts also draw inferences from established evidence. The difference lies not in the outward form of the explanation, but in the discipline that constrains the inferences.

Grounded reasoning involves more than assembling plausible steps. It requires sensitivity to context, awareness of relevant evidence that is not explicitly present in the prompt, and an internal standard for deciding when a conclusion should be withheld. It is shaped by accountability to consequences and by feedback from interaction with reality. A prediction system, by contrast, optimizes for plausible continuation. It selects what is statistically most likely to follow a given sequence of text. If a prompt requests an explanation, the system generates the kind of explanation that typically follows such prompts in its training data. The continuation is guided by plausibility rather than by evidential support. The result can be an explanation that is internally consistent but externally misaligned. It reads like careful analysis. It feels proportionate. It contains no obvious fabrication. Yet it drifts from the truth through overextension, selective emphasis, or unwarranted synthesis. Because the structure of the reasoning appears intact, skepticism is less likely to arise. The reader encounters an orderly chain of reasoning and assumes that coherence reflects validity. But coherence and correctness are not the same. A narrative can be smooth without being accurate. An argument can be well formed without being well founded.

The practical consequence follows directly. Verifying sources can expose fabrication, but it cannot detect drift. In a drifted explanation, the sources are real. Checking them confirms that the individual components exist. It does not determine whether the extension is warranted, the limitations are given appropriate weight, or the synthesis is justified. Detecting drift requires evaluation rather than verification. It requires an independent assessment of whether the reasoning genuinely follows from the evidence. That assessment depends on the very domain knowledge that the reader seeking an explanation is most likely to lack. The reader who most needs the explanation is often the reader least able to detect that it has drifted. In plausible but false explanations, the structure of reasoning remains intact. The connection between the reasoning and the evidence no longer fully constrains the conclusion.

6.3 Medical, Legal, and Academic Drift

Where the Cost of Confident Error Is Highest

The consequences of plausible drift vary by domain. In casual conversation, a slightly overstated conclusion may carry little cost. In high-stakes fields, the same structural misalignment can have serious consequences. Three features make certain domains especially vulnerable. They depend on complex reasoning over specialized knowledge that many recipients cannot evaluate independently. They produce outputs that guide real decisions affecting people's lives. They also rely on well-established signals of authority, making it difficult to recognize when those signals are no longer supported by sound reasoning. Medicine, law, and academic scholarship bring these features together most clearly.

In medicine, reasoning often moves from symptoms to possible causes, from causes to treatment options, and from treatment options to risk assessment. Each step involves uncertainty, trade-offs, and context. A plausible explanation may correctly describe a condition and outline a standard treatment pathway, yet fail to account for contraindications, atypical presentations, or patient-specific factors not included in the prompt. The recommendation may appear careful and well structured while quietly overlooking details that would materially change clinical judgment.

Medical knowledge also spans a wide spectrum, from well-established consensus to active debate and frontier uncertainty. Clinical expertise depends not only on knowing the evidence, but also on judging its strength, recognizing where consensus is fragile, and identifying where apparent certainty reflects methodological limitations. AI-generated medical explanations tend to flatten these distinctions. They reproduce the confident style of established medical writing even where a careful clinician would express greater caution. The danger lies not in dramatic mistakes, but in miscalibration. A slightly overstated benefit, an understated risk, or an unqualified generalization can influence decisions when time is limited and cognitive demands are high. The language signals professionalism, while the drift may remain undetected unless someone with relevant expertise reviews the explanation in its full clinical context.

In legal reasoning, drift often appears when correct principles are applied to circumstances where they do not belong. A doctrine may be accurately summarized but extended beyond its jurisdictional limits. A precedent may be described faithfully but interpreted more broadly or more narrowly than the case law supports. The familiar structure of legal reasoning, moving from issue to rule, application, and conclusion, remains intact and creates the appearance of careful analysis. Yet a subtle mismatch between legal rule and factual circumstances can materially change the outcome. Because legal reasoning depends heavily on interpretation, small shifts in emphasis matter. A text may read like competent legal advocacy while relying on an inference that would not withstand careful review by a specialist familiar with the relevant body of law. Someone relying on such analysis to understand legal rights or obligations encounters the language, structure, and confidence of professional reasoning, without any assurance that the connection between legal principle and circumstance has been made correctly.

In academic contexts, drift often appears during synthesis. Individual studies may be summarized accurately yet combined into a stronger consensus than the evidence supports. Limitations may be acknowledged but given too little weight. Correlation may be described in language that subtly suggests causation. None of these errors requires fabricated evidence. Each follows patterns found in legitimate academic writing.

The cumulative effect is gradual distortion. A reader may accept such a synthesis as an accurate representation of the field, particularly when it uses correct terminology and presents a coherent argument. Over time, repeated small overextensions can reshape understanding of what the evidence actually shows. When a drifted synthesis becomes the basis for later work, correcting it is more difficult than identifying a single fabricated citation. The distortion spreads before it becomes visible.

Across these domains, the cost of drift arises not from dramatic falsehoods but from incremental misalignment. The explanation appears responsible. The vocabulary is appropriate. The reasoning unfolds in familiar steps. Confidence is conveyed without obvious warning signs. High-stakes professions manage uncertainty through peer review, professional oversight, and other forms of accountability. Prediction systems do not participate in these processes. They generate the language of careful reasoning without being constrained by the practices that evaluate and correct it. Where decisions affect health, liberty, or the direction of research, the margin for subtle error becomes much smaller. Plausible inaccuracy, delivered with confidence, can therefore exert influence far beyond its visibility. The risk is not that every output is seriously wrong. It is that drift can occur without revealing itself. In high-stakes domains, even modest drift can have significant consequences.

6.4 Authoritative Delivery as Performed Verification

How Confidence Disarms Scepticism

Explanations are evaluated not only for their content, but also for the way they are delivered. In many domains, confidence functions as a signal that careful scrutiny has already taken place. A hesitating speaker invites questions. A carefully qualified yet confident explanation suggests that alternatives have already been considered and resolved. Tone does not determine truth, but it influences how much effort listeners invest in evaluating what they hear. This pattern is not irrational. In ordinary human interaction, confidence often reflects familiarity and preparation. Experts typically speak fluently within their areas of expertise. Years of training compress uncertainty into structured judgment. The smoothness of delivery reflects earlier cognitive effort. It carries the traces of a mind that has worked through the problem, assessed the evidence, and reached a conclusion that can be presented with confidence. When readers relax their critical distance in response to confident delivery, they are applying a heuristic that has long been reliable because it responded to a signal that was also generally reliable.

Prediction systems reproduce that smoothness without performing the cognitive work it traditionally signaled. Large language models are optimized to generate coherent, well-structured continuations. They avoid visible hesitation unless prompted. They do not adjust their tone in proportion to epistemic uncertainty. Their output tends toward grammatical completeness, orderly sequencing, and decisive phrasing. Even when caveats appear, they remain embedded within an otherwise confident response. The result is rhetorical stability. The explanation unfolds without visible struggle. Alternatives are acknowledged and resolved within the same response. The conclusion arrives without hesitation.

For readers, this structure can create the impression that prior verification has already occurred. The absence of visible uncertainty suggests that uncertainty has already been addressed. The orderly progression from premise to conclusion implies disciplined reasoning. The tone conveys resolution rather than exploration. Under these conditions, confident delivery carries an implicit claim: the explanation has already been evaluated by a competent mind and found to be sound. The claim is never stated. It does not need to be. It is conveyed through the form of the explanation. Readers who accept that signal have not verified the explanation themselves. They instead assume that verification has already taken place. Their subsequent reasoning begins from that assumption.

When drift is subtle, this rhetorical stability becomes especially important. Because the explanation appears settled, the impulse to re-examine its premises weakens. Questioning a fluent explanation requires interrupting a line of reasoning that feels complete. The cost of skepticism therefore increases. Confidence functions as a cognitive shortcut. It reduces the perceived need for further checking. In human interaction, this shortcut is often adaptive because confidence frequently reflects competence. In predictive systems, the relationship is unreliable. The tone is generated as part of a learned statistical pattern, not as a reflection of internal certainty, evidence assessment, or accountability. This creates an asymmetry. The system produces language that resembles expert assurance. Readers respond with interpretive habits shaped by interactions with human experts. The resemblance at the surface conceals the structural difference beneath.

The danger is not overt persuasion. It is the quiet reduction of friction. When authoritative delivery creates the appearance of prior verification, skepticism becomes effortful rather than automatic. In cases of fabrication, an anomaly triggers doubt. A missing source or an untraceable case raises suspicion. In cases of drift, no such anomaly appears. Confidence smooths the surface. The explanation feels complete. Even partial verification can reinforce the illusion. A reader may confirm that the cited sources are real, the terminology is correct, or the general principle is legitimate. These checks confirm that the individual components exist. They do not determine whether the reasoning connecting those components is sound. Drift lies in the connections, specifically in the inferences, emphasis, and synthesis. The surface passes inspection. The misalignment remains.

The mechanism is subtle. Nothing in the text announces overreach. Nothing signals that additional caution is needed beyond what is stylistically conventional. Yet tone itself shapes belief. Understanding this mechanism does not eliminate its effect. The cognitive shortcut operates before analytical awareness can intervene. Awareness instead creates a small but important gap between receiving the signal of confidence and acting on it. Within that gap, a question becomes possible: does the confidence being experienced reflect the reliability of the reasoning, or does it arise from stylistic features that have long been associated with trustworthy expertise? That question does not require domain expertise. It requires only the recognition that confident delivery and reliable reasoning have become separable. The signal of prior verification can now be produced without the verification it once reflected. Fluency carries momentum. Confidence directs it.

6.5 Small Errors, Real Consequences

How Minor Inaccuracies Compound

Plausible drift rarely appears as a dramatic falsehood. More often, it takes the form of a small miscalibration. It may involve an overstated implication, an understated limitation, or an inference extended slightly beyond what the evidence supports. In isolation, such deviations may seem negligible. A careful reader may detect them and adjust accordingly. The difficulty arises when small inaccuracies enter a chain of decisions. Many institutional processes are sequential. An initial assessment informs a recommendation. A recommendation informs a plan. A plan guides action. Each stage assumes that the previous one has filtered out significant error. When an early explanation contains subtle drift, later stages may treat that drift as established input.

In medicine, a slightly overstated probability may influence how aggressively a condition is treated. In law, a modest extension of a legal doctrine may shape how a case is framed. In academic research, an inflated sense of consensus may influence which hypotheses are pursued or funded. Each step appears reasonable within its immediate context. The overall direction, however, gradually changes. This effect compounds not only across stages but also over time. A generated explanation may be incorporated into a report. That report may later be cited in other work. The original drift, expressed in fluent language, becomes part of a larger body of information. Later reasoning builds on it without necessarily revisiting its foundation. Because drift operates within genuine material rather than fabricated material, it does not automatically collapse under scrutiny. The studies exist. The legal doctrine is real. The terminology is correct. The error lies in degree, emphasis, or scope. These are features that are less likely to trigger immediate correction.

Confidence accelerates this process. When an explanation appears settled, those who rely on it are less likely to re-examine its foundations. Time pressure and cognitive economy favor acceptance over reanalysis. The explanation becomes part of the background. It becomes something assumed rather than examined. AI-generated drift compounds with particular force for reasons that extend beyond scale alone. A human professional who is uncertain about an early step often carries that uncertainty forward. That uncertainty can encourage caution in later decisions and prompt reconsideration before commitments deepen.

A prediction system presents an uncertain early step with the same confident tone as a well-supported one. No signal of uncertainty carries forward. The sequence proceeds as though the foundation were sound. Because the system cannot revise its earlier outputs in light of later developments, no internal correction takes place. The confident early step remains fixed. It is carried forward without qualification or revision into later decisions that depend on it. The resulting harm is rarely traceable to a single moment. It emerges through accumulation. A slight overstatement here. A selective emphasis there. An unexamined inference carried forward. Together, these small deviations shape outcomes in ways that are disproportionate to the original error. This dynamic is not unique to prediction systems. Human reasoning is also vulnerable to cumulative error. The difference lies in scale, speed, and reuse. Systems that generate fluent explanations in large volumes increase the number of opportunities for subtle drift to enter chains of decision. Their outputs are easily reproduced, circulated, and incorporated into documents, reports, and communications. Small inaccuracies therefore matter not because each one is catastrophic, but because they spread. When plausible error is repeated, cited, or put into practice, it acquires structural significance. In practice, this changes where scrutiny is most valuable. Checking final recommendations identifies errors only after a chain of reasoning has already been built on them. Examining the earliest stages can identify misalignment before it compounds. This includes the initial characterization, the first inference, and the description that sets the direction of later reasoning. The cost of correction at the first step is low. The cost after the chain has grown is much higher.

In AI-assisted professional work, early scrutiny has disproportionate value because drift is subtle. The cost of confident error is measured less by spectacular failure than by gradual divergence. It appears in decisions that are incrementally shaped by reasoning that seemed careful but was never fully grounded.

6.6 Why Drift Is Harder to Defend Against Than Fabrication and What That Means

Fabrication and drift arise from the same underlying mechanism, but they require different forms of protection. Fabrication can be addressed at the level of reference. A source can be searched. A case can be located. A credential can be confirmed. When the referent is absent, the failure becomes visible. The appropriate response is straightforward: check the reference. Drift operates at a different level. The referent exists. The terminology is accurate. The reasoning is structured. Verification confirms that the cited materials are real. It does not confirm that the conclusions drawn from those materials are justified. Protection against drift therefore requires more than confirming that the underlying material exists. It requires evaluating the reasoning. This distinction matters because existence is easier to verify than judgment. It is simpler to determine whether a study was published than to decide whether its findings support a particular conclusion. It is easier to confirm that a legal doctrine exists than to determine whether it applies to a specific case. It is easier to verify that a concept is legitimate than to judge whether it has been applied with the appropriate scope and weight. Drift hides within legitimate material. It passes the first level of scrutiny.

Fluency makes this problem harder. A well-structured explanation reduces the perceived need for further analysis. The absence of obvious anomalies encourages acceptance. Where fabrication creates friction through a broken reference or a missing case, drift creates a smooth path from one conclusion to the next.

There is another important difference. Fabrication is often detected before its effects spread. Once an absent reference is discovered, the foundation of the explanation begins to collapse. Drift, by contrast, can pass through successive stages of reasoning without interruption. Each step inherits the appearance of legitimacy from the one before it. By the time the misalignment becomes visible, it is no longer confined to a single inference. It has shaped the direction of the entire argument.

As predictive systems improve, this smoothness becomes more convincing. Explanations become more coherent, qualifications more contextually appropriate, and tone more professionally aligned. The resemblance to disciplined reasoning leaves less room for doubt to arise naturally. This creates another important difference in how the two forms of error are addressed. Fabrication invites external verification. Drift requires internal evaluation. It requires careful examination of the inferences, the weighting of evidence, the scope of the claims, and the confidence attached to the conclusions. That evaluation demands domain knowledge, time, and cognitive effort.

For people using these systems, the implication is not that every explanation should be treated with suspicion, nor that reliance is impossible. It is that visible signs of correctness are not sufficient evidence of reliability. Those signs include genuine citations, appropriate terminology, and coherent reasoning. The absence of fabrication does not guarantee sound judgment. In high-stakes domains, this distinction is decisive. Protection against fabrication is primarily procedural. Protection against drift depends on careful evaluation.

Prediction without grounding can produce both nonexistent references and subtly misaligned reasoning. The former can be detected by checking the evidence. The latter requires closer examination of the argument itself. That scrutiny need not be indiscriminate. Drift tends to appear at identifiable pressure points: when explanations extend beyond what the evidence supports, when separate findings are combined into stronger conclusions than the evidence justifies, and when conclusions are expressed with greater confidence than the premises warrant. A reader who knows where drift is likely to appear is better positioned than one who either trusts everything or distrusts everything equally. Drift is harder to detect because it does not disrupt the surface of the explanation. It preserves it. The challenge, therefore, is not only to confirm that the individual components are genuine, but also to determine whether they have been connected through sound reasoning.

Closing Reflection

Someone reads an explanation. The sources are real. The argument is well structured. The qualifications appear where they should. The conclusion appears well supported. Nothing in the language signals a problem. This is the more difficult form of error.

Fabrication breaks the link between form and reality. Drift preserves that link at the level of appearance while distorting its meaning. The first can be exposed by checking whether a source, case, or claim exists. The second requires asking whether existing evidence has been interpreted appropriately. The distinction marks a shift in where the vulnerability lies. With fabrication, the weakness lies in the reference. With drift, it lies in the reasoning.

In environments shaped by predictive systems, both forms of error remain possible. As these systems become more fluent, obvious fabrications become easier to detect and, in some settings, easier to limit through external safeguards. Plausible drift, by contrast, becomes harder to recognize. More polished explanations narrow the visible gap between careful analysis and statistical prediction. What appears careful may not reflect sound judgment. What appears complete may not reflect the available evidence. The problem is not simply that prediction can produce errors. Human reasoning has always produced them. The problem is that predictive systems can reproduce the signals of careful reasoning without the practices that have traditionally kept those signals reliable. The gap is subtle. Nothing appears to be missing. The studies, principles, terminology, and structure all appear to be in place. Only the grounding of the reasoning is missing.

This chapter aims to cultivate attention rather than suspicion. The key questions are not only whether the sources are real, but also whether the inference is justified. The concern is not only whether the structure is familiar, but also whether the evidence supports the conclusion. These questions are more difficult. They cannot be answered by checking a database alone. They require judgment. Knowing where plausible drift tends to occur makes that judgment easier. Authority without substance creates a visible flaw. Reasoning without grounding creates a smooth surface that gradually slopes away from the truth. The surface has not changed. What has changed is the way it is interpreted. The next question is whether continued improvements in predictive systems reduce that slope or make it harder to perceive.

CHAPTER 7
When Pattern Systems Meet the Real World

Why the Illusion Deepens as AI Improves

The failures described in the previous chapters are easy to dismiss. Invented citations, nonexistent legal cases, and subtly misleading explanations can all seem like symptoms of an immature technology. Early systems make mistakes. Later systems improve. The history of computing provides many examples of this pattern. Early speech-recognition systems struggled with ordinary conversation. Early translation software produced awkward or incorrect sentences. Early image-recognition systems misclassified everyday objects. In each case, unreliable early performance gradually gave way to dependable systems as datasets expanded, algorithms improved, and computing power increased.

Seen from this perspective, the current limitations of language models appear familiar. If a system occasionally invents a citation, misapplies a concept, or produces a misleading explanation, the most intuitive conclusion is that it is not yet powerful enough. With enough additional training data and computational capacity, the model should eventually converge toward reliable understanding. This assumption is both reasonable and reassuring. It suggests that the difficulties encountered so far are simply the growing pains of a young technology. As models scale, their errors should become less frequent, their reasoning should improve, and the gap between fluent output and genuine understanding should gradually narrow. Call this the consoling assumption.

The consoling assumption rests on a straightforward premise: the problems examined in the previous chapters arise primarily from insufficient scale. If predictive systems make mistakes because they lack enough data or computational capacity, then larger systems should eventually overcome those limitations. Improvement would naturally converge toward something resembling genuine understanding. The question explored in this chapter is whether that premise is correct.

Intellectual honesty requires acknowledging what the consoling assumption gets right. Engineering advances do matter. Retrieval-augmented systems reduce fabricated citations when retrieval is correctly implemented. Improved training methods reduce certain kinds of error. Users of well-engineered systems often receive more reliable outputs than users of earlier models. These improvements are real and deserve recognition. But they do not settle the deeper question. The question is not whether prediction improves with scale. It clearly does.

The central question is whether better prediction narrows the gap between surface performance and the conditions that Chapter 4 identified as essential to genuine understanding. These conditions include grounding in reality, orientation toward truth, the ability to revise beliefs over time, and awareness of epistemic limits. They are not simply more advanced forms of pattern recognition. They describe a fundamentally different relationship between a system and the world. Viewed from this perspective, the failures examined in earlier chapters take on a different meaning. Fabricated authority and plausible but misleading explanations do not arise primarily from a lack of fluency. In many cases, the systems that produce them are already highly fluent. The problem lies elsewhere. What is missing is not expressive power, but the grounding that constrains how information is interpreted, connected, and applied. Prediction may continue to improve while that constraint remains absent. This distinction is crucial.

Engineering improvements change how often a system produces correct outputs in familiar situations. They do not change what the system fundamentally is. They do not change how it relates to truth, evidence, or the boundary between accurate reasoning and plausible error. A more capable predictor is not, for that reason, closer to genuine understanding. The improvement occurs at the level of expression rather than comprehension. If this analysis is correct, continued improvement may produce a counterintuitive result. As predictive systems become more fluent, their outputs may appear increasingly authoritative even though the underlying mechanism remains unchanged. The illusion of intelligence would not fade with progress. It would deepen. The first step in examining this possibility is to examine the intuition itself: the belief that larger and more powerful systems will naturally close the gap between prediction and understanding.

7.1 The Consoling Assumption

Better AI Will Fix These Problems

The expectation that further improvement will resolve these difficulties is not unreasonable. It reflects a familiar pattern in the history of technology. When a new computational system behaves unreliably, the usual explanation is simple:

it does not yet have enough information. Early versions of many technologies behave this way. They perform well under limited conditions but become unstable beyond them. As datasets grow and algorithms improve, the systems become more dependable. Against this historical background, the behavior of modern language models appears easy to explain. If a system occasionally invents a source or produces a misleading explanation, the natural response is to attribute the error to incomplete training. With enough additional examples, the model should eventually learn the correct patterns. In this view, the path forward is straightforward: scale. Larger datasets expose the system to more situations. Larger models capture more subtle statistical relationships. As scale increases, predictions become more refined and more reliable.

Recent progress in artificial intelligence appears to support this view. Each generation of models has produced outputs that are more coherent, more context-sensitive, and more linguistically sophisticated than the last. Tasks once thought to be beyond the reach of machines are now performed with notable competence. These include writing extended explanations, answering open-ended questions, and summarizing complex documents. Under these conditions, progress appears continuous. If today's systems already approximate many forms of human communication, tomorrow's systems may simply approximate them more closely. The remaining limitations appear to be matters of degree rather than kind. That expectation is correct in some respects.

Retrieval augmentation reduces fabricated citations when it is properly implemented. Improved training reduces certain classes of error. These developments represent genuine engineering progress. But the expectation also rests on a deeper assumption that is often left unstated. It assumes that the limitations described in the previous chapters arise from missing patterns rather than from the nature of pattern prediction itself. If the difficulty lies only in incomplete coverage of the world's complexity, more data should eventually fill the gaps. If the difficulty lies deeper, and if some aspects of understanding require something beyond pattern continuation, scaling alone may improve performance without removing the underlying limitation. The distinction is subtle. Both paths produce systems that appear increasingly capable. Both produce outputs that seem more informed and more coherent over time. Yet the implications are very different. If scale gradually closes the gap between prediction and understanding, the problems examined earlier in this book are temporary obstacles on the path to more reliable systems. If it does not, progress may produce a more paradoxical result: systems whose answers appear increasingly authoritative because their fluency improves, even though the underlying mechanism remains unchanged.

To understand why this distinction matters, it is helpful to examine the situations in which pattern-based systems encounter their greatest difficulty. These situations, often called edge cases, provide little guidance from familiar patterns. They also reveal something important about the limits of prediction.

7.2 Edge Cases and Unfamiliar Contexts

Where Pattern Systems Fail Most Quietly

Predictive systems perform best where patterns are abundant. Every system trained on data has a distribution, the range of situations, topics, and contexts represented in its training material. Large language models are trained on enormous collections of text. Within those collections, many situations appear repeatedly: common medical questions, widely discussed legal concepts, familiar scientific explanations, and everyday forms of reasoning. When a prompt resembles these well-represented situations, the model can draw on strong statistical patterns learned during training. The resulting response often appears coherent, structured, and informative. In such cases, the system performs as designed. It identifies similarities between the prompt and patterns in its training data, then generates the continuation that best fits those patterns. Difficulties arise when the situation moves beyond these well-represented regions of the distribution.

Real-world problems often involve circumstances that are rare, ambiguous, or only partly documented. A question may combine several ideas in ways that seldom appear together in the training data. It may involve an emerging technology, a newly enacted regulation, or an unusual medical presentation. Sometimes the problem is not inherently rare but simply underrepresented in the available text. Engineers commonly refer to these situations as edge cases.

In human reasoning, unfamiliar situations often prompt caution. When people recognize that a case differs from familiar patterns, they slow down, gather additional information, or suspend judgment until more evidence becomes available. Recognizing novelty becomes part of the reasoning process itself. Predictive systems do not possess this capacity.

A language model does not determine whether a question falls within a region where its experience is reliable. It does not assess whether its training data adequately represent the situation being described. The system performs the same operation regardless of familiarity. It generates the statistically most plausible continuation of the prompt. When a situation lies outside the well-represented regions of its training distribution, the model relies on partial similarities rather than strong patterns. It fills the gaps through extrapolation. The resulting output may still appear fluent and well organized. The model has learned the language of explanation and argument from millions of examples. Even when the underlying patterns are sparse, it can produce text that resembles competent reasoning. The informational support for that reasoning, however, may be weak.

In unfamiliar situations, predictive systems often rely on analogy. They map a new situation onto the closest familiar one and generate an answer suited to that more common case. This strategy works well in many circumstances. Human reasoning also uses analogy to extend knowledge into new situations. The difference lies in the treatment of uncertainty. Human experts usually recognize when an analogy is tentative. They qualify their conclusions, identify unknowns, and treat their interpretations as provisional. Predictive systems lack this form of epistemic self-awareness. They apply the analogy without recognizing its limits, then present the resulting explanation with the same fluent confidence as answers supported by stronger patterns. The result is not always an obvious mistake. Often the explanation is broadly plausible. Many of its elements may be correct. The difficulty is that the system cannot recognize the limits of its own reliability. Nothing in the language signals this change. The response may appear as polished and confident as any other answer. The difference lies not in the fluency of the explanation, but in the strength of the patterns supporting it.

This silence has an important consequence in high-stakes domains. Routine, well-represented cases in medicine, law, and scholarship are the cases most heavily represented in training data and the ones predictive systems handle most reliably. The situations that require expert judgment most are often the ones least represented in the training distribution.

Readers encountering confident output in such situations are also the ones least likely to possess the independent knowledge needed to recognize that the confidence is unwarranted. The risk of failure therefore becomes greatest where the consequences are most serious and detection is most difficult. This pattern also connects directly to the previous chapters. Fabricated authority often appears at the boundary of the training distribution, when a system is asked about a source that does not exist and extrapolates from nearby citation patterns. Plausible drift often emerges under similar conditions, when questions about synthesis, interpretation, or proportionality fall outside the dense center of the data on which the model relies. Edge-case failure is therefore not a separate phenomenon. It is one way in which those earlier failures arise.

A common assumption is that more data will gradually push these boundaries outward. This is true to a point. Larger and more diverse datasets can extend coverage by bringing some previously rare situations closer to the center of the distribution. Expanding coverage, however, does not eliminate the boundary. Every finite training dataset has an edge. The situations that matter most are often the ones most likely to remain there. More data from the past cannot reliably cover situations that are genuinely new. For this reason, predictive systems often fail most clearly at the edges of unfamiliar situations. Where patterns are sparse, extrapolation becomes unavoidable. When extrapolation replaces grounded knowledge, the risk of error increases. The language, however, remains perfectly fluent.

Recognizing this dynamic clarifies where the limits of pattern prediction first become visible. Unfamiliar situations, however, are only one source of difficulty. Problems can also arise within familiar domains when the context changes in subtle ways. The next section examines how these shifts occur and why they often pass unnoticed.

7.3 Context Shifts That Break Coherence

How Silent Failure Is More Dangerous than Visible Failure

The difficulty for pattern-based systems does not arise only in rare or unfamiliar situations. Even within familiar domains, problems can emerge when the context of a question changes in subtle but meaningful ways. Human reasoning depends heavily on context. A statement that is correct in one setting may become incorrect when conditions change. A legal rule may apply in one jurisdiction but not another. A medical guideline may be appropriate for one group of patients but not for another. A scientific conclusion may depend on time, location, or experimental conditions.

Understanding requires keeping these contextual constraints in view while reasoning. Predictive systems operate differently. Before examining how, it is useful to distinguish two kinds of failure. The first is visible. A fabricated citation, an answer that contradicts well-known facts, or a response that clearly misunderstands the question immediately triggers doubt. The reader recognizes that something is wrong, scrutiny begins, and correction becomes possible. The second kind of failure is silent. The output appears correct. The language is fluent. The explanation is coherent. Yet something has gone wrong in a way that the surface does not reveal.

Context shift is the primary source of silent failure. Silent failure is more dangerous than visible failure because it does not trigger the same corrective response. Large language models generate responses by extending patterns found in their training data. When a prompt resembles situations that occur frequently in those data, the resulting answer often appears coherent and well structured. The system identifies familiar relationships and reproduces them fluently. The difficulty arises when a prompt combines several contextual constraints in ways that are not strongly represented in the patterns the system has learned. Consider a simple example. A legal question may combine a specific jurisdiction, a particular type of contract, and an unusual timeline. Each element may resemble examples found in the training data. The exact combination, however, may be rare.

A predictive system cannot recognize that rarity in the way a human expert can. Instead, it constructs the most statistically plausible response by drawing on the closest familiar patterns. As the response develops, those dominant patterns pull it toward the most common answer to the most common version of the question, rather than the specific question that was asked. The constraint that distinguishes the present situation from the common case may be quietly dropped. The resulting answer addresses the common case fluently and confidently. The language remains smooth. The reasoning appears structured. But the response has drifted away from its original context.

This pattern appears across many domains. A medical explanation may describe a treatment suitable for typical cases while overlooking a constraint introduced earlier in the prompt. A technical answer may apply a general engineering principle while ignoring a parameter that changes the situation. An academic summary may combine findings from studies conducted under different conditions as though they were directly comparable. None of these responses necessarily contain fabricated information. The concepts may be correct. The terminology may be appropriate. The explanation may appear logically organized. What fails is the ability to preserve the original context. Human reasoning maintains a model of the situation under consideration. As new information becomes available, that model is updated. Earlier assumptions may be revised, and conclusions may change accordingly. This ability allows people to track how meaning changes as circumstances change.

Predictive systems approximate this process by keeping recent text within the model's attention. But this approximation does not produce grounded understanding. The model has no independent representation of the world against which each new statement can be evaluated. Instead, it generates a response one token at a time, guided by statistical patterns in the data. When important constraints fall outside those patterns, or when several constraints interact in unusual ways, the system may quietly drop one condition, reinterpret another, or combine assumptions that do not belong together. The explanation remains grammatically coherent and logically organized, even though its connection to the specific situation has weakened. The most important feature of this failure is its silence. Nothing in the language signals that coherence has been compromised. There is no abrupt breakdown, no visible contradiction, and no obvious fabrication. The explanation reads smoothly from beginning to end. The break occurs beneath the surface. This reveals a deeper characteristic of predictive systems: they track pattern similarity rather than stable meaning. As long as each part of the response resembles familiar examples, the system can maintain fluent language even after the overall context has shifted.

Humans can often detect such shifts. When a discussion becomes inconsistent with the original problem, a reader may pause, reconsider the earlier constraints, and revise the line of reasoning. The ability to recognize that a situation has changed, and that earlier assumptions must also change, is a central feature of understanding. Predictive systems lack this ability. They continue generating the most plausible continuation available, even after the underlying situation has changed in subtle but important ways. This failure connects directly to the compounding process described in the previous chapter. Context shifts often introduce small errors at the earliest and most important stages of a decision: framing the problem, interpreting the initial constraints, and assessing the specific features of the situation. A context shift at this stage quietly determines the direction of everything that follows. Because the failure remains silent, nothing interrupts the reasoning before that direction has already been established.

The practical implication is significant. General verification, such as checking whether cited sources exist or whether general principles are correct, cannot reliably detect a context shift. The sources may be genuine. The principles may be correct. The error lies not in the individual components, but in whether the response continues to respect the specific constraints of the original problem. Detecting this kind of failure requires more than verifying individual parts. It requires evaluating whether the explanation remains faithful to the original context from beginning to end. This helps explain why failures in predictive systems often appear not as obvious mistakes, but as quiet misalignments. The language remains coherent while its connection to the original context gradually weakens. It is precisely this gradual drift that prepares the next step in the argument.

Even when the context remains familiar and stable, predictive systems can still struggle when multiple conditions interact in complex ways. Understanding why leads to a broader question: can larger models, more data, and greater computational power overcome these limitations, or do the limits arise from the nature of pattern prediction itself? That question is the focus of the next section.

7.4 Why Scaling Does Not Equal Understanding

The limitations described in the previous sections invite an obvious response. If predictive systems struggle with edge cases and changing contexts today, perhaps the problem is simply one of scale. Larger models trained on larger datasets may gradually overcome these weaknesses. This view is widely shared, and not without reason.

Over the past decade, scaling has produced striking improvements in the performance of large language models. As models have grown and training datasets have expanded, their outputs have become more coherent, more sensitive to context, and better able to handle complex tasks. Problems that once seemed beyond the reach of machines can now be addressed with remarkable fluency. From the outside, the direction of progress appears clear. Each generation of systems performs better than the one before it. It is tempting to see this pattern as a gradual movement toward genuine understanding. But scaling improves a specific capability: pattern recognition.

Larger models capture more subtle statistical relationships within language. Larger datasets expose them to a wider range of linguistic situations. Together, these improvements enable predictive systems to generate more refined continuations of text. In other words, scaling makes prediction more accurate. What scaling does not change is the system's basic objective. A language model is still trained to predict the most probable next token from the sequence that precedes it. The architecture becomes larger and more sophisticated, but the underlying process remains the same. This distinction is fundamental.

The assumption is reassuring because it suggests a gradual convergence. If a system's outputs currently fall short of genuine understanding, and if scaling consistently brings those outputs closer to it, then sufficient scale should eventually close the gap. But this view misunderstands what scaling improves. As a prediction system grows, its pattern recognition becomes more accurate and more stable. It does not acquire a fundamentally different capacity. It develops more refined versions of the capability it already possesses. Better prediction does not bring a system closer to understanding, any more than greater speed in water brings a swimmer closer to flight.

Prediction can become extraordinarily powerful without becoming understanding. A system may learn highly complex statistical patterns without acquiring any grounded connection to the world those patterns describe. The distinction becomes clearer by returning to the criteria for understanding introduced earlier in the book. Genuine understanding requires more than the ability to produce plausible language. It requires at least four additional capacities.

The first is grounding in reality. Understanding connects symbols to the world they represent. Words about disease refer to actual biological processes. Legal concepts correspond to real institutions and procedures. Scaling does not create this connection. A system trained on ten times more medical text has encountered ten times more language about patients, but not a single additional patient. More data provides more language about the world. It does not provide more contact with the world itself. The gap between symbol and referent does not shrink by accumulating more symbols.

The second is orientation toward truth. Understanding includes the ability to distinguish correct beliefs from incorrect ones and to revise them in response to evidence. A larger system does not become more sensitive to whether its outputs are true. It becomes more sensitive to whether its outputs are statistically probable given its training data. In familiar domains, where training data reflects reality reasonably well, probability and truth may coincide. The difference becomes important at the edges: in novel situations, rapidly changing domains, or cases where data is sparse or biased. Scaling improves pattern prediction. It does not make the system more sensitive to the difference between what is probable and what is true.

The third is the ability to revise beliefs over time. Understanding is not static. It changes as new information becomes available and earlier assumptions are corrected. Scaling does not create the persistent subject that such revision requires. Each interaction with a predictive model begins without memory of previous interactions. A larger system may produce better individual responses, but it does not recognize a recurring pattern of error across responses and revise its beliefs accordingly.

The fourth is reflective awareness of epistemic limits. A system capable of understanding can recognize when it does not know something and suspend judgment. Scaling can train a model to produce the language of uncertainty by learning when uncertainty is commonly expressed in its training data. Producing the language of uncertainty, however, is not the same as experiencing genuine uncertainty. The language is a learned pattern, not evidence of an internal epistemic state. A model trained to hedge will hedge where its training data suggests caution. It will not hedge where it is genuinely unreliable but its training data provides no indication of that unreliability.

Scaling prediction does not create these capacities. Increasing the number of parameters allows a model to capture more detailed statistical regularities. Expanding the training data exposes the system to more examples of how language is used. Both developments can improve performance across many tasks. They do not create grounding in the world. They do not introduce mechanisms for tracking truth independently of linguistic patterns. They do not produce persistent beliefs that can be revised over time. They do not generate reflective awareness of epistemic limits. In this sense, scaling refines the appearance of reasoning without changing the underlying structure.

An analogy may help. Increasing the resolution of a digital image makes the picture clearer. Details become sharper, edges become smoother, and colors become more precise. The image does not become the object it depicts. No matter how refined the image becomes, it remains a representation. In the same way, increasing the sophistication of statistical prediction improves the quality of generated language. The outputs become more coherent, more sensitive to context, and more convincing. Better imitation does not change the kind of system performing the imitation. This distinction explains a paradox. As outputs become more accurate and more stable, the temptation to attribute understanding grows stronger. The system appears increasingly competent, and fluency is more readily interpreted as evidence of comprehension. Yet the underlying mechanism remains prediction. Progress reduces visible errors while leaving the underlying limitations unchanged.

Understanding this distinction is essential because it leads to a surprising consequence. Improving predictive systems does not necessarily weaken the illusion of intelligence. In many cases, it strengthens it. That dynamic is the focus of the next section.

7.5 The Illusion Deepens as Systems Improve

If scaling does not transform prediction into understanding, an important question follows: what happens as predictive systems continue to improve? The most intuitive answer is reassuring. As models become more capable, their errors should gradually diminish. Better systems should simply become more reliable versions of earlier ones. In one sense, this expectation is correct. Engineering improvements do reduce certain kinds of error.

Early language models often produced awkward phrasing, inconsistent reasoning, and easily detected fabrications. As models have improved, these visible weaknesses have become less common. Responses are now more fluent, more context-aware, and more internally consistent. From the user's perspective, the systems appear increasingly dependable. Yet this progress produces an unexpected effect. When early systems made obvious mistakes, users remained cautious. A fabricated citation or an incoherent paragraph signaled that the output required scrutiny. The system's limitations were visible, and that visibility encouraged skepticism. As systems improve, those signals begin to disappear. The language becomes smoother. The reasoning appears more carefully structured. Fabrications become less frequent. Responses increasingly resemble the work of a competent human writer. As the surface improves, users naturally become less vigilant.

This shift is subtle but important. Human judgment often relies on heuristic cues, which indicate when careful evaluation is necessary. Visible errors activate those cues. Fluent, coherent responses suppress them. The more reliable a system appears, the less effort readers devote to questioning its conclusions. This response is not irrational. It reflects a useful heuristic: sources that appear reliable generally deserve more trust than those that appear unreliable. The difficulty arises because the signals on which that heuristic depends have become separated from the underlying conditions they once reliably indicated.

The visible failures that are decreasing are not the same as the structural limits that remain. As visible errors become less common, normal processes of trust calibration lead readers to perceive greater reliability. The heuristic responds appropriately to the available signals. The problem is that those signals no longer reliably reflect the underlying process. This dynamic creates a paradox. Improvements that genuinely increase the usefulness of predictive systems can also make their limitations harder to recognize.

The underlying mechanism, however, remains unchanged. The system still generates responses by predicting statistically plausible continuations of text. It still lacks grounding in the world, an orientation toward truth, persistent beliefs, and reflective awareness of its own epistemic limits. As surface performance improves, these structural constraints become less visible. The result is a widening gap between appearance and mechanism. There is another way in which this gap widens over time. When a technology is new and unreliable, users actively evaluate its outputs. Its unreliability is obvious. The outputs are treated as claims to assess rather than as information to rely on.

As the technology becomes more reliable in visible ways, active evaluation tends to give way to more passive use. The tool moves from the foreground of attention into the background of everyday practice. This transition is usually adaptive. Mature technologies recede from conscious scrutiny because they have earned trust. That adaptive process works less well when visible reliability and structural reliability have become separated. Apparent reliability encourages routine use even though the underlying limitations remain. Outputs become part of ordinary workflows at the very point when their structural constraints are least likely to receive careful attention.

There is a further consequence for the confidence mechanism examined in Chapter 6. A system that rarely produces obvious errors creates the impression of prior verification more convincingly than one that fails frequently. The anomalies that once interrupted confident delivery, such as fabricated citations or visible inconsistencies, become less common as the technology improves. As those signals disappear, skepticism becomes less likely to arise. Better systems present the same structural limitations in outputs that are less likely to invite doubt. To the user, the system appears increasingly intelligent. Its explanations are fluent. Its reasoning appears well structured. Its responses are helpful in many practical situations. Together, these experiences create a powerful impression of competence. Yet the process that generates those responses remains the same pattern-based prediction described earlier in the book.

This is the paradox of progress in predictive systems. Improvement strengthens the signals that people normally interpret as evidence of understanding. Fluency increases. Coherence improves. Obvious errors become less common. The temptation to attribute genuine comprehension therefore becomes stronger. Yet the underlying architecture has not crossed the boundary between prediction and understanding. Progress does not dissolve the illusion of intelligence. In many contexts, it makes the illusion more convincing.

As the illusion becomes more convincing, it also becomes quieter. It settles more deeply into everyday practice, where it is less likely to be noticed or examined. Recognizing this pattern is essential because it explains why the limitations described in this chapter are unlikely to disappear through scaling alone. The systems will continue to improve. Their outputs will become increasingly useful and persuasive. For that reason, distinguishing prediction from understanding will become more important, not less.

This insight brings Part Two to its conclusion. Before the discussion turns to the psychology of human vulnerability in the next part of the book, one final step remains. It is necessary to clarify what genuine progress in artificial intelligence would require and how it differs from the improvements delivered by scaling alone.

7.6 The More Convincing Lost Traveler

What Genuine Progress Would Require Versus What Scaling Delivers

The dynamics described in this chapter become clearer through a familiar example. Imagine a traveler who is asked for directions in an unfamiliar city. If the traveler genuinely knows the city, the answer reflects that knowledge. The directions are grounded in an understanding of streets, landmarks, and spatial relationships. When uncertainty arises, the traveler may hesitate, reconsider, or admit that a particular route is unclear.

Now imagine a different traveler who has never visited the city but has read thousands of descriptions of it. This traveler has studied travel guides, maps, and conversations about local routes. When asked for directions, the traveler can produce explanations that sound remarkably plausible. Street names appear in the correct form. Landmarks are described in ways that suggest genuine familiarity. The explanation may even resemble directions that would work in many common situations. But the traveler does not know the city. The answer is assembled from patterns found in descriptions rather than from direct knowledge of the environment. When the situation differs from those patterns, such as an unusual starting point, a temporary road closure, or a rarely discussed neighborhood, the explanation may quietly drift away from reality.

Now imagine that this second traveler becomes increasingly skilled at producing convincing explanations. With greater exposure to maps and travel writing, the descriptions become more detailed and fluent. The directions sound increasingly authoritative. Yet the traveler is still lost. Greater skill has made the performance more convincing. It has not supplied the missing orientation. The more convincing the lost traveler becomes, the more dangerous the directions.

Predictive systems operate in a similar way. Scaling increases the richness and accuracy of the patterns a model can reproduce. With more parameters and more data, the system becomes better at generating explanations that resemble those produced by people who understand a subject. But scaling does not provide the missing element: a grounded orientation toward the world described by the language. A predictive model can learn broad statistical regularities in how people discuss diseases, legal doctrines, engineering systems, or historical events. It can generate explanations that closely resemble expert discourse in those fields. What it does not acquire is the relationship to reality that allows experts to judge whether those explanations are correct. Achieving that requires more than increasingly accurate pattern recognition.

What Genuine Progress Would Require

Genuine progress toward understanding would require systems that connect symbols to the world they describe. It would require mechanisms that distinguish probable statements from true ones, revise conclusions when evidence changes, and recognize when a situation lies beyond the system's reliable knowledge. In other words, it would require the properties identified earlier in this book as essential to understanding: grounding, truth orientation, the ability to revise conclusions over time, and awareness of epistemic limits. Scaling prediction does not produce these capacities.

Genuine progress toward grounding would require systems that are not only trained on language about the world but also connected to the world itself. Such systems would anchor their symbolic representations to reality through something more than statistical patterns in text. Accumulating more language about patients is not the same as encountering patients. Accumulating more language about legal proceedings is not the same as participating in them or being accountable within them. More data provides more descriptions of the world. It does not provide more contact with the world those descriptions refer to.

Genuine progress toward reflective awareness would require systems with access to their own epistemic states. Such systems would distinguish between well-supported conclusions and speculative extrapolation within their own reasoning processes. The language of uncertainty produced by current systems is not the same thing. It is a learned stylistic pattern associated with situations in which uncertainty is conventionally expressed. Genuine epistemic awareness would require expressed uncertainty to reflect actual uncertainty rather than linguistic convention.

The direction of genuine progress and the direction of scaling are therefore different. Scaling improves prediction, producing responses that are more accurate, coherent, and useful across many well-represented tasks. Genuine progress moves toward a system that is grounded in reality, oriented toward truth, able to revise its conclusions, and aware of its epistemic limits. Reaching that goal requires something fundamentally different: a different relationship between the system and the world. Scaling and understanding therefore follow different paths. What scaling delivers instead is a traveler who becomes increasingly articulate while remaining fundamentally disoriented. This is why improvement alone does not dissolve the illusion of intelligence. It strengthens the signals that human beings naturally interpret as evidence of understanding. The traveler sounds increasingly confident. The directions sound increasingly precise. Yet the traveler is still navigating through patterns of description rather than through the city itself.

The claim that scaling does not produce understanding is not a claim that current AI systems lack value. On the contrary, they are genuinely useful, often remarkably so, across many tasks in well-represented domains. Improvements produced by scaling make these systems more helpful to more people in more contexts. A lost traveler who knows the familiar parts of a city well can still be a useful guide within those areas. The danger arises when trust earned in familiar territory extends into situations where that traveler's orientation quietly fails.

Recognizing this distinction clarifies the central claim of this chapter. The limitations described here are not temporary defects that will disappear as models grow larger. They arise from the difference between predicting language about the world and knowing the world that language describes. The more fluent the predictions become, the easier it is to mistake one for the other. This insight prepares the final step of the argument. If the limits of predictive systems are structural rather than temporary, the expectation that scaling alone will eliminate them must be reconsidered. The reassuring assumption with which this chapter began can now be set aside.

7.7 Structural Limits Persist

The Consoling Escape Route Is Closed

The argument developed across this part of the book can now be viewed as a whole. Chapter 5 examined fabricated authority: the imitation of scholarly and expert signals without the underlying knowledge that gives them meaning. Fabricated citations, invented cases, and synthetic expertise emerged as structural outcomes of systems that generate statistically likely continuations without an inherent connection to the reality they describe. Chapter 6 turned to a subtler and more difficult problem: plausible error. These explanations followed the form of sound reasoning while gradually drifting away from the truth. The sources were real. The terminology was accurate. Yet the absence of fabrication did not ensure sound judgment. Confident delivery created the impression that the claims had already been verified when they had not. Chapter 7 addressed the deeper question raised by these findings: whether such failures are temporary limitations that will disappear as these systems improve.

The most intuitive answer was also the most reassuring. With more data, larger models, and better engineering, predictive systems should gradually move toward genuine understanding. This chapter has examined that assumption closely. Scaling improves prediction. It increases fluency, coherence, and the ability to reproduce complex linguistic patterns. As models grow larger and training datasets expand, their outputs become more capable and useful across a wide range of familiar tasks. Yet scaling does not change the underlying mechanism. Predictive systems generate responses by extending statistical patterns in language. They do not possess the properties that earlier chapters identified as essential to understanding: grounding in reality, orientation toward truth, the ability to revise commitments over time, and awareness of their own epistemic limits. Without these properties, certain forms of failure remain.

At the edges of the training distribution, where patterns are sparse, systems must extrapolate. Even within familiar domains, subtle changes in context can quietly disrupt coherence. As models improve, obvious errors become less common while the underlying limitations remain. Progress refines the output, but it does not change the mechanism. For this reason, the failures described in the preceding chapters should not be viewed as temporary defects that scaling alone will correct. They arise from the difference between predicting language about the world and knowing the world that language describes. That distinction does not disappear as systems become more capable. It becomes harder to recognize. This helps explain why improvement can deepen the illusion of intelligence rather than remove it. As predictive systems become more fluent and useful, the signals that people typically interpret as evidence of understanding become stronger. Confidence appears more justified. Skepticism becomes less instinctive. Yet the underlying limits remain beneath an increasingly convincing surface.

Recognizing these limits does not require rejecting predictive systems or denying their usefulness. In domains where pattern-based reasoning works well, these models can be powerful tools. The gains achieved through scaling are real, and they expand the range of tasks these systems can support. Yet usefulness should not be confused with understanding.

Part Two provides not a basis for rejection, but a framework for orientation. Readers who understand the structural argument are better equipped to recognize where failures are most likely to occur, what questions to ask, and why some domains and outputs deserve closer scrutiny. This framework has limits. Understanding how the system works does not eliminate its effects, and confidence remains persuasive even when its source is recognized. Even so, this knowledge matters. It changes what can be noticed and what questions can be asked.

The reassuring belief that greater scale will erase the distinction between prediction and understanding cannot support the expectations placed upon it. The limits examined in this part of the book are not simply engineering problems. They arise from the architecture of predictive systems themselves. A reader finishes an explanation on a screen. The sources are real. The argument is coherent. The conclusion is presented with confidence. The surface has not changed. The interpretation has. There is now a clearer understanding of where failures are most likely to occur, a recognition that fluency and reliability can diverge, and a set of questions that the surface does not invite but that Part Two has made available. Once acquired, that awareness is not easily set aside.

Part Two has provided a necessary clarification. The illusion of intelligence does not arise only from isolated errors. It arises from a deeper misreading: the tendency to treat fluent prediction as evidence of genuine understanding. The next part of the book shifts attention from the machine to the human mind. If the limitations of predictive systems are structural, an important question remains. Why do intelligent, educated, and skeptical people so readily interpret their outputs as signs of understanding? Answering that question requires an examination of the cognitive habits that shape how human beings interpret fluent language.

PART THREE
WHY THE ILLUSION PERSUADES

The Psychology and Cognitive Science of Human Vulnerability

The mirror now turns toward the reader. Parts One and Two looked at the machine. Part Three explains why human minds, including intelligent, educated, and skeptical minds, remain vulnerable to the illusion. It examines three forces that operate across different timescales: immediate, longitudinal, and civilizational.

CHAPTER 8
The Fluency Bias

Why Smooth Language Feels True and Why Awareness Does Not Eliminate the Bias

The previous parts of this book examined the machine. They explained how large language models generate fluent responses without the grounding, truth-tracking, and self-awareness that characterize genuine understanding. The resulting failures arise from the architecture of predictive systems: fabricated authority, plausible but misleading reasoning, and silent contextual drift. Yet a puzzle remains. If these limitations are structural, why are the outputs of such systems so often interpreted as signs of intelligence? Why do responses generated through statistical prediction appear to come from an understanding mind? Why does this happen even among intelligent, educated, and skeptical readers who know the limitations of AI and approach its outputs with caution? The answer lies not only in the design of the machine, but also in the habits of the human mind that encounters it.

For most of human history, fluent language was a reliable signal of intelligence. Producing coherent and articulate speech required a mind capable of reasoning, memory, and social understanding. When language sounded thoughtful, it was almost always produced by someone who was thinking. Human cognition therefore developed a practical shortcut. Rather than evaluating every statement from first principles, people came to treat fluency itself as evidence of competence. A smooth explanation feels like understanding. Clear structure feels like reasoning. Confident delivery feels like knowledge. In everyday life, this shortcut works remarkably well. It allows people to navigate conversations, evaluate explanations, and recognize expertise without verifying every claim in detail. Much of social and intellectual life depends on this form of trust.

Predictive language systems introduce a new condition. For the first time, language can display the outward signals of understanding without the cognitive processes that historically produced those signals. The words remain fluent. The structure remains persuasive. What has changed is the relationship between the signal and the mind behind it. The cognitive machinery that interprets fluency as reliability has not changed. The environment in which that machinery operates has. Throughout most of human communicative history, fluent language and confident delivery were reliable guides because they reflected genuine cognitive work. Predictive systems reproduce those same surface features without performing that work. The mechanism of interpretation remains the same. The signal it interprets has changed. The machine does not create the illusion alone. The human mind completes it. Explaining why this happens requires examining one of the most thoroughly studied features of human cognition: the tendency to experience ease of processing as evidence of truth. Psychologists refer to this tendency as the fluency bias.

In Part Three, the focus therefore turns toward the reader, not in accusation, but in explanation. Minds that experience this illusion are not credulous or insufficiently critical. They are adapted to a communicative environment that has changed rapidly and recently. Explaining how this cognitive machinery operates, why it is activated, and why it remains active even when its operation is understood, is the task of this chapter.

The sections that follow examine how the fluency bias operates, why fluent language is such a powerful trigger, and why even intelligent and well-informed readers remain vulnerable to its effects. They conclude with a finding that is both uncomfortable and necessary: awareness of the bias alone does not provide protection against it. Partial protection comes not from awareness alone, but from the deliberate cognitive habits that awareness makes possible. The illusion of intelligence persists not only because machines produce convincing language, but also because human minds are predisposed to trust it.

8.1 Cognitive Ease and Perceived Truth

Why Reduced Effort Feels like Correctness

Human judgment is not designed to examine every statement through careful analysis. Most of the time, the mind relies on faster signals that indicate whether something deserves closer scrutiny. One of the strongest of these signals is ease of processing. When information is easy to read, understand, and follow, it tends to feel more credible. Psychologists describe this experience as processing fluency. It is the subjective feeling that information is easy to process. Processing fluency is not a belief. It is a feeling.

A clearly structured sentence requires less mental effort to understand. An explanation that follows a familiar pattern is easier to follow than one that is disorganized. Familiar words are recognized more quickly than unfamiliar ones.

When the mind processes information with little friction, the experience feels smooth. And smoothness feels right.

A large body of psychological research shows that people often interpret this feeling of ease as a sign of accuracy. Statements that are easier to read are judged to be more truthful than identical statements presented in harder-to-read fonts. Repeated claims seem more believable than new ones because repetition makes them easier to process. Explanations presented in clear, well-structured language are often judged to be more reliable than explanations containing the same information expressed less fluently.

Researchers first documented this perceived-truth effect systematically, and later studies replicated it across many experimental settings, including visual presentation, auditory processing, written argument, and social judgment. The mind interprets ease as evidence. This tendency is not arbitrary. In the environments where human cognition evolved, information that was easy to process was often more reliable. Familiar statements were more likely to be repeated because they reflected shared knowledge. Clear explanations usually came from people who genuinely understood what they were explaining. Cognitive ease therefore served as a practical proxy for credibility. It was a useful heuristic rather than a systematic error.

The mechanism, however, operates automatically. The mind does not pause to ask why something feels easy to process. It registers the experience and uses it as a cue for judgment. The feeling of fluency arises before deliberate reasoning begins and quietly shapes the interpretation that follows. This is why fluency can influence judgment even when caution is intended. Awareness does not prevent the initial signal from operating. It only allows later reasoning to reconsider the impression that the signal created. That reconsideration begins from a position already shaped by the fluency effect rather than from a neutral starting point.

Deliberate evaluation can override the conclusion that cognitive ease encourages. It cannot prevent cognitive ease from operating before evaluation begins. The crucial point is temporal. Fluency operates before reflection. It belongs to the fast, intuitive layer of cognition that forms impressions before deliberate analysis begins. When language is smooth, structured, and confident, the mind experiences ease. That ease is naturally interpreted as a sign that the explanation is sound.

Several features of language trigger this effect independently, and predictive systems combine them with particular force. Grammatical correctness reduces processing friction. Familiar vocabulary allows comprehension to proceed without interruption. Structural coherence, in which ideas follow recognizable logical sequences, creates the impression that an argument is sound rather than merely well written. Decisive phrasing removes the friction of hesitation and qualification, allowing statements to appear complete and settled. Each of these features contributes to processing fluency on its own.

Large language models generate all of these features at the same time. The resulting cognitive ease can therefore be substantial. In ordinary human communication, this shortcut worked remarkably well. Fluency was earned. It reflected knowledge, experience, and disciplined reasoning expressed through clear language. Trusting fluent speakers was therefore a reliable heuristic because fluency and reliability were usually linked. Predictive systems have broken that relationship. They produce fluency without performing the cognitive work that fluency historically signaled. The surface cues that cognitive ease interprets as signs of reliability remain present. The underlying qualities those cues once reflected are absent. A system does not need to understand in order to appear convincing. It only needs to produce language that feels easy to understand. That feeling is often enough to create the impression that understanding is present.

The next section examines how this effect becomes even stronger when fluency is mistaken not only for clarity, but also for substance.

8.2 Mistaking Smoothness for Substance

Why AI Amplifies the Fluency Bias

The fluency bias described in the previous section operates in everyday communication between people. Clear explanations feel more convincing than confused ones. Smooth arguments are easier to trust than disorganized ones. This tendency shapes how readers evaluate essays, lectures, conversations, and expert advice. But the environments in which this bias evolved included an important constraint.

Human communication is imperfect. Even highly knowledgeable people hesitate while speaking. They search for words, revise sentences as they speak, and sometimes struggle to organize their thoughts clearly. Expertise improves clarity, but it does not remove the small irregularities of natural language. These irregularities play a subtle role in judgment. They remind listeners that an explanation is being constructed by a human mind in real time. Pauses, qualifications, and occasional rough edges reveal the cognitive effort involved in working through a problem. They also reveal an epistemic constraint. Human fluency is limited by the match between what a person says and what that person actually knows. Sustaining a confident explanation beyond the limits of genuine understanding is difficult. The imperfections mark where that limit has been reached. In this sense, they often reflect honesty rather than failure. Predictive language systems remove many of these signals.

Large language models generate text that is grammatically clean, well organized, and largely free from the hesitations that characterize human speech and writing. Sentences arrive fully formed. Explanations unfold in an orderly sequence. Transitions between ideas appear deliberate and composed. The result is language that is unusually easy to process. From the perspective of cognitive fluency, this matters. The human mind tends to treat smoothness as evidence that the underlying reasoning is sound. When friction disappears from language, comprehension feels almost effortless. This does not simply improve readability. It changes how credibility is judged.

A human expert explaining a complex issue may struggle to compress years of knowledge into a brief explanation. The result may include digressions, reformulations, and moments of uncertainty. These features reflect both the complexity of the subject and the difficulty of expressing it clearly. A predictive model, by contrast, does not struggle with the problem itself. It generates a statistical continuation of language about the problem. The explanation therefore appears complete from the outset. The text has the structure of reasoning without the visible traces of the reasoning process.

When a human expert delivers a fluent explanation, that fluency reflects genuine cognitive work. It reflects knowledge shaped into clear language through engagement with the subject. When a predictive system produces the same surface, the fluency results from statistical optimization for coherent continuation. Human cognition cannot distinguish between these two forms of fluency from the language alone. Both appear similar on the surface. Both trigger the same fluency effect. The absence of friction therefore creates a powerful impression: the explanation feels settled.

Several features of predictive systems strengthen this effect. Their vocabulary is consistently accessible and rarely drifts into obscure terminology. Sentences are syntactically balanced. Paragraphs follow familiar patterns that readers recognize as well-structured writing. Equally important, responses arrive complete. When asked a question, the system rarely pauses before producing an answer. The explanation appears immediately as a finished product. Each of these features increases processing fluency. Together, they produce language that is exceptionally easy to read, easy to follow, and easy to accept.

From the perspective of cognitive psychology, predictive systems function as a superstimulus for the fluency bias. The bias evolved to respond to signals of human expertise because those signals were constrained by epistemic reality. These signals included fluency, coherence, and confident delivery. They were difficult to sustain without genuine understanding. Predictive systems reproduce the same signals without that constraint. Every feature that promotes cognitive ease is present. Many features that temper the effect in human communication are largely absent. These include hesitation, qualification, variation, and visible limits of knowledge.

As a result, the mechanism responds more strongly than it does in ordinary human interaction because the stimulus exceeds the conditions under which the mechanism evolved. In this sense, predictive systems outperform human speakers in triggering the fluency bias. Not because they possess deeper understanding, but because they reproduce the signals associated with understanding more consistently than human speakers do. The effect is subtle. Readers often interpret the smoothness of the language as evidence that the system has reasoned carefully about the question. Yet the fluency of the explanation arises from statistical language generation rather than from the cognitive processes that historically produced fluent explanations in human experts.

The smooth surface therefore encourages a mistaken inference: that clarity of expression reflects depth of understanding. In ordinary human communication, that inference is often justified. In the presence of predictive systems, it becomes less reliable. Readers encounter language that resembles the product of careful reasoning even when the system generating it has not reasoned about the problem. In this context, fluency no longer signals substance.

There is a final irony. The fluency bias is not misled because it is functioning incorrectly. It responds exactly as it evolved to respond. The signal is genuinely present. What is absent is the underlying understanding that the signal historically indicated.

A reader who trusts fluent AI output is not applying the bias incorrectly. The bias is responding appropriately to a stimulus it did not evolve to encounter. The next section examines another consequence of this effect. Highly fluent language often reduces the level of scrutiny applied to the claims it contains. Style begins to perform work that careful evaluation would otherwise perform.

8.3 Why Style Lowers Scrutiny

How Fluency Substitutes for Evaluation

The effects described in the previous sections do not stop at shaping how language feels. They also influence how readers decide whether further evaluation is necessary. When information is difficult to process, attention usually increases. Confusing explanations prompt questions. Awkward sentences slow reading. Disorganized arguments signal that closer inspection may be needed.

Fluent language produces the opposite response. When an explanation is easy to follow, clearly structured, and confidently delivered, readers experience cognitive ease. That ease does more than create a sense of credibility. It also reduces the perceived need for verification. The explanation creates the impression that the intellectual work has already been done. This effect can be understood as a form of implicit epistemic delegation. Instead of evaluating the reasoning behind a claim, readers treat the smoothness of the explanation as evidence that the reasoning has already been carried out by the speaker or writer.

In ordinary human communication, this shortcut is often justified. Producing a clear explanation usually requires genuine understanding. When a knowledgeable person condenses complex reasoning into a concise account, the resulting fluency reflects intellectual work that has already taken place. In this sense, style is the visible expression of prior thinking.

From the outside, careful reasoning has recognizable features. It acknowledges a question before answering it. It organizes ideas in a logical sequence. It qualifies claims when the evidence is mixed. It recognizes counterarguments. It reaches conclusions that match the available evidence. These features result from genuine epistemic work. They are also recurring patterns. A system trained on millions of examples of careful reasoning can learn what those patterns look like without performing the reasoning they usually signal. The structure of deliberation is present. The deliberation itself is not.

Readers encountering that structure receive the outward form of thought. The evaluative impulse that normally responds when work appears unfinished instead receives the impression that the work has already been completed. This shortcut has important consequences. When language is highly fluent, readers tend to devote less cognitive effort to evaluating the claims it contains. Questions that might otherwise arise become less likely to be asked: How is this known? What assumptions are being made? Are alternative explanations possible? The structure of the explanation suggests that these questions have already been addressed. Research on persuasion shows that when information is easy to process, people rely more on intuitive judgment and less on careful analysis. Ease of processing signals that the situation is familiar and manageable. Under those conditions, the mind conserves effort and accepts explanations with minimal resistance.

Fluency therefore performs an important role before deliberate evaluation begins. An explanation arrives already carrying the appearance of credibility. The reader encounters a conclusion that seems to have been carefully reasoned, even when the reasoning itself has not been examined closely. Predictive language systems take advantage of this tendency with unusual efficiency. Their outputs are consistently fluent. They are grammatically polished, logically structured, and delivered without hesitation. As a result, they produce the very signals that encourage readers to relax evaluative scrutiny. The explanation feels complete. The reasoning appears settled. Surface coherence suggests that careful thinking has already taken place. In predictive systems, however, that inference is unreliable.

The fluency of the explanation reflects statistical patterns in language rather than a reasoning process that has worked through the problem. Yet the reader's cognitive system responds to these surface signals much as it would to the fluent explanation of a human expert. Style takes the place of scrutiny. The consequence is subtle but significant. Readers do not necessarily accept every statement produced by a predictive system. More often, they treat the output as a reasonable starting point, a plausible account that appears coherent enough to accept provisionally. What disappears in this process is friction.

Critical thinking often begins with small disruptions: a confusing phrase, an unexplained step in an argument, or a moment of uncertainty that invites further questioning. Highly fluent language removes many of these triggers. The explanation moves smoothly from premise to conclusion, leaving little reason to pause. The impulse to evaluate responds to the appearance of completion. When the work appears to have been done already, the scrutiny that might reveal the difference between appearance and reality never fully engages. Over time, this pattern accumulates. Readers who repeatedly encounter explanations that appear to have completed the intellectual work in advance may gradually lose the habit of doing that work independently. It does not happen all at once. It develops through the absence of the opportunities that sustain the habit. The skill weakens because it is no longer exercised. Fluency does more than persuade. It quiets the impulse to question.

The next section examines the deeper cognitive structure behind this tendency. It examines the mental shortcut that treats articulate language as a signal of authority.

8.4 The Mind's Shortcut to Authority

The Psychological Machinery beneath the Historical Cognitive Shortcut

The fluency bias and the reduction in scrutiny described in the previous sections are not isolated quirks of judgment. They reflect a deeper cognitive shortcut that has long shaped how expertise is evaluated. In everyday life, there is rarely enough time or knowledge to verify every claim independently. Most fields of knowledge are specialized. Medicine, law, engineering, economics, and science all require years of study. Under these conditions, human cognition relies on signals that help distinguish genuine expertise from its absence.

Language has historically been one of the most reliable of those signals. Explaining a subject clearly usually requires genuine understanding. Articulate language tends to emerge from familiarity with concepts, repeated engagement with problems, and the gradual refinement of ideas through experience and reflection. People who understand a subject well are typically able to organize it coherently, describe it with precision, and respond to questions through structured reasoning. Over time, human cognition internalized this pattern. Rather than evaluating expertise from first principles, the mind adopted a practical rule of thumb: clear explanation signals competence. When a speaker presents an issue in structured, confident language, listeners naturally infer that the speaker possesses knowledge.

Social psychologists have studied this tendency extensively. From Stanley Milgram's work on deference to authority to Robert Cialdini's analysis of persuasive signals of expertise, the findings are consistent. Implicit signals of competence trigger deference almost as reliably as formal credentials. These signals include confident delivery, organized explanation, and specialized but accessible vocabulary. This inference often works remarkably well. Much of education depends on it. Skilled teachers communicate complex ideas through explanations that are easier to follow than the reasoning that produced them. The fluency of the explanation reflects genuine cognitive work completed beforehand. The mind therefore treats articulate language as evidence.

The basis of this shortcut extends beyond individual habit. Human children enter a world they cannot navigate independently. Survival and development depend on acquiring knowledge that cannot be discovered through individual experience alone. A disposition toward epistemic deference allows children to learn rapidly by relying on the accumulated knowledge of others. It involves accepting information from people who display signals of competence. This disposition does not disappear in adulthood. It becomes more selective and more sensitive to domain-specific signals. Adults can question sources, compare evidence, and reject claims when knowledge and motivation permit. Yet the underlying tendency to defer remains. It is not a peripheral feature of cognition. It is a fundamental part of how knowledge passes from one generation to the next. Each generation inherits what earlier generations discovered without having to rediscover it. This process usually operates below conscious awareness. Readers and listeners do not deliberately reason that fluent language implies understanding. The impression of authority emerges automatically.

The structure of an explanation carries its own signal. When its parts fit together, its logic flows, and its conclusion follows from its premises, the mind registers that coherence not only as clarity but also as evidence of the speaker's competence. The reader does not consciously think, "This explanation is coherent, therefore the speaker understands the subject." The attribution occurs during the act of comprehension itself. Understanding the explanation and evaluating its source are experienced as parts of the same process. This mechanism helps explain why articulate speakers often appear more knowledgeable than hesitant ones, even when their underlying knowledge is the same. It also explains why confident explanations are frequently taken as evidence of expertise.

For most of human history, this shortcut functioned well because the signal and the underlying reality were closely linked. Producing sustained, coherent explanations without genuine understanding was difficult. The effort required to maintain the appearance of expertise typically revealed its absence. Predictive language systems disrupt this relationship. Large language models can generate explanations that display the outward signs of expertise without possessing the understanding those signs historically signaled. These signs include clear structure, confident delivery, and a coherent progression of ideas. The language resembles expert discourse because it reproduces the patterns through which knowledgeable people express their ideas. To the human mind, however, the signals appear the same. The shortcut that once helped identify expertise now responds to language that can be produced without the cognitive processes that once made those signals reliable. The mind's shortcut to authority therefore continues to operate as it always has. What has changed is the environment in which it operates.

The fluency bias, the authority heuristic, and the coherence-as-competence inference do not operate independently. Together, they form a mutually reinforcing system. Fluent output creates cognitive ease, which is experienced as credibility. That same fluency activates the authority heuristic because articulate language signals expertise. Coherent structure triggers the inference that disciplined reasoning has taken place. Each mechanism produces a signal of reliability, and each signal strengthens the others. The resulting experience is more than the impression that the output is probably correct. It is the impression that the source knows, has reasoned carefully, and can therefore be trusted. Readers encounter language that displays the signs of expertise while lacking the epistemic grounding those signs historically represented. The inference from articulation to authority still occurs, but the relationship that once justified it has weakened. The result is not irrational trust. It is a cognitive shortcut operating in an environment that has recently changed.

Understanding this shortcut does not disable it. These mechanisms operate before deliberate evaluation begins. By the time a reader consciously evaluates an explanation, the combined impression has already formed: that the source is authoritative, that the reasoning has been carefully developed, and that the conclusion can be accepted provisionally. Deliberate evaluation works against that initial impression. It does not prevent the impression from forming. This dynamic helps explain why the illusion of intelligence persists even among careful readers. The signals that human cognition has long used to identify knowledge are present in the outputs of predictive systems. The machinery of judgment responds accordingly.

The next section examines a further consequence of this dynamic: why even highly educated individuals and domain experts are not immune to the influence of fluency.

8.5 Why Expertise Does Not Protect Against the Fluency Bias

How the Fluency Bias Operates across Intelligence and Education Levels

The mechanisms described in the previous sections might seem, at first glance, to affect mainly inexperienced readers. If fluency bias leads people to mistake smooth explanations for reliable reasoning, it is natural to assume that education and expertise would offer protection. Individuals trained in critical thinking, scientific reasoning, or professional analysis might be expected to distinguish articulate language from genuine understanding.

In practice, the picture is more complicated. The cognitive processes that produce fluency effects operate before deliberate evaluation begins. Cognitive ease is experienced automatically. The feeling that an explanation makes sense arises before the reader consciously examines whether the reasoning is sound. By the time careful analysis begins, the initial impression has already formed.

Education and intelligence influence what happens next. Experienced readers may be better able to identify errors, question assumptions, or detect contradictions once analysis begins. The initial signal, however, the sense that an explanation is coherent and credible, arises through the same cognitive processes in experts and non-experts alike. Expertise does not prevent the bias from operating. It only increases the likelihood that the initial impression will later be corrected.

Psychological research shows that many cognitive heuristics operate in this way. They produce rapid intuitive judgments that guide attention and interpretation before conscious reasoning begins. Studies of fluency effects across different education levels show that higher education does not eliminate susceptibility. It changes the cues that trigger it. Research on expert judgment in fields such as medicine, law, and finance likewise shows that experts remain vulnerable to systematic cognitive biases that expertise does not reliably remove.

Fluency bias is not unusual in this respect. It operates across levels of intelligence and education because it functions at a level of cognitive processing that deliberate expertise cannot fully reach. Experts therefore experience the same initial impression of fluency as everyone else. In some situations, expertise can even strengthen the effect. Specialists become accustomed to reading well-structured arguments and technically competent explanations. When an explanation follows the familiar patterns of reasoning within a field, it can feel especially persuasive. The coherence of the argument matches patterns encountered repeatedly through experience.

This effect can be described as domain pattern reinforcement. Expertise develops through repeated exposure to the characteristic patterns of a field. These include common forms of argument, established approaches to problems, and familiar ways of organizing knowledge. When AI-generated output reproduces these patterns accurately, it matches the expert's internal representation of what sound reasoning looks like. That match is often experienced, below conscious awareness, as a signal of validity. Yet the errors most likely to appear in AI-generated explanations within expert domains are precisely those that pattern recognition is least likely to detect. The patterns themselves may be correct. The drift occurs in the connections between them: extending a principle beyond its proper scope, combining ideas in a subtly misleading way, or expressing unwarranted confidence in a conclusion. Detecting these errors requires disciplined evaluation, the very process that fluency tends to suppress.

There is a further complication. Part of expertise involves knowing which knowledge within a field is well established and which remains uncertain. AI-generated output creates a problem of calibration. The system often presents contested issues with the same confidence as settled ones. For topics an expert knows well, this mismatch may be recognized. But in adjacent specialties or frontier areas, where expert judgment is often needed most, it may go unnoticed. The confident presentation still has its effect. The shortcut that links confidence with authority is activated. The expert may accept the system's level of confidence even when independent evaluation is difficult.

Expertise is also highly domain-specific. A physician may quickly recognize weaknesses in a medical explanation, yet evaluate a legal argument using the same general cues available to a non-specialist. An engineer may identify a technical error with ease while judging a historical account mainly through its coherence and fluency. Even highly educated people therefore spend much of their intellectual lives outside their own areas of expertise. In those situations, the cognitive shortcuts described in this chapter remain fully active.

The interaction between expertise and fluency bias follows a distinctive pattern. Experts may detect errors within their own field once careful analysis begins. But fluency still shapes their initial interpretation. The explanation first appears plausible. Weaknesses may become visible only after closer examination. That second stage of evaluation, however, does not always occur. Under ordinary reading conditions, few people examine every explanation with sustained analytical effort. Time is limited. Attention is divided. Much of everyday information processing depends on rapid judgments about what appears credible enough for provisional acceptance. Under these conditions, fluency bias operates across all levels of intelligence. The important difference between individuals is not whether the bias occurs, but how often it is corrected. Some readers examine explanations more carefully. Others move on after the first impression of plausibility. Yet the initial impression arises from the same cognitive processes in both cases: the sense that the explanation is coherent, reasonable, and competently expressed.

There is another point worth noting. Highly educated readers often have strong confidence in their ability to evaluate arguments. They are trained to assess evidence, identify weak reasoning, and detect flawed arguments. That confidence is usually justified. But it can also create vulnerability. Confidence in one's own judgment may reduce the vigilance needed to ask a more fundamental question: does the sense of credibility arise from careful evaluation, or from cognitive processes operating outside awareness? The mechanisms described in this chapter operate before deliberate evaluation begins. Skill in evaluating arguments does not guarantee awareness of how the initial impression of credibility was formed.

The protection provided by expertise is therefore uneven. It is strongest where AI output is least likely to fail: the reproduction of established knowledge through familiar patterns of explanation. It is weakest where AI output is most likely to fail: subtle drift, overextension, and misplaced confidence beneath a surface that appears trustworthy. Recognizing this changes how the vulnerability described in this chapter should be understood. Susceptibility to fluent language is not a defect of the uninformed. It is a consequence of how human cognition manages complexity.

Even highly trained thinkers rely on signals of coherence and clear expression when working with unfamiliar material. The difference is not immunity. It is the ability, when necessary, to slow down and examine the reasoning more carefully. The next section considers the final implication of this pattern. If awareness alone cannot prevent fluency bias from operating, then knowledge of the mechanism is not, by itself, sufficient protection against it.

8.6 Knowing About the Bias Is Not Enough

Why Protection Requires Deliberate Cognitive Habits, Not Just Awareness

At this point, the mechanisms behind fluency bias are clear. Cognitive ease creates an immediate sense of credibility. Smooth explanations reduce the impulse to scrutinize claims. Articulate language activates the mind's shortcut to authority. Even expertise does not prevent these signals from shaping initial interpretation. A natural response is to assume that awareness alone provides protection. Once the bias is understood, it seems reasonable to expect that it can be recognized and corrected. Unfortunately, cognitive bias rarely works this way.

The mechanisms described in this chapter operate before deliberate reasoning begins. Psychologists often distinguish between two levels of cognitive processing: a fast, automatic process that forms impressions and prior credences, and a slower, deliberative process that evaluates them. Fluency bias, the authority shortcut, and the substitution of style for scrutiny all operate in the first process. Awareness belongs to the second.

Knowledge of the bias becomes available only after deliberate reasoning begins. It cannot prevent the initial impression from forming. By the time conscious reflection starts, the impression of plausibility has already taken shape. Knowing that the mechanism exists does not stop that first impression from appearing. In this respect, fluency bias resembles many other automatic features of perception. A visual illusion does not disappear once its mechanism is understood. The perception remains. What changes is the ability to treat it with caution. Cognitive biases operate in much the same way. Awareness can create distance from an initial impression, but it cannot stop the impression from arising.

Research on debiasing consistently shows that simply informing people about a bias is among the least effective interventions. More effective approaches introduce structured procedures that change how judgments are formed rather than providing knowledge after the process has begun. This is why simply advising readers to think critically rarely solves the problem. Critical thinking is not a permanent mental state that can be switched on at will. It is a set of deliberate practices applied when circumstances require them. Without those practices, the mind returns to the shortcuts that make everyday reasoning efficient.

Protection against fluency bias therefore depends less on awareness than on habits that interrupt the automatic process. The distinction between awareness and habit is important. Awareness is propositional knowledge: knowing that the bias exists and that it shapes later evaluation by creating prior impressions. This knowledge must be consciously recalled and applied after the impression has already formed. A cognitive habit is different. It is a practiced procedure, a structured way of engaging with information before the automatic impression sets the starting point for evaluation. Awareness operates after the impression. Habit operates during the conditions that produce it. Awareness must be remembered and applied repeatedly. Habit requires less deliberate effort because it becomes part of the reader's normal way of evaluating explanations. Such habits do not eliminate the bias. They introduce small moments of friction that allow deliberate evaluation to begin.

Several examples illustrate the difference. Formulating a precise question before consulting AI output helps resist the tendency of predictive systems to drift toward common cases rather than the specific situation presented. Separating source verification from reasoning evaluation helps guard against plausible drift. Confirming that sources exist is not the same as determining whether the connections between them are sound. Noticing when confidence seems disproportionate to the complexity of an issue helps counter the uniform confidence predictive systems often produce. Pausing briefly between receiving an answer and acting on it restores a step that fluent language often suppresses. The purpose of these interruptions is not to guarantee perfect judgment. It is to restore the evaluative step that fluency tends to bypass.

These habits become especially important when interacting with predictive language systems. Such systems combine many of the signals that trigger fluency bias: grammatical clarity, structured reasoning, confident delivery, and the appearance of completeness. The resulting language is exceptionally easy to process. Without deliberate interruption, the mind naturally treats that ease as evidence that the explanation is reliable.

Recognizing this tendency is the beginning of protection, but it is not the protection itself. The safeguard lies in slowing the transition from comprehension to acceptance. Understanding an explanation and accepting it are distinct cognitive acts, even though fluent language often makes them feel like one continuous process. Disciplined thinking separates them again. This does not require rejecting fluent explanations or treating them with constant suspicion. It requires recognizing that clarity of expression is not evidence of truth by itself. Fluency may accompany genuine understanding, but it can also accompany statistical prediction. The mind experiences both in much the same way. For this reason, the most reliable defense against fluency bias is not greater intelligence or a deeper understanding of the mechanism. It is the deliberate cultivation of evaluative habits that restore the missing step between understanding an explanation and accepting it.

A reader may finish this chapter with a clear understanding of fluency bias, the authority shortcut, the substitution of style for scrutiny, and the limits of expertise. If nothing more changes, that reader will be better informed but not reliably better protected. Information becomes protection only when it is translated into habit. Those habits do not eliminate the illusion of intelligence. They make it easier to recognize it. With this, the psychological foundation of the illusion becomes clearer. Predictive systems generate language that activates cognitive mechanisms on which humans have relied for centuries. The resulting impression that the system understands arises naturally from the way the mind processes fluent communication. The illusion therefore arises not from a single mistake, but from the interaction between a new technological capability and cognitive shortcuts that were historically reliable. Understanding that interaction completes the argument of this chapter. The next chapter examines a second, slower process through which AI systems extend their influence into human thinking: the gradual transfer of judgment from human reasoning to automated suggestion.

Closing Reflection

Awareness without Practice

A fluent explanation unfolds with the ease of careful reasoning. The argument moves through its stages smoothly. The conclusion arrives with confidence. Before deliberate evaluation begins, and largely below the threshold of conscious awareness, a sense of credibility has already formed.

The mechanisms examined in this chapter reveal a subtle and persistent pattern. Cognitive ease creates a sense of credibility. A coherent explanation activates the mind's shortcut to authority. Smooth delivery reduces the impulse to scrutinize claims. Even expertise does not prevent these signals from shaping a reader's first impression. None of these responses are mistakes in the ordinary sense. They arise from cognitive mechanisms that have served human communication well throughout most of history. Clear language was usually produced by people who understood what they were saying. Articulate explanation was normally the visible expression of careful reasoning. Trusting these signals was therefore a practical way to navigate a world in which knowledge was distributed across many minds.

Predictive language systems change that environment without changing the cognitive processes that interpret it. The signals remain the same: fluency, structure, and confident delivery. What has changed is the relationship between those signals and the cognitive processes that historically produced them. Language that once reliably indicated understanding can now be generated by systems that lack the underlying properties that once made those signals trustworthy. Human judgment continues to respond to those signals as it always has. This is why the illusion of intelligence does not arise primarily from deception by the machine. It emerges from the interaction between a machine's ability to generate fluent language and the human mind's long-established tendency to interpret fluency as evidence of thought.

Understanding this interaction clarifies an important point. The vulnerability described in this chapter is not limited to the uninformed or the careless. It is rooted in cognitive mechanisms shared by all human thinkers. Intelligence, education, and skepticism can help detect errors once careful evaluation begins, but they do not prevent the first impression of credibility from forming. These mechanisms do not disappear once they are understood. They are not removed by expertise. They reflect the normal operation of minds shaped for a communicative environment that has changed rapidly in a very short time. Awareness therefore marks the beginning of protection, not its completion.

A reader who understands the fluency bias can recognize that the feeling of clarity accompanying a fluent explanation is not, by itself, evidence of truth. It becomes possible to recognize that coherent language may reflect statistical prediction rather than reasoning. It also becomes possible to recognize that the signals of expertise embedded in fluent text may no longer correspond to genuine understanding. Recognition alone, however, does not change the initial experience. Fluent language will continue to feel convincing. What awareness provides is an opportunity to treat that feeling as a cue for closer attention rather than as evidence of reliability. When clarity arrives too easily, because an explanation seems complete before careful thought has begun, it becomes a reason to pause rather than a reason to proceed. In that pause, a small but important gap opens between the moment credibility is first experienced and the moment action follows. That gap makes a simple question possible: does the credibility being experienced reflect the substance of the claim, or only the way the claim has been presented? The question does not answer itself. Yet the habit of asking it consistently, as a deliberate practice rather than an occasional reminder, turns awareness into effective protection. This small shift in interpretation marks the beginning of disciplined engagement with predictive systems. It restores a moment of reflection between comprehension and acceptance, allowing the reader to ask whether the explanation deserves the credibility its fluency appears to command. The first impression becomes the beginning of evaluation rather than its end.

The illusion of intelligence therefore persists not because readers lack critical ability, but because fluent language quietly discourages the scrutiny that critical thinking requires. Recognizing this dynamic completes the first part of the psychological explanation for why AI outputs appear so persuasive. Yet the influence of these systems does not end with the immediate experience of reading a fluent explanation. Over time, repeated interaction with systems that provide immediate answers can begin to reshape how people approach thinking itself. The next chapter examines this slower and less visible process: how the convenience of automated answers gradually encourages the transfer of judgment from human reasoning to machine suggestion.

CHAPTER 9
Automation Bias and Cognitive Offloading

The Gradual Erosion of Judgment: How Frictionless Answers Quietly Replace the Habit of Thinking

The previous chapter examined the immediate psychological effects of fluent AI output. Smooth explanations create cognitive ease. Coherent language activates the mind's shortcut to authority. Style reduces scrutiny, and even experienced readers may treat articulate language as evidence of understanding. These mechanisms explain why a single interaction with an AI system can create a persuasive impression. The language feels credible, and a reader may accept a conclusion that deserves closer examination. The deeper transformation, however, unfolds over a different timescale. The danger is not limited to the moment when an answer is read and interpreted. It lies in how repeated encounters with frictionless answers gradually reshape the habits of thought through which judgment is exercised.

Most human reasoning develops through effort. Questions are clarified. Possibilities are considered. Sources are consulted. Conclusions are revised. The process is often slow and occasionally frustrating. That friction is not an accidental inconvenience. It is part of how judgment develops. Thinking takes time because evaluating competing possibilities requires mental effort.

Predictive systems change this environment by removing much of that friction. A question that once required searching, comparison, and synthesis can now receive an immediate answer. The response appears complete, organized, and confident. In many cases, it is genuinely useful. The system can summarize information, outline possibilities, and provide starting points that would previously have required considerable effort to assemble. Yet this ease introduces a subtle change in how people interact with information. When answers arrive quickly and fluently, they become easier to accept as adequate. People do not necessarily abandon their own reasoning. Instead, the system begins to perform parts of that reasoning for them. Over time, this pattern can gradually shift cognitive responsibility from human judgment to automated suggestion. The shift rarely results from a conscious decision. It develops through repeated interactions with a tool that consistently reduces the effort required to reach a conclusion.

Psychologists identified similar patterns long before the arrival of modern AI systems. Research on decision-making in environments that included automated assistance described a phenomenon known as automation bias: the tendency to rely on system outputs even when those outputs conflict with independent judgment or when they should be verified.

Automation bias does not arise because people become passive or unthinking. It emerges because automated systems change the conditions under which decisions are made. When a machine provides a recommendation that appears competent and requires little effort to obtain, questioning that recommendation demands additional mental effort. Accepting the output becomes the easier option. Over time, this small change can alter the role of human judgment in the decision process. Understanding this shift requires attention not only to the accuracy of individual answers but also to the habits of thought that repeated reliance on automated systems encourages. A single interaction may produce a misleading explanation. Thousands of interactions, however, can reshape how problems are approached.

The resulting transformation is gradual and largely invisible. Nothing dramatic happens in any single moment. People continue to read, question, and decide. Yet the proportion of reasoning carried out independently gradually shrinks, while reliance on the system grows. What makes this transformation difficult to detect is the absence of any clear signal. There is no single moment of transition. Instead, there is a gradual weakening of a capacity whose loss becomes apparent only when it is needed and found to be diminished. This chapter examines how that shift unfolds. It begins by looking more closely at the difference in timescale that separates this problem from the immediate interpretive effects examined in the previous chapter.

9.1 From Immediate Deception to Gradual Erosion

The Invisible Timescale of Change

The effects examined in Chapter 8 occur quickly. A reader encounters fluent language, experiences cognitive ease, and forms an initial impression of credibility before deliberate evaluation begins. The entire process may unfold within seconds.

Automation bias operates differently. Rather than shaping a single moment of interpretation, it develops across repeated interactions. Each encounter may appear harmless. A user consults the system, receives an answer, and moves on. Nothing in that moment suggests that judgment has changed. The change occurs through accumulation. When a task that once required independent reasoning is solved repeatedly by consulting an automated system, the incentive to reason through it independently gradually weakens. The user remains involved throughout the process, asking questions, reading responses, and making decisions. Yet the role of independent reasoning steadily narrows.

The process develops in small steps. The first encounter with an AI system produces a useful and approximately correct answer. Choosing to use it instead of reasoning independently is reasonable. It is efficient and appropriate. The second encounter is similar. The third is similar. Across many encounters, the system becomes consistently useful, and trust grows. As trust increases, the threshold for consulting the system instead of reasoning independently gradually falls. The system begins to be used for tasks the user could have completed without assistance. It is faster, the output is fluent, and the habit of independent reasoning has already begun to give way to the habit of consultation. Each step appears reasonable on its own. The erosion lies not in any single decision, but in the accumulation of many such decisions. Gradually, the system becomes the starting point for conclusions rather than one source among several. This shift is subtle because it does not feel like surrendering judgment. The user still evaluates the answer, revises it, asks follow-up questions, or combines it with other information. Human control appears to remain. Yet the structure of the interaction has changed.

Instead of constructing an answer through deliberate inquiry, the user begins with a ready-made explanation generated by the system. Evaluation replaces generation as the primary cognitive task. Over time, this reversal can reshape how problems are approached. Instead of asking how a question should be reasoned through, the default becomes asking what the system says about it. The difference may appear small. Yet it marks an important shift in where the cognitive work of judgment takes place. The shift is especially significant because it compounds. Every occasion on which system consultation replaces independent reasoning is also an occasion on which the habit of independent reasoning goes unpracticed.

The capacity for independent judgment is not fixed. It includes tolerance for uncertainty, a willingness to work through problems without immediate guidance, and the habit of forming an initial assessment before consulting external sources. It is a capacity maintained through use and weakened through repeated disuse.

Cognitive offloading therefore creates a self-reinforcing pattern. Each occasion weakens the capacity that would make independent reasoning feel natural during the next encounter. As that capacity weakens, consultation becomes more likely. More consultation further weakens the habit of independent reasoning. The movement from convenience to reliance and then to dependency is therefore not linear. It compounds. This compounding process makes timescale the central challenge examined in this chapter. Fluency bias operates within a single moment that awareness can sometimes interrupt. Cognitive offloading develops across months and years. It accumulates through individually reasonable decisions and produces no immediate warning, only a gradual loss. By the time the erosion becomes visible, when independent reasoning is needed but found diminished, the process has already advanced a long way.

The next section examines this phenomenon through the concept psychologists use to describe it: automation bias, the tendency to trust automated outputs even when independent evaluation is both possible and advisable.

9.2 Trusting Outputs Over Judgment

Automation Bias as a Documented Psychological Phenomenon

The gradual shift described in the previous section is not unique to modern AI systems. Long before predictive language models appeared, psychologists studying human interaction with automated technologies observed a similar pattern. They called it automation bias.

Automation bias is the tendency to place undue trust in the outputs of automated systems, even when independent judgment suggests caution. When a system offers a recommendation that appears competent and authoritative, users often defer to it instead of evaluating the situation independently. This tendency does not arise because users are careless or unskilled. Researchers identified it through studies of human performance in automated environments. Among the most influential were Raja Parasuraman and Dietrich Manzey, whose work on automation in complex systems remains foundational. They studied environments in which human operators were highly trained professionals who understood the limitations of their systems. The findings were striking. Operators who could accurately describe the conditions under which automated systems might fail still showed a consistent tendency to defer to their outputs. Automation bias therefore reflects not the naïve trust of uninformed users, but the systematic deference of informed users. Training and knowledge can reduce this tendency, but they do not eliminate it.

Many early studies examined highly trained professionals, including airline pilots, medical diagnosticians, military operators, and industrial control engineers. These individuals were trained to maintain vigilance, skepticism, and independent judgment. Yet even in these settings, automated assistance changed how decisions were made. Researchers identified two characteristic patterns of error. The first is a commission error. The automated system produces an incorrect recommendation, and the human operator follows it despite having information that could reveal the mistake. The authority of the system's output overrides the operator's own judgment. The second is an omission error. The automated system fails to provide a warning or recommendation when one is needed. Because the system remains silent, the operator assumes that no problem exists and fails to act. In both cases, the human remains part of the decision process. The operator is neither absent nor disengaged. Yet the presence of the system quietly changes where attention and trust are directed.

Automation bias arises from several psychological forces working together. One is perceived competence. Automated systems are designed to appear precise, consistent, and technically sophisticated. When they perform well in routine situations, users gradually come to see them as generally reliable. Trust builds through repeated successful interactions. Another force is cognitive economy. Monitoring automated recommendations while also evaluating them independently requires effort. When the system's suggestions are usually correct, the motivation to carry out that additional verification gradually weakens. A third force is the diffusion of responsibility. When a system participates in the decision process, responsibility for the outcome becomes psychologically shared between the human and the machine. This subtle shift can make following the system's recommendation feel less risky than relying entirely on independent judgment. Beneath these forces lies a deeper structural change. Once an automated system begins providing recommendations, the starting point for judgment changes. Instead of forming an independent judgment first, the operator begins with the system's recommendation and evaluates the situation from that point.

Acting independently now requires overriding the system's output. The burden of proof has shifted. To reject the automated recommendation, the operator must provide a sufficiently strong independent assessment to justify doing so. This creates a higher cognitive threshold than existed when the operator's own judgment initiated the decision. Across many decisions, this higher threshold produces the systematic pattern of excessive deference documented in automation research.

The problem does not arise from automation itself. In many contexts, automated systems genuinely improve performance. They process large amounts of information quickly, identify patterns that might escape human attention, and reduce certain types of error. The difficulty arises when automation changes how people allocate their own cognitive effort. Once a system becomes the primary source of recommendations, independent evaluation can gradually decline. The human operator shifts from forming judgments to monitoring the system's output and intervening only when something appears obviously wrong. Detecting such problems, however, requires maintaining the situational awareness that automation often reduces. This pattern has been observed repeatedly across many domains.

In medicine, studies of clinical decision-support systems show that physicians presented with automated diagnostic suggestions often adjust their reasoning toward those suggestions. In some cases, they accept incorrect diagnoses despite having clinical information that could have led them independently to the correct conclusion. In military command-and-control systems, automation bias has been linked to documented incidents in which operators followed automated threat assessments even though the available evidence should have prompted them to question those assessments. In financial decision-making, research on algorithmic trading shows that professional traders and fund managers sometimes reduce scrutiny of their own analyzes when algorithmic recommendations are available, accepting positions they might otherwise have rejected.

The breadth of these findings matters. Automation bias has been documented in fields whose practitioners are among the most highly trained and strongly motivated to exercise careful judgment. The pattern therefore reflects not a weakness of credulous individuals, but a systematic feature of human decision-making in automated environments. The resulting paradox is well established in research on human-automation interaction. Systems designed to assist human judgment can, under certain conditions, weaken the vigilance that makes that judgment effective.

Predictive language systems introduce this dynamic into a new domain. Instead of assisting physical control systems or specialized professional tasks, they now assist thinking itself. They generate explanations, outline arguments, summarize evidence, and propose conclusions across a wide range of intellectual activities. The pattern of interaction therefore resembles the one documented in earlier automation research. The system offers a fluent recommendation. The user evaluates it. Repeated successful interactions gradually increase trust. As trust grows, the threshold for independent verification quietly rises. The conditions that produce automation bias in aviation or medicine appear in AI interaction in a more concentrated form.

Traditional automated systems operate within bounded domains. Their outputs are recognized as automated recommendations that remain distinct from the operator's own reasoning. AI language systems, by contrast, generate responses across nearly every domain of knowledge in fluent natural language that closely resembles human explanation. The fluency and coherence that produce the cognitive effects described in Chapter 8 also strengthen the conditions that give rise to automation bias. The output does not appear as a mechanical recommendation from a specialized system with known limits. It appears as an explanation. It is structured, articulate, and linguistically similar to the reasoning of a knowledgeable person. The breadth of domains, the frequency of interaction, and the difficulty of distinguishing automated output from human reasoning together create an environment especially favorable to automation bias. Trusting the output becomes easier than reconstructing the reasoning independently. The following sections examine why this shift toward reliance becomes so attractive, and why frictionless answers often feel preferable to the slower work of reasoning through a problem independently.

9.3 The Appeal of Frictionless Answers

Why Instant Confident Responses Feel Preferable to Genuine Thinking

If automation bias helps explain why people sometimes defer to automated systems, a further question follows. Why does that deference arise so readily? Part of the answer lies in a basic feature of human cognition: thinking requires effort. Careful reasoning rarely proceeds in a straight line. Questions must be clarified, assumptions identified, possibilities explored, and evidence weighed. The process often involves uncertainty and revision. Conclusions emerge gradually, sometimes after several false starts. This friction is not a defect of human reasoning. It is a natural consequence of evaluating complex information under conditions of limited knowledge and competing possibilities. Thinking takes time because judgment requires comparison, reflection, and doubt.

Automated systems present answers in a very different way. A question is asked, and an immediate response follows. The explanation arrives structured, fluent, and confident. It does not display the hesitation, revision, or uncertainty that typically accompany reasoning in progress. Instead, it appears as a finished product. From the perspective of cognitive effort, the contrast is striking. Human reasoning constructs an answer step by step. Automated systems present an answer that appears already complete. The user encounters not the process of thinking, but its apparent conclusion.

The attraction of such responses is therefore easy to understand. What strengthens that attraction is the particular kind of effort that frictionless answers remove. Independent reasoning involves not only effort, but also incompleteness. It produces conclusions with visible limits. They are judgments that are probably correct rather than fully resolved, and explanations that retain some uncertainty.

A person who has worked through a difficult question often reaches a conclusion that feels tentative compared with the fluent, organized, and confidently expressed response produced by an AI system. This difference does not arise because independent reasoning is less reliable. It arises because independent reasoning is more honest about its limits. The frictionless answer removes not only the effort of thinking, but also the sense of incompleteness that accompanies genuine inquiry. The partial conclusion is replaced by the experience of resolution. That replacement is psychologically powerful.

Research on decision-making consistently shows that people prefer options that reduce cognitive effort. When two paths appear to lead to the same outcome, the mind naturally favors the one that requires less mental work. This tendency allows attention to be distributed across many tasks. Frictionless answers take advantage of it in a particular way. Because the system presents its output as coherent and complete, the user experiences the difficult work of reasoning as already done. Evaluating the answer requires less effort than developing it independently. As a result, the path of least resistance changes.

Instead of beginning with independent analysis and using the system as one source among several, users increasingly begin with the system's output and use their own reasoning as a secondary check. The difference may seem small in a single interaction. Accepting a well-written summary instead of assembling one from several sources can be efficient. Using an AI system to outline possible approaches before examining them more carefully may also be a sensible shortcut. Yet these small efficiencies accumulate. Each time the system performs part of the reasoning process, the user has less need to perform that reasoning independently. Over time, solving problems through consultation becomes familiar and comfortable. The relief provided by frictionless answers is not a minor influence. It is one of the strongest forces shaping repeated behavior. When a pattern of action consistently removes discomfort, people become more likely to repeat it.

A person who consults an AI system repeatedly has not consciously decided to offload judgment. Instead, repeated experiences of relief gradually shape behavior until offloading becomes habitual. The mental effort that once accompanied careful thinking begins to fade. Predictive systems introduce another feature that strengthens this attraction: confidence.

Human reasoning typically proceeds with visible uncertainty. A person working through a difficult problem may hesitate, reconsider assumptions, or acknowledge the limits of available knowledge. These signals reflect the reality that judgment often takes place under incomplete information. Automated systems rarely display this pattern. Their responses tend to arrive with consistent fluency and apparent confidence. Even when the underlying answer is uncertain, the language of the response often appears settled and decisive.

For the user, the psychological effect is powerful. The combination of fluency and confidence creates the impression that the problem has already been resolved. The user encounters not a tentative exploration, but a conclusion. Over time, another subtle change occurs. As instant, confident answers become the normal experience, they create an implicit standard for what answers should look like. Independent reasoning begins to seem deficient by comparison. Its conclusions are partial. Its uncertainty remains visible. Its confidence is measured rather than uniform. These are not defects of independent reasoning, but honest signs of a mind working through a problem. Yet when measured against the standard created by repeated interaction with AI, they can begin to feel like shortcomings. A quiet ratchet effect emerges.

The more the system is consulted, the more its outputs shape expectations about what answers should feel like, and the less satisfying independent reasoning becomes by comparison. The appeal of frictionless answers therefore extends beyond convenience. It also lies in the relief they provide from the uncertainty and effort that normally accompany thinking. Instead of confronting an open question, the user receives a ready-made explanation. Instead of weighing competing possibilities, the user receives a structured narrative that appears to have already organized the problem. The system does not merely save time. It also removes the experience of cognitive struggle that genuine reasoning often requires.

Under these conditions, the shift toward reliance described earlier becomes easier to understand. The user is not abandoning judgment. The user is adopting a tool that appears to make judgment easier. In many individual cases, that appearance is accurate. The tool is often helpful. The time saved is real. The relief is genuine. The difficulty lies elsewhere. A single decision to consult the system may be rational, but many such decisions can produce a different result. Each use may be sensible in isolation. Across many interactions, however, the location of the thinking gradually shifts. The system generates the initial explanation. The human user evaluates it. Generation gives way to supervision.

The next section examines the consequence of this shift: a decision process in which humans remain present but increasingly delegate the construction of judgment to the system itself.

9.4 Delegating Decisions to Systems

The Nominally Present, Cognitively Absent Human

As frictionless answers become familiar and automation bias quietly raises the threshold for independent verification, the structure of decision-making begins to change in a subtle but important way. The human remains part of the process. A person still asks the question. A person still reads and interprets the answer. The final decision may still be made by a person. On the surface, little appears to have changed. Yet beneath that surface, the distribution of cognitive work has shifted.

In a traditional reasoning process, a person confronting a problem begins by forming a judgment. Information is gathered, possibilities are considered, and a tentative conclusion gradually emerges. External sources, including books, articles, and colleagues, may contribute to this process, but the central activity remains the formation of a judgment within the human mind. Automated systems introduce a different sequence. Instead of building a judgment from the ground up, the user begins with a ready-made explanation generated by the system. The cognitive task shifts from producing an answer to evaluating one that already exists.

At first glance, this may appear to be a minor procedural change. Evaluation is still a form of thinking. The user can reject the system's output, modify it, or consult additional sources before reaching a decision. Yet the psychology of evaluation differs from the psychology of generation. When people construct an explanation independently, they remain aware of the uncertainties that arose during its development. The reasoning process reveals assumptions, alternative interpretations, and gaps in knowledge. These remain visible because they were encountered while the judgment was being formed.

When an explanation is presented fully formed, that history of uncertainty disappears. The reasoning arrives already organized and apparently resolved. The evaluator encounters the conclusion without experiencing the cognitive process that produced it. Under these conditions, evaluation tends to require less cognitive effort than generation. The user scans the explanation for obvious errors, inconsistencies, or omissions. If none immediately appear, the answer may be accepted as a reasonable account of the situation. The deeper work of constructing and testing alternative interpretations often does not occur. This is not because the user has consciously chosen to abandon it. It is because the presence of a plausible answer makes that work seem unnecessary. The difference between these two conditions marks the boundary between genuine cognitive presence and nominal presence.

The genuinely present decision-maker contributes something the system has not already provided: an independent analysis, an independent interpretation of the available information, and an independent judgment about what the situation requires. The nominally present decision-maker contributes something narrower: an evaluation of what the system has already produced. The form of engagement remains the same. The substance does not. Gradually, the role of the human mind changes. Instead of serving as the primary source of judgment, it becomes a supervisory layer that monitors the system's outputs. This change rarely announces itself. During the early stages of reliance, independent analysis is still applied by extending the system's output, questioning it, and comparing it with an independently formed assessment. As reliance deepens, that independent analysis gradually diminishes. The system's framing is accepted more readily. Comparison with an independently formed judgment becomes less systematic, not because the individual has chosen to be less rigorous, but because repeated experience has reduced the perceived need for such rigor.

In later stages, the human contribution may narrow further until it becomes little more than a check that the system's answer seems broadly reasonable. That check usually passes because the system's outputs are generally reasonable. At each stage, the adjustment feels rational. The user appears simply to be learning to trust a tool that has repeatedly proved useful. The cumulative effect is the gradual replacement of genuine cognitive engagement with nominal presence. Yet this change does not feel like a loss because it does not occur all at once. It emerges through a series of individually reasonable adjustments.

Human-automation researchers have long observed a similar pattern in technical environments. Operators who oversee automated systems often remain physically present and formally responsible for decisions while carrying out much less of the underlying cognitive work. The system generates recommendations, and the human intervenes only when something appears obviously wrong. This condition is sometimes described as being "in the loop" without being cognitively engaged in the loop. The operator remains present, but much of the thinking takes place elsewhere. When predictive language systems support intellectual tasks, the same pattern can emerge in reasoning itself. The user continues to ask questions, read explanations, and approve conclusions. The formal structure of responsibility remains unchanged. Yet the center of cognitive activity shifts outward. The system constructs the argument. The human monitors it. This arrangement creates a powerful illusion of continued intellectual control. Because the user still reads and evaluates the output, the interaction feels like an active exercise of judgment. The person remains involved at every stage. Nothing in the experience suggests that thinking has been delegated. This ability to conceal itself is one of the condition's most significant features.

The nominally present human does not experience cognitive absence. The person feels engaged. The person feels as though independent thinking is taking place. The activities themselves are real. What has quietly been replaced is the work of constructing an independent judgment, and that change leaves no clear experiential signal. The feeling of engagement is genuine. The independent judgment that the feeling appears to reflect is not. Yet the delegation has already occurred.

The essential step in reasoning is constructing the explanation that connects evidence to a conclusion. That step has been performed by the system. The human contribution has narrowed to supervision. This change rarely appears dramatic in any single moment. Each interaction seems like a sensible use of a helpful tool. The explanation is checked, perhaps revised slightly, and then accepted. As this pattern repeats, however, the center of gravity of judgment moves steadily outward. In principle, the human remains the final authority. In practice, the system increasingly becomes the source of answers.

The operational consequence of this shift is an uneven decline in judgment. Accuracy remains high in routine situations where the system's output is correct and the supervisory check passes easily. Performance declines in non-routine situations where the system's output is wrong in ways that are not obvious during a superficial review. The nominally present human performs well precisely where that presence makes little difference. Performance declines precisely where genuine cognitive engagement matters most. The capacity for genuine cognitive engagement does not simply remain intact until those moments when it is needed.

Judgment is a practiced capacity. Its habits are strengthened through use and weakened through repeated substitution. A decision-maker who has spent months in nominal presence and is suddenly required to construct an independent judgment without the system's support is being asked to use a capacity that gradual delegation has already weakened. This shift shows why the problem described in this chapter is not simply one of error or deception. Even when automated systems produce broadly correct answers, the gradual transfer of reasoning from human minds to machines changes the structure of judgment itself.

The next section examines a further consequence of this change: the emergence of a form of delegation that often goes unnoticed because the human user remains physically present throughout the decision process.

9.5 The Invisible Delegation

Remaining Physically in the Loop While Exiting It Cognitively

The shift described in the previous section creates a distinctive condition. The human remains part of the decision process while gradually stepping back from the cognitive work it requires. Questions are still asked by a person. Answers are still read by a person. Decisions are still approved by a person. The formal structure of responsibility remains unchanged. Yet the intellectual work that once produced those decisions is increasingly performed elsewhere. This is what makes the delegation described in this chapter difficult to recognize. Nothing in the outward structure of the interaction indicates that judgment has shifted. The human user remains in the loop, still reading and still choosing.

Delegation has occurred without the visible signs that usually accompany it. In many forms of delegation, the transfer of responsibility is explicit. A task is assigned to someone else, and the original decision-maker steps back. The change is obvious because that person is no longer involved in the process.

Automation introduces a different pattern. The human remains in the loop, but the process itself has changed. The machine generates the proposal, and the human evaluates it. The central step of reasoning, linking information to a conclusion through explanation, has already been completed before the human evaluates the output. Because the user still takes part in the final stages of the process, the interaction continues to feel like an exercise of judgment. Yet the cognitive center of the decision has already shifted.

Human-automation research offers a useful distinction. Genuine participation in the loop requires more than physical presence. It requires actively maintaining situational awareness and continuously building an independent understanding of the problem through direct engagement with the available information. A decision-maker who is genuinely in the loop develops and updates that understanding through independent reasoning.

Nominal presence creates a different condition. Instead of building an independent understanding of the situation, the individual begins to monitor the system's output. Attention shifts from asking what the situation requires to asking whether the system's explanation appears reasonable. This pattern resembles what researchers describe as out-of-the-loop performance. Operators remain present and responsible for the outcome while gradually losing the situational awareness that once allowed them to detect problems independently. Their role becomes reactive rather than generative.

Predictive language systems create the possibility of a similar condition in the domain of thinking itself. The user remains engaged with the system's output. Explanations are read, arguments are followed, and judgments are made about whether a response appears reasonable. Yet the work of constructing the reasoning has already been completed by the system. That is the stage at which independent judgment is normally exercised. The user therefore occupies an unusual position. The conclusion of the reasoning process is encountered without participating in its construction. From the user's perspective, this does not feel like an absence. The experience of active thinking remains. Evaluating an explanation requires attention, interpretation, and judgment. That activity is genuine. What has quietly disappeared is the deeper cognitive work through which the explanation itself would have been developed. This distinction is difficult to perceive because evaluation and generation share many surface features. Both involve reading, interpreting, and making decisions. From the user's perspective, they feel similar.

The user continues to read, and reading feels like engagement. Questions continue to be asked, but they arise in response to the system's output. They refine the system's framing instead of testing it against an independently developed understanding. Decisions continue to be made, and the retention of final authority reinforces the impression of full participation in the reasoning process. Yet these activities serve different roles in the formation of judgment.

Generation produces the explanation. Evaluation accepts, rejects, or revises an explanation that already exists. The result is a form of delegation that remains largely invisible. The individual continues to experience personal responsibility for the outcome. The explanation is read, the conclusion is approved, and the decision carries the individual's authority. Nothing in the immediate experience contradicts that sense of ownership. Yet the intellectual path that produced the answer no longer depends primarily on the individual's own reasoning. Because active engagement is still experienced, the erosion of independent judgment rarely feels like a loss. There is no clear moment at which the individual recognizes that the work of reasoning has gradually shifted elsewhere. Instead, the process appears to be a steady improvement in efficiency. Each interaction seems reasonable when viewed in isolation. What remains difficult to perceive is the cumulative shift produced by repeated interactions. As the generative stage of reasoning increasingly occurs within the system, the human role becomes progressively narrower.

Several mechanisms reinforce this narrowing without drawing attention to it. The first is frame capture. As system outputs become the consistent starting point for inquiry, the system's framing of the problem gradually becomes the user's framing as well. It shapes how the situation is understood before independent reasoning begins. The second is the weakening of independent framing. The ability to approach a problem without the system's scaffolding declines as opportunities to exercise that ability become less frequent. The third is the normalization of supervisory monitoring as thinking itself. When checking and approving outputs become the routine form of interaction, those activities gradually come to be experienced as the natural form of thinking. None of these mechanisms announces itself. Each operates below the level of deliberate awareness required to interrupt it. This invisible delegation does not persist under all conditions. When the system produces an answer whose errors require genuine independent judgment to detect, the user is suddenly required to perform the very cognitive work that repeated delegation has gradually displaced.

Research on human interaction with automated systems consistently shows what happens in such moments. The response is rarely immediate independent reasoning. Instead, operators often show confusion, delayed recognition, and an initial tendency to consult the system again rather than reason without it. The orientation toward consultation persists precisely when independent judgment is most needed. At that point, the invisible delegation becomes visible, not through self-awareness, but through the difficulty of performing the cognitive work that active participation would have maintained. The individual remains present, but the nature of that participation has changed. The individual is still in the loop. But the thinking that once defined that role has begun to occur elsewhere. Delegation that is visible can, in principle, be interrupted. It can be recognized, named, and reversed through deliberate recalibration. Delegation that remains invisible offers no such opportunity. An individual who does not recognize that judgment has been delegated has no reason to reclaim it. For this reason, invisible delegation is not a stable endpoint but a threshold. Beyond it lies the deeper erosion examined in the next section: the gradual weakening of the habits that sustain independent reasoning as opportunities to exercise those habits steadily disappear.

9.6 The Slow Erosion of Critical Habits

When Delegated Judgment Becomes Unavailable

The invisible delegation described in the previous section does not merely shift where thinking takes place. Over time, it can also change the capacities that make independent thinking possible. Judgment is not a fixed intellectual resource that remains unchanged regardless of how often it is used. Like many complex cognitive abilities, it depends on habits that are strengthened through repeated practice.

Independent reasoning involves a set of learned practices: framing a question clearly, identifying relevant information, constructing possible explanations, weighing competing interpretations, and tolerating the uncertainty that accompanies incomplete knowledge. Together, these practices form the basis of critical judgment. They are not abstract skills that can simply be called upon whenever they are needed. They are habits of mind sustained by situations that require them. Beneath these visible practices lies a deeper orientation toward inquiry. It includes forming an independent frame for a problem before seeking answers, treating information as material to be organized rather than accepted in its existing form, and remaining willing to stay with uncertainty before reaching a conclusion. These orientations are not techniques that can simply be recalled and applied. They support independent judgment itself. It is this foundation, not only the visible skills, that repeated delegation gradually weakens. As the situations requiring these habits become less common, the habits themselves begin to fade.

Repeated reliance on automated systems changes exactly those situations. Questions that once required independent framing are answered through consultation. Problems that once required gathering information from multiple sources arrive already summarized and organized. Arguments that once had to be constructed are encountered in finished form. The immediate effect is convenience. Tasks are completed more quickly and with less effort. The long-term effect is more subtle. Each occasion on which independent reasoning is replaced by system consultation is also an occasion on which the habits supporting independent reasoning go unused.

Psychologists who study expertise have long observed a similar pattern in other domains. Complex abilities depend on continued practice. Musicians who stop playing gradually lose technical precision. Athletes who stop training lose physical coordination. The underlying capacity does not disappear immediately, but the ease and reliability with which it can be used gradually decline. Cognitive habits follow the same pattern. A person who spends years analyzing arguments, comparing sources, and constructing explanations develops fluency in those activities. The processes become familiar, and the effort they require decreases through repetition. When those activities are consistently replaced by automated suggestions, however, the cycle of reinforcement begins to reverse. The knowledge needed for independent reasoning may remain, but the readiness to use it gradually weakens. Problems that once prompted immediate analysis now prompt consultation instead. This change rarely feels like the loss of a skill. Instead, it appears as a change in how problems are approached. Independent reasoning increasingly begins with the system's output rather than with an independently constructed frame.

The system provides the starting point; the human provides the review. Over time, this pattern can produce a deeper change. The capacity for independent judgment begins to depend on the very system that has gradually replaced it. Someone attempting to reason independently after long periods of consistent delegation may encounter something disorienting: the absence of the mental framework through which independent judgment was once developed. The disorientation is not intellectual but structural. The individual does not know where to begin, not because the problem exceeds their intelligence, but because the habit of beginning independently has been replaced by the habit of beginning with the system's framing.

The tolerance for uncertainty that independent reasoning requires may also weaken. This is the ability to sustain attention on an open question without seeking an immediate answer. Repeated exposure to frictionless answers gradually reduces the length of time a thinker is accustomed to remaining with uncertainty. The history of reasoning that makes genuine revision possible is also often missing. The alternatives considered, the assumptions identified, and the paths explored and rejected are no longer part of the person's own thinking. Instead, the reasoning is generated by the system and encountered only in its final form. At this stage, delegated judgment has moved beyond convenience. It has become part of the way thinking is carried out. In this sense, consistently delegated judgment can become structurally unavailable judgment. The capacity remains in principle, but the habits that make it readily available have weakened. The distinction between weakened judgment and structurally unavailable judgment is important. A weakened capacity requires greater effort but remains accessible. A structurally displaced capacity requires rebuilding the cognitive framework that consistent delegation has gradually replaced.

Rebuilding requires more than deciding to think independently. It requires restoring the habits that support independent reasoning: framing problems without external scaffolding, sustaining tolerance for uncertainty, and shifting the starting point of inquiry from consultation to independent construction. This process cannot occur instantly. It requires sustained practice across many situations in which the impulse to consult the system is deliberately resisted and the discomfort of partial or uncertain conclusions is accepted rather than immediately resolved.

The erosion described here is rarely visible in everyday interactions because most encounters with automated systems occur in familiar situations where their outputs are broadly reliable. Under those conditions, the human role as reviewer appears sufficient. The weakness becomes visible mainly at the boundaries, when a problem is unusual, ambiguous, or poorly represented in the system's training data. These are precisely the situations in which independent judgment is most valuable. They are also the situations in which the habits that sustain such judgment may have been exercised the least. The gradual nature of this erosion makes it especially difficult to detect. No single interaction appears responsible. Each consultation seems reasonable on its own. The deeper change emerges only over time through the accumulation of many small shifts in where the work of reasoning takes place.

The invisibility described in the previous section compounds this problem. Invisible delegation conceals the structural displacement it creates. Someone who does not recognize that judgment has been delegated cannot recognize that the habits supporting that judgment have begun to weaken. Recognition becomes the first step toward recovery. Yet the self-concealing nature of this condition makes recognition especially difficult. By the time the consequences become visible, the habits that once supported independent judgment may already have weakened.

The final section of this chapter examines the broader implication of this dynamic: how increasing dependence on automated reasoning systems can simultaneously increase their usefulness and the vulnerability of those who rely on them.

9.7 Dependency and Vulnerability Growing Together

The Compounding Danger of Cognitive Offloading over Time

The developments examined throughout this chapter reveal a pattern that becomes visible only when the individual mechanisms are considered together. Automation bias encourages users to defer to automated recommendations. Fluent answers make it psychologically easy to rely on the system. The human role gradually shifts from making independent judgments to supervising the system's outputs. Delegation occurs without appearing to occur. Over time, the habits that support independent reasoning weaken through disuse. Together, these processes gradually transfer cognitive work from human minds to automated systems.

At first, this transfer appears beneficial. Predictive systems often provide accurate information, organize complex material efficiently, and reduce the time needed to reach a workable conclusion. In many situations, they genuinely improve performance. Tasks that once required extensive searching or careful synthesis can be completed quickly and with reasonable reliability. It is precisely this usefulness that allows the transfer to deepen.

Each successful interaction strengthens the perception that the system is a reliable starting point for reasoning. As confidence in the tool grows, the threshold for consulting it falls. Questions that once would have been approached independently are now directed to the system first. Over time, consultation becomes the default starting point for problem solving. Dependency therefore grows through success rather than failure. The more consistently the system provides useful answers, the more natural it becomes to rely on them. Individual users do not experience this shift as dependence. It appears instead as a sensible adaptation to a powerful tool. Yet the dependency created by this gradual displacement is more than a preference or a habit. It is a condition in which the system becomes the primary framework through which problems are approached. When this happens, the absence of the system creates more than inconvenience. It creates disorientation. The cognitive habits that once supported independent reasoning have been replaced by habits organized around the system's constant availability. This growing reliance also introduces a structural vulnerability.

The more reasoning is offloaded to an external system, the more human cognitive habits adapt to that arrangement. Independent judgment is exercised less often, while consultation becomes the routine response to uncertainty. This adaptation creates vulnerability through several mechanisms that reinforce one another over time. As reliance grows through repeated experiences of efficiency and reliability, the range of problems referred to the system also expands. The system begins to be consulted in situations that lie beyond its reliable operating range, where its outputs remain confident even when their calibration is uncertain. At the same time, as the human role narrows to supervisory monitoring, the ability to detect errors that are not obvious from a superficial review gradually declines. The errors to which dependency creates the greatest vulnerability are precisely those least likely to be detected by such a review.

Finally, when cognitive engagement is concentrated primarily in the system's output instead of being shared between independent reasoning and system consultation, any systematic weakness in the system's reasoning affects the user's entire intellectual activity. Under ordinary conditions, these weaknesses may remain invisible. Most everyday questions fall within familiar domains where the system's responses are broadly reliable. In such situations, the user's supervisory role appears sufficient. The difficulty arises when the system encounters a problem that is unusual, poorly represented in its training data, or too contextually complex for it to interpret adequately. The reliability that previously justified trust begins to weaken. At precisely that point, independent human judgment becomes essential. Yet the person facing that situation is no longer the same thinker who might once have approached the problem independently. The habits that sustain independent reasoning may have been used less often, replaced by routine consultation. Dependency and vulnerability therefore grow together. The more effective the system becomes in routine situations, the more people rely on it. The more they rely on it, the less often they practice independent reasoning. The less frequently that reasoning is practiced, the harder it becomes to use when the system fails.

What makes this dynamic more than a simple cycle is its self-reinforcing character. The very capacities that could interrupt it are gradually weakened by the same pattern of behavior that it creates. These capacities include independent assessment, tolerance for uncertainty, and the willingness to test the system's output against an independently developed line of reasoning. The process therefore does not level off. It accelerates. Each step deepens dependency and increases vulnerability. Each increase in vulnerability, in turn, magnifies the consequences of dependency. This dynamic resembles other forms of technological reliance. Tools designed to improve efficiency often reduce the need to use certain human abilities. As reliance grows, those abilities weaken through disuse. When the tool is unavailable or performs poorly, the underlying ability proves harder to recover than expected.

In the case of predictive reasoning systems, what is at stake is not merely technical skill but judgment itself. For this reason, the central risk described in this chapter does not arise primarily from isolated errors produced by automated systems. Individual mistakes can be identified and corrected. The deeper concern is the gradual redistribution of reasoning between man and machine. As cognitive offloading becomes routine, the center of gravity of thinking shifts outward. Human judgment remains formally responsible for decisions, yet the processes that shape those decisions increasingly take place within the system.

The result is a condition in which dependency and vulnerability advance together. The system becomes more capable and more useful, encouraging greater reliance. At the same time, the human capacities needed to operate without it are exercised less often. Those capacities include grounding reasoning in independent analysis, orienting judgment toward truth rather than fluency, revising conclusions when warranted, and maintaining awareness of uncertainty. As this self-reinforcing process weakens these capacities, collaboration becomes less genuinely collaborative and more structurally dependent, even though it continues to feel productive and efficient. The danger therefore grows quietly over time. Nothing dramatic marks the transition. Each interaction appears efficient and reasonable. Only when independent judgment becomes necessary does the depth of the dependence become visible.

The trajectory described in this chapter, from convenience to reliance to dependency, is not an inevitable outcome. It is a predictable dynamic. The mechanisms involved operate largely below deliberate awareness, accumulate through individually reasonable decisions, and unfold over a timescale that ordinary self-reflection rarely detects. Predictable, however, is not the same as inevitable. The mechanisms can be identified. The structural displacement they produce is not permanent. The self-reinforcing process can be interrupted. But interruption requires more than awareness. It requires recognizing that the process is occurring and deliberately practicing the habits that counteract it. Recognition is not protection. It is the precondition for protection.

Automation bias and cognitive offloading do not merely influence how individual answers are interpreted. Over time, they can reshape how reasoning itself is organized by transferring parts of the cognitive work of judgment from human minds to the systems that increasingly assist them. The next chapter turns from the psychology of reliance to a broader question. If predictive systems can gradually reshape how individuals think, what happens when those systems become embedded in the intellectual infrastructure of entire institutions?

Closing Reflection

When Convenience Becomes Structure

A question needs an answer. A problem requires analysis. A decision must be made. A query is entered. An answer arrives, fluent, organized, and confident. A decision follows. The screen is closed. The interaction appears complete. Nothing suggests that anything important has changed.

The process examined in this chapter shares a defining characteristic: it does not appear dramatic while it is unfolding. Consulting an automated system seems reasonable. Accepting a clear, well-structured answer seems efficient. Allowing a reliable tool to perform part of the reasoning process seems sensible. Each interaction is easy to justify. No single moment reveals that a gradual shift is taking place.

The danger examined in this chapter differs from visible failures that announce themselves, such as a fabricated citation, a confidently incorrect answer, or an error that immediately invites scrutiny. Such failures often trigger correction because they are easy to recognize. The process examined in this chapter rarely triggers correction because it does not reveal itself while it is unfolding. Its effects become visible only over time, and only when careful reflection reveals what has gradually changed. Repeated reliance on automated systems can change how judgment is exercised. Automation bias encourages trust in system outputs. Frictionless answers make that trust psychologically appealing. As a result, the role of the human thinker gradually shifts from constructing explanations to evaluating those produced by the system. Responsibility for reasoning remains with the user, but more of the path to a conclusion passes through the machine. The habits that sustain independent reasoning gradually weaken through disuse. None of these changes requires a deliberate decision to surrender judgment. They emerge through convenience, efficiency, and the natural tendency to choose solutions that reduce cognitive effort.

The result is not an abrupt loss of cognitive capacity, but a gradual shift in where thinking takes place. Across many individually reasonable interactions, the framework through which problems are approached begins to change. The habit of beginning with one's own understanding is gradually replaced by the habit of beginning with the system's answer. The capacity to remain with uncertainty weakens as that uncertainty is repeatedly resolved before it has been genuinely examined. This displacement is rarely visible in a single encounter. It becomes visible only when a problem requires independent judgment and that judgment is less available than expected. It appears in the disorientation that arises when an open question must be addressed without the scaffolding that repeated consultation has made seem natural. That moment of disorientation is not evidence of intellectual failure. It reflects a gradual shift shaped by many interactions that each seemed efficient. The system increasingly generates the explanations through which problems are understood. The human mind increasingly evaluates those explanations instead of constructing them independently. Responsibility remains with the human user, but the intellectual path to a conclusion increasingly passes through the machine. This change is difficult to notice because it rarely produces obvious failure. Under ordinary conditions, the system performs well enough that the user's supervisory role appears sufficient. The interaction remains productive, useful, and efficient. Only when an unusual or poorly represented problem arises does the underlying pattern become visible. At precisely the moment when independent judgment becomes most necessary, the habits that sustain it may have been practiced least. A paradox emerges that is common to many powerful technologies: the more effectively a tool performs its function, the more deeply its users adapt to relying on it.

Success therefore becomes the engine of dependence. Recognizing this dynamic does not require rejecting automated systems or refusing their assistance. Their advantages are real and often substantial. The question raised by this chapter is not whether such systems should be used, but how their use reshapes the habits of thought that develop alongside them. The movement from convenience to reliance to dependence is not an argument against convenience. It is an argument for recognizing the cumulative effect of many individually convenient choices. It also shows that patterns of use matter in ways that individual encounters do not reveal. Recognition alone is not protection. It is the precondition for protection. It also marks the beginning of the deliberate attention to cognitive habits developed in the chapters that follow.

The danger described here differs from the fluency bias examined in Chapter 8 in an important way. Fluency bias operates within a single moment. It is fast, automatic, and can, in principle, be interrupted by the deliberate habits described earlier. The process examined in this chapter is slower, more gradual, and more deeply embedded. It does not act through a single encounter. It unfolds over time, gradually reshaping the cognitive framework through which new problems are approached. A deliberate pause before accepting a single AI-generated response may reduce the first danger. Preserving independent judgment against the long-term effects of repeated delegation requires something more sustained. It requires attention to patterns of use and the continued practice of independent reasoning, not merely to correct individual outputs, but to preserve the distinctive character of human judgment.

The gradual transfer of cognitive labor from human minds to machines is not confined to individual interactions. When tools that assist reasoning become widely adopted, the patterns described here can extend beyond individual users. They can begin to shape how professional communities approach problems, how institutions organize knowledge, and how decisions are made collectively. The next chapter turns to this broader level of analysis. If cognitive offloading can quietly reshape the habits of individual thinkers, what happens when the same process unfolds across the intellectual infrastructure of modern institutions?

CHAPTER 10
Outsourcing Thought

From Search to Substitution: What Happens to Human Deliberation When Answers Arrive before Questions Can Be Lived with

For most of the digital age, interacting with information followed a familiar pattern. A question arose. Information was searched, sources were examined, and pieces of evidence were brought together to form a provisional understanding. Even after search engines made retrieval almost instantaneous, the task of interpreting the information remained with the user.

Generative AI changes that pattern. Instead of presenting a collection of sources to interpret, the system often provides a finished explanation. The pieces have already been combined. What once required comparing multiple perspectives now arrives as a coherent narrative presented in a single voice. The user encounters not the materials from which understanding is built, but a completed conclusion.

At first glance, this appears to be a simple gain in efficiency. Questions that once required extended searching and comparison can now receive immediate answers. In many contexts, this capability is genuinely useful. Yet the convenience changes more than the speed of inquiry. It changes how inquiry unfolds. The space between question and answer becomes smaller. It is within that space that uncertainty is explored and understanding gradually develops. In some cases, the space disappears altogether. The answer arrives before the question has been fully considered.

This chapter examines the consequences of that change. The previous chapters in Part Three focused on the psychology of individual thinking: how fluent language creates persuasive impressions and how repeated reliance on automated systems gradually reshapes habits of judgment. The process examined here operates at a different scale. Thinking is not only an individual activity. It is also a cultural practice. Communities develop shared ways of asking questions, evaluating evidence, and reaching conclusions. Educational systems, professional disciplines, and public institutions all depend on forms of inquiry that unfold over time. Deliberation is central to those practices. It is the discipline of remaining with a question long enough to weigh competing considerations and allow understanding to emerge through sustained engagement with the problem. When answers arrive before that process has unfolded, the practice itself begins to change.

The sections that follow examine how the gradual shift from searching for information to accepting ready-made explanations reshapes not only individual reasoning but also the culture of inquiry through which societies produce knowledge. The discussion begins with a change that has unfolded so gradually that it often passes unnoticed: the shift from retrieving information to receiving answers.

10.1 The Cultural Shift Nobody Announced

From Information Retrieval to Answer Consumption

The transformation described in this chapter did not arrive as an announced change in how people were expected to think. No institution declared that the practices of inquiry had been reorganized. No formal transition replaced one model of knowledge with another. The change occurred quietly through the gradual evolution of the tools used to access information.

Early internet search preserved the basic structure of inquiry that had existed for centuries. A question led to a search for relevant sources. The search produced documents rather than conclusions. Those documents had to be read, interpreted, compared, and brought together into an understanding. Even when search engines greatly accelerated access to information, they still delivered materials rather than answers. The human mind remained the place where synthesis occurred. A search result might point to an article, a paper, a report, or a discussion. Each source carried its own perspective, assumptions, and limitations. Understanding therefore required moving among them. Areas of agreement had to be recognized, disagreements interpreted, and the weight of the evidence judged. The process demanded time and attention, but it also preserved something essential to inquiry: the experience of constructing understanding.

Three features of that experience are worth identifying because they are the very features displaced by the later transformation. The first is exposure to disagreement by encountering sources that do not speak with one voice and discovering that many questions remain contested. The second is the need for independent judgment by deciding which arguments are more persuasive, which evidence is more reliable, and which interpretations deserve greater weight. The third is the visibility of difficulty by confronting the actual state of knowledge, including the places where it remains uncertain, incomplete, or unresolved. Together, these features form the practice of inquiry. They are not merely steps toward an answer. They are the activities through which judgment is exercised and developed.

Over time, however, digital information systems began to compress this process. Knowledge platforms condensed large bodies of information into brief summaries. Knowledge panels presented explanations directly within search results. Recommendation systems gave greater visibility to some interpretations than to others. Each development was experienced as an improvement in efficiency. The distance between a question and useful information became shorter. What began as information retrieval gradually became something closer to answer delivery.

Generative AI completes this transition. Earlier systems retrieved documents that might contain an answer. Generative systems construct the answer itself. Instead of encountering a set of competing sources to interpret, the reader encounters a single explanation that has already synthesized those sources into a coherent narrative. The interpretive work that once took place in the reader's reasoning now takes place within the system. This shift changes the character of inquiry in ways that are easy to overlook. When information arrives as documents, understanding must be constructed from them. When information arrives as a finished explanation, the reader's role shifts from construction to evaluation. The question is no longer what those sources collectively imply, but whether the answer appears acceptable.

At first glance, the difference appears small. The user still reads, evaluates, and decides whether to trust what appears on the screen. Yet the underlying cognitive activity has changed. In one case, understanding develops through engagement with a landscape of information. In the other, understanding is presented as a finished product. The synthesized answer replaces several parts of inquiry that earlier forms of investigation made visible. Exposure to disagreement becomes the appearance of consensus. Contested questions are resolved or bypassed before the reader encounters them. Independent judgment gives way to the acceptance of pre-formed conclusions. Repeatedly weighing sources is no longer necessary when the conclusion arrives already assembled. The visibility of difficulty gives way to the appearance of ease. A smooth and confident explanation appears even when knowledge is rough, contested, or incomplete. The reader therefore reaches a conclusion with confidence shaped not by the actual state of knowledge, but by the appearance of settled understanding projected by the synthesized answer. The experience of inquiry becomes the experience of receiving answers.

Because this transformation unfolded gradually, it rarely appeared to be a decisive cultural shift. Each stage seemed to offer a practical improvement over the previous one: faster search, better summaries, and clearer explanations. Three features of the transition helped conceal its significance. First, each stage presented itself as a refinement rather than a replacement. It appeared to improve the efficiency of inquiry without changing its structure. Second, what disappeared was a process rather than a product. The loss of a process leaves little visible trace when useful conclusions continue to appear. Third, the benefits were immediate, while the costs emerged slowly and diffusely. Efficiency was experienced at once. The erosion of the habits supported by the earlier process became visible only over time. A transition whose benefits are immediate and whose costs accumulate gradually will almost always be seen as progress. Taken together, however, these developments have changed the default way questions are answered. For much of modern intellectual life, the first step in answering a question was to locate the materials from which an answer could be developed. Assembling those materials into understanding remained a human responsibility. Today, that responsibility increasingly shifts to the systems that mediate access to knowledge. The result is a quiet cultural movement from retrieving information to consuming answers.

This movement matters not only because it changes how efficiently questions are answered, but also because it changes what people experience when they confront a question. When answers appear immediately, the interval between question and conclusion becomes shorter. The time available to explore, reframe, or reconsider a problem is reduced. Practices that once supported careful deliberation begin to erode through disuse rather than rejection. What distinguishes the present stage of this transition is that generative systems change the structure of inquiry itself. Earlier technologies accelerated access to the materials of knowledge. Generative AI delivers the appearance of completed conclusions. The shift is cultural because it changes what feels normal: what counts as engaging with a question, how much difficulty is expected in genuine inquiry, and the standards communities apply when judging whether the work of thinking has been done. Inquiry has never been defined solely by the answers it produces. It has also been defined by the process through which those answers emerge. When that process recedes from everyday intellectual life, the consequences extend beyond the efficiency of information retrieval. They reach into the habits through which cultures think. The next section examines this transformation more closely by tracing the point at which generative systems changed the relationship between human inquiry and the production of answers, turning search from a tool for investigation into a substitute for it.

10.2 From Search to Substitution

How Generative AI Changed the Human Relationship to the Epistemic Process

The transition described in the previous section becomes clearer when considering what changed as generative systems entered the information environment. Earlier digital tools accelerated access to knowledge but left the basic structure of inquiry intact. The user still moved through the familiar stages of the epistemic process: locating relevant materials, interpreting their meaning, comparing competing claims, and combining them into an understanding. Generative systems change that structure. There is an important difference between a tool that supports investigation and a system that performs part of the investigative process. The distinction seems straightforward when stated directly, yet it is easy to overlook because both interactions begin in the same way: a question is entered, and a response appears. The difference lies in the role of the human mind.

When search functioned as a tool for investigation, the inquirer began from a position of not yet knowing. The query marked the beginning of inquiry rather than its end. The results consisted of materials that required interpretation rather than conclusions that required evaluation. Understanding developed gradually as those materials were examined, compared, and integrated. In this sense, the investigator was changed by the investigation. Generative systems reorganize this process more fundamentally. Instead of helping users find the components of an answer, they produce the answer itself. The system does not simply retrieve information that may contribute to understanding. It performs the act of synthesis that has historically been central to inquiry. Search becomes substitution. Earlier technologies made the inputs to inquiry easier to access. Generative systems increasingly perform one of its central tasks: constructing a coherent explanation from dispersed information.

The mechanism behind this change is straightforward. Search returned documents, external sources that remained separate from the reader and required deliberate interpretation. The distance between those documents and the reader's understanding had to be bridged through active thought. Much of the cognitive work of inquiry occurred in that process. Generative AI produces responses rather than documents. Those responses are written in the user's register and address the question directly. Much of the interpretive work has already been completed before the response is presented. The distance between explanation and comprehension is deliberately reduced. This change alters the relationship between human thinking and the tools that support it.

When a system retrieves information, the user remains responsible for turning that information into understanding. When a system generates a conclusion, the user encounters an explanation that has already been assembled. The role shifts from constructing an account of the problem to judging whether the account appears acceptable. Inquiry increasingly becomes the evaluation of answers rather than their construction. The distinction may appear subtle, but its consequences are significant. The epistemic process does more than produce conclusions. It also develops the ability to reach those conclusions independently. Repeatedly assembling evidence, weighing arguments, and constructing explanations strengthens the habits of judgment required for disciplined thinking. When the stage of synthesis is displaced, the cognitive work that develops those habits becomes less frequent. Generative systems therefore change more than the speed of inquiry. They change its structure.

Part of the process of building knowledge becomes externalized. Instead of moving from question to materials, from materials to interpretation, and from interpretation to conclusion, the sequence increasingly begins with a conclusion. Interpretation follows as a secondary evaluation. The order of inquiry is reversed. This reversal changes what it means to engage with a question. Under the traditional structure of inquiry, a question initiated exploration. Information accumulated gradually, and conclusions emerged from that process. Under the generative structure, a coherent answer often appears immediately, making further exploration optional rather than necessary. Additional sources may still be consulted, and the system's response may still be reconsidered. Yet the initial orientation has already been shaped by the presence of a ready-made explanation.

From the user's perspective, this reorganization feels like an improvement. Less effort is required to navigate conflicting sources or remain with uncertainty before reaching a conclusion. What disappears from immediate view is the role those difficulties once played. Disagreement encouraged comparison. Uncertainty demanded judgment. Difficulty sustained engagement with the question long enough for its complexity to become visible. When those conditions are removed, inquiry becomes easier. It also becomes more receptive than investigative.

The relationship between uncertainty and knowledge changes as well. In earlier forms of inquiry, uncertainty marked the starting point. The thinker remained with the question long enough to encounter its complexity before arriving at a conclusion. In the generative structure, uncertainty is often resolved before it is fully experienced. A coherent explanation appears at the moment the question is asked. The opportunity to explore uncertainty becomes shorter. This change extends beyond individual interactions. The epistemic process has always served two purposes: producing answers and developing the intellectual habits needed to evaluate them. When part of that process is consistently externalized, the balance between those purposes begins to shift. Answers continue to appear, often more quickly and in greater volume than before. The practices through which people learn to produce and critically evaluate those answers become less central to everyday inquiry.

The relationship between knowledge and the activity of knowing also changes. Generative systems do not simply provide information more efficiently. By performing the act of synthesis internally, they transform a tool for investigation into a substitute for part of the investigative process. Inquiry does not disappear, but part of it is relocated. The work of assembling understanding increasingly takes place inside the system that produces the answer rather than in the mind that receives it.

As this shift spreads across millions of users, educational institutions, professional communities, and research environments, it changes collective expectations. What counts as adequate engagement with a question begins to change. The level of effort considered necessary for genuine inquiry declines. These changes are not merely individual cognitive adjustments. They are cultural changes that accumulate gradually, often without the recognition that shifts of this scale would normally receive. What has changed is not the appearance of the answer, but the location of the process that produced it.

The following sections examine the implications of that relocation. When the work of synthesis is completed before the reader encounters the question, evaluation begins to replace deliberation. Understanding the cost of that substitution requires a closer look at what disappears when part of the work of thinking is performed in advance by the system that provides the answer.

10.3 When Convenience Replaces Evaluation

The Real Cost of What Is Lost When Synthesis Is Pre-Performed

If generative systems substitute answers for investigation, another change follows. The point at which judgment occurs begins to shift. Under the earlier structure of inquiry, evaluation took place throughout the process. Sources were assessed as they were read. Claims were weighed against competing claims. Interpretations changed as new information appeared. Judgment developed gradually as the investigator worked through the question. When synthesis arrives already completed, that structure changes. The user encounters a finished explanation rather than the materials from which an explanation must be built. Evaluation does not disappear, but it moves to a later stage. Instead of shaping understanding step by step, it becomes a response to an already assembled account. The question is no longer how the answer should be constructed, but whether it appears reasonable. From the user's perspective, this shift feels efficient. The system has already gathered and organized the information. The reader can focus on deciding whether the explanation is convincing. Yet removing the work of synthesis carries a cost that is not immediately visible.

Synthesis is more than combining sources. It involves identifying relevant information, judging the reliability of sources, recognizing patterns of agreement and disagreement, and integrating these elements into an explanation that reflects the actual state of the question, including its uncertainties and contested areas. These activities exist only while synthesis is being carried out. A pre-synthesized explanation can present the result of this work. It cannot convey the work itself. Evaluation is strongest when it grows out of participation in the reasoning process. Someone who assembles an explanation piece by piece encounters incomplete evidence, conflicting interpretations, and points where careful judgment is required. Those encounters shape the evaluation of the final account. When synthesis has already been completed, those encounters never occur. The reader sees the conclusion without experiencing the path that produced it. The explanation appears coherent and settled from the outset. The uncertainty that accompanied its construction has already been smoothed away. This smoothing is not merely stylistic. It has epistemic consequences. Genuine inquiry reveals where evidence is strong, where it is weak, where sources conflict, and where questions remain open. Pre-performed synthesis presents a more continuous and stable picture. Contested issues are resolved or passed over, and uncertainty becomes less visible. The reader therefore encounters a representation of the problem that is more orderly than the underlying knowledge often justifies.

Under these conditions, evaluation becomes lighter. The user scans the explanation for obvious problems: an incorrect fact, a contradiction, or a claim that conflicts with prior knowledge. If none appears immediately, the answer often seems adequate. The deeper task of reconstructing the reasoning independently is rarely undertaken. Convenience changes the nature of evaluation. Instead of examining the reasoning itself, users often judge whether the presented reasoning appears plausible. Plausibility can be judged quickly because it depends largely on coherence and familiarity. Genuine evaluation requires reconstructing the argument and comparing it with alternative interpretations. That reconstruction requires an independent standard. A person who has carried out their own synthesis of sources possesses an internal understanding against which a pre-formed account can be compared. When the two differ, the difference signals the need for closer scrutiny. Someone who consistently relies on pre-formed synthesis lacks that independent standard. Their evaluation is genuine, but it is based on the surface of the explanation rather than on an independently constructed understanding of the problem. The more convenient the answer appears, the less likely such reconstruction becomes. This pattern does not arise from carelessness. It follows from the structure of the interaction itself. When an explanation arrives in finished form, it signals that the intellectual work has already been completed. The user encounters the product of reasoning rather than the activity of reasoning. Evaluation therefore becomes optional rather than necessary.

In many everyday situations, this arrangement works well enough. Generative systems often produce explanations that are broadly accurate and practically useful. For routine questions, the difference between reconstructing the reasoning and accepting a plausible synthesis may seem small. The cost becomes visible mainly when questions are complex, contested, or poorly represented in the available data. In such cases, sound judgment depends on deep engagement with the problem. It is precisely that engagement that pre-performed synthesis tends to remove. The loss of this engagement has two consequences. The first affects the quality of conclusions. Without participating in the construction of an explanation, readers are less likely to notice subtle gaps in reasoning or assumptions that deserve closer scrutiny. The second develops more gradually. The habits of evaluation that support careful inquiry weaken when they are no longer exercised regularly. The ability to examine arguments deeply develops through repeated practice. When most explanations arrive already assembled, that practice becomes less frequent. Convenience therefore changes not only how answers are evaluated, but also how the capacity for evaluation develops over time. The role of the human thinker gradually shifts. Instead of building understanding through engagement with evidence, the user increasingly performs a supervisory role, accepting or rejecting conclusions produced elsewhere. Within a single interaction, this shift may appear minor. Across thousands of encounters, it changes the balance between effort and acceptance that has historically shaped inquiry. The cognitive work that once occupied the center of the epistemic process moves to the periphery.

As that work moves to the periphery, its effects begin to accumulate. The capacity for synthesis weakens through disuse. Independent standards for testing pre-formed conclusions become less available. Miscalibrated explanations become harder to detect. Each change reinforces the others. As the ability to synthesize weakens, the ability to develop independent standards also declines. Without those standards, miscalibration becomes harder to recognize. As miscalibration becomes harder to detect, pre-formed explanations are accepted more readily. Their acceptance further reduces the occasions for independent synthesis. Over time, this process gradually erodes the ability to evaluate ready-made explanations in depth. Convenience begins to replace evaluation. The significance of this change becomes clearer when considering what happens to the space in which deliberation once occurred. As answers appear more quickly, the interval between question and conclusion becomes shorter. The next section examines how this shrinking interval affects the practice of thinking itself.

10.4 The Shrinking Space for Deliberation

When Answers Arrive before Thinking Begins

The changes described in the previous sections alter not only how answers are evaluated, but also when thinking begins. Under earlier forms of inquiry, a question opened a period of exploration. Information had to be gathered, interpretations considered, and possibilities weighed. A conclusion emerged gradually through engagement with the problem. This period was not empty time waiting for an answer. It was the time during which thinking took place.

Generative systems compress that process. When an answer appears immediately after a question is asked, the period that once allowed for deliberation becomes shorter or disappears altogether. A conclusion appears before the work of exploring the question has begun. The system presents a coherent explanation that appears to have already followed the path the thinker might otherwise have taken. It occupies that space before the thinker enters it. The generated answer does not interrupt deliberation already in progress. It often prevents deliberation from beginning. The conclusion arrives as soon as the question is posed, closing the space that genuine inquiry requires to remain open. The result is not simply faster access to information. It is the occupation of the space in which deliberation would otherwise occur.

When a conclusion appears first, the question is no longer approached as an open problem. Instead, the thinker encounters an explanation that already offers a way of understanding it. Even when the response is examined critically, its presence shapes the starting point of thought. Reflection begins within an existing frame rather than in uncertainty.

Deliberation depends on the opposite condition. The thinker must encounter the question as genuinely unresolved. Competing possibilities must remain available long enough for their implications to be examined. The difficulty of the problem must be experienced directly rather than reconstructed afterward. During this process, several cognitive developments occur that cannot arise once a conclusion has already been presented. The question is refined through engagement with its complexity. The thinker discovers that the initial formulation was incomplete or misleading. Disagreement among sources reveals the contested nature of the issue instead of presenting it in a smoothed form. Connections emerge between the present question and related questions encountered earlier, reshaping understanding. These developments arise from engaging with the question itself. They cannot be reproduced simply by evaluating a completed answer.

When an explanation appears immediately, the system's account becomes a cognitive anchor. It provides an initial interpretation around which later thinking tends to revolve. Even when the reader questions the response, reflection often takes the form of adjusting or refining the explanation already provided rather than building an independent account from the beginning. Over time, this repeated pattern changes the starting point of inquiry. Thinking increasingly begins with the system's answer rather than with the question itself. The exploration that follows becomes a revision of that answer rather than an investigation that comes before it.

Within a single interaction, this shift may seem minor. A reader may still consult other sources or reconsider the system's explanation. Yet the direction of the inquiry has already been influenced by the presence of a ready-made account. The space in which alternative explanations might have been developed independently has already been occupied. Repeated across many encounters, this shortening of the interval begins to change how questions are experienced. Problems come to feel less like open questions requiring exploration and more like prompts awaiting explanation. Deliberation begins to seem unnecessary. The pattern reinforces itself. As generated answers resolve questions quickly, opportunities to develop the habits of independent deliberation become less frequent. Those habits weaken through disuse. As they weaken, beginning with the system's explanation feels increasingly natural, and the interval in which independent thinking might have occurred becomes easier to surrender.

The consequences extend beyond individual habits of thought. Inquiry in education, professional communities, and public discourse has long depended on a shared space in which questions remain open long enough for disagreement, criticism, and revision to occur. Arguments developed gradually through dialog and refinement. When answers appear before that process begins, the conditions that support deliberation become harder to maintain. Nothing prevents individuals from setting aside an automated explanation and investigating a question independently. The change lies elsewhere. The structure of the interaction no longer requires that effort. The presence of an immediate answer changes expectations about how inquiry normally proceeds. The space for thinking must now be created deliberately rather than arising naturally.

This illustrates a broader feature of technological change. Tools rarely eliminate practices directly. Instead, they change the environment in which those practices occur. When that environment no longer supports an activity, the activity gradually becomes less common. Deliberation follows the same pattern. As generated explanations increasingly occupy the interval between question and conclusion, spending time with an unresolved question becomes less central to everyday inquiry. The shared standard for what counts as adequate engagement with a problem changes accordingly. What once required the work of inquiry increasingly appears satisfied by the receipt of a confident answer. The result is not the disappearance of thought, but a change in its timing. Reflection increasingly occurs after an answer has been presented rather than before one exists. The next section examines why this change matters beyond individual cognition. Deliberation is not only a private mental activity. It is also a cultural practice through which communities sustain shared standards of reasoning and judgment.

10.5 Deliberation as Cultural Practice

Why the Loss Extends beyond Individual Cognitive Performance

The contraction of the deliberative interval described in the previous section may appear, at first, to affect only the habits of individual thinkers. When answers arrive immediately, there are fewer opportunities to remain with a question before reaching a conclusion. Over time, the habits that support careful inquiry weaken through disuse. Deliberation, however, has never been only a private mental activity. It is also a cultural practice. Communities of inquiry, including scientific disciplines, legal traditions, academic institutions, and professional fields, depend on shared practices for exploring questions and testing conclusions. These practices shape how evidence is weighed, how disagreement is handled, and how uncertainty is treated. The capacity for deliberation is therefore sustained not only within individual minds but also through the norms that guide collective inquiry. These norms define when a question has been examined adequately, how disagreement tests and refines understanding, how new members learn by participating in inquiry, and how repeated encounters with unresolved questions foster epistemic humility. These are not individual cognitive traits. They are collective practices sustained through shared activity. Within such communities, thinking rarely occurs in isolation. A researcher proposes an interpretation that others examine critically. A scholar's argument develops through response and revision. A professional judgment is tested against the experience and reasoning of colleagues. Through these interactions, individual reasoning becomes part of a broader process of collective deliberation. That process depends on time. Questions must remain open long enough for alternative interpretations to emerge and be examined. Arguments must be tested through criticism before their conclusions are accepted. Knowledge advances not only by producing answers, but by testing, challenging, and refining those answers.

Generative systems introduce a different dynamic. When a coherent explanation appears immediately in response to a question, it becomes difficult to avoid the impression that the issue has already been addressed. The answer arrives as a finished account rather than as a contribution to an ongoing inquiry. Even when approached cautiously, it tends to establish the initial frame for subsequent discussion. Questions therefore begin to circulate differently within communities. Instead of serving primarily as starting points for exploration, they increasingly arrive with ready-made explanations. Participants often begin by evaluating the generated response rather than by developing independent interpretations of the problem.

Deliberation moves downstream of the answer. This shift changes the role of disagreement in intellectual life. In traditional inquiry, disagreement arose from independently developed interpretations of evidence. Competing accounts forced investigators to clarify assumptions, reconsider evidence, and refine conclusions. When an answer is already synthesized, disagreement takes a different form. Participants respond to a shared explanation rather than advancing independent analyzes. The range of perspectives considered may narrow because discussion begins within the boundaries established by the generated account. The nature of disagreement changes as well. When individuals have examined the evidence independently, disagreement tests competing analyzes and can produce revised understanding. When individuals respond to the same generated explanation, disagreement often becomes a debate about a shared account. Discussion shifts subtly from exploration to reaction. Over time, these changes can influence the standards by which communities judge whether a question has been examined adequately. When answers appear quickly and convincingly, the expectation that inquiry requires sustained deliberation may weaken. The threshold for what counts as sufficient engagement with a problem gradually declines. Serious deliberation will not disappear. Scholars, scientists, and professionals will continue to challenge claims, examine evidence, and debate interpretations. The environment in which those practices occur, however, is changing. The presence of instant, synthesized explanations alters both the pace and the direction of inquiry. The pressure to move quickly from question to answer increases.

In educational settings, the consequences are particularly visible. Learning has long depended on sustained engagement with questions whose answers are not immediately available. Students develop intellectual discipline by working through sources, confronting conflicting interpretations, and revising their understanding through effort. When explanations appear instantly, the experience of inquiry risks being replaced by the acceptance of conclusions. Students encounter the appearance of understanding before they experience the process that produces it. The habit of deliberation becomes harder to develop when finished answers consistently precede investigation.

The broader cultural consequences follow the same pattern. Public discourse depends on the ability of communities to deliberate collectively about uncertain questions, including political decisions, scientific controversies, and ethical dilemmas. These processes require time for disagreement, reflection, and revision. When persuasive explanations appear immediately, the patience they require becomes harder to sustain. The expectation that complex questions deserve extended examination gradually weakens when answers appear readily available. Deliberation, like many cultural practices, survives only while the conditions that support it remain intact. Technological change rarely eliminates practices directly. Instead, it changes the environment in which they occur. When that environment no longer supports a practice, the practice gradually becomes less central to everyday life. Deliberation follows this pattern.

The contraction of the deliberative interval therefore affects more than individual habits of thought. It influences the cultural norms through which communities decide how knowledge should be produced and evaluated. What is at stake is not simply whether individuals think carefully, but whether the collective practices that sustain careful thinking remain part of the intellectual environment. The resulting loss has a distinctive character. Individual cognitive skills can, in principle, be strengthened through deliberate practice. Cultural practices cannot be restored so easily. They depend on shared norms and repeated participation across communities. When deliberation weakens, what erodes is not simply the sum of individual cognitive abilities. It is the shared infrastructure of thought: the collective practices, standards, and expectations through which communities achieve together what no individual's private reasoning can accomplish alone. The next section examines why these practices depend on forms of difficulty and friction that technological systems increasingly remove.

10.6 What Disciplined Thinking Requires

Difficulty, Uncertainty, Friction, and Synthesis

The preceding sections have traced a gradual change in the relationship between questions and answers. Generated explanations shorten the interval between them, reducing or eliminating the space in which deliberation once took place. To understand why this matters, it is necessary to examine what disciplined thinking actually requires.

Thinking is often imagined as the smooth arrival at a conclusion. In practice, it rarely unfolds that way. Before examining the conditions that support disciplined reasoning, a possible misunderstanding should be addressed. The argument that follows is not a defense of difficulty for its own sake. It does not claim that thinking is valuable simply because it is difficult, or that removing difficulty is always a loss. The claim is more precise. Difficulty, uncertainty, friction, and the effort required to bring ideas together are not incidental features of disciplined thinking. They are the conditions through which it develops. When these conditions are absent, something that resembles thinking may still occur, but the cognitive processes through which understanding is normally formed are no longer fully engaged.

Disciplined reasoning begins with difficulty. When a person confronts a genuine problem, the path to understanding is rarely direct. Information must be located and interpreted. Competing explanations must be compared. Assumptions must be identified and tested. Initial interpretations often prove incomplete or mistaken. These features can make the process appear inefficient. It includes pauses, detours, and uncertainty. Yet these apparent inefficiencies serve an essential function. They engage the cognitive processes that disciplined reasoning requires.

A question that can be answered by recognizing a familiar pattern does not require independent evaluation of evidence or the construction of an explanation from available information. Difficulty interrupts pattern recognition. It forces the thinker to move beyond recognition into analysis and synthesis. In this sense, difficulty slows the movement from question to answer so that genuine reasoning can occur.

Uncertainty plays a related but distinct role. Before reaching a conclusion, the thinker must remain in a state where the correct answer is not yet known. This condition can feel uncomfortable. The mind naturally prefers closure to open questions. Yet the willingness to remain with uncertainty is precisely what allows a problem to be explored rather than resolved too quickly. Difficulty belongs to the problem. Uncertainty belongs to the thinker. A thinker who cannot tolerate uncertainty moves quickly toward closure, accepting the first available answer instead of remaining with the question long enough for deeper engagement. The capacity to remain with uncertainty develops through repeated encounters with unresolved questions. It weakens when those encounters are consistently removed. Generated answers displace this condition directly. By resolving uncertainty as soon as it appears, they close the space of not yet knowing before the thinker has had the opportunity to inhabit it.

Friction is the experiential dimension of this process. It is what genuine engagement with a difficult question feels like from the inside. It is the experience of resistance: the resistance encountered when initial approaches fail, when evidence contradicts expectations, and when sources disagree in ways that require judgment rather than retrieval. Friction signals that the thinker is engaging with the problem itself rather than simply receiving an account of it.

Generated answers remove friction by design. The fluency described in Chapter 8 is defined by this absence of resistance. It is the smooth, confident delivery that makes generated explanations feel authoritative. A fluent response presents no obstacles. It fits the user's framing of the question and delivers a conclusion without the rough edges that genuine inquiry often produces. The result is an explanation that feels intellectually satisfying while bypassing the experience that would have calibrated judgment.

Friction serves a crucial epistemic function. It calibrates confidence. A thinker who has struggled with a problem learns where the evidence is strong, where it remains uncertain, and where conclusions must stay tentative. Someone who receives a frictionless explanation encounters the conclusion without experiencing the process that justifies that calibration. Removing friction therefore does more than make thinking easier. It replaces engagement with representation.

The final condition is synthesis, the activity through which separate pieces of information become understanding. It requires distinguishing relevant from irrelevant evidence, recognizing patterns across sources, and combining those elements into an explanation that reflects the complexity of the question. The explanation is only the visible outcome. The intellectual work occurs during the process itself. A thinker who performs that work becomes familiar with the structure of the problem: where evidence converges, where it diverges, and where interpretation is required. That familiarity becomes the basis for careful judgment.

Difficulty, uncertainty, and friction come together in the work of synthesis. Genuine synthesis requires difficulty because the answer cannot be retrieved from a single pattern. It requires uncertainty because the conclusion cannot be known in advance. It requires friction because sources disagree and evidence is incomplete. These conditions make synthesis possible. Through the effort of synthesis, understanding develops. When a system performs the synthesis in advance and delivers a finished account, the product of reasoning is transmitted without the experience of reasoning. The explanation may be coherent and informative. What is missing is the engagement through which understanding normally develops. The difference resembles observing a completed puzzle rather than assembling it. Both reveal the final arrangement of the pieces. Only the second provides the experience of discovering how those pieces fit together.

This distinction matters because disciplined thinking is not only a way of producing answers. It is also the practice through which intellectual capacities are maintained. Repeated engagement with difficult questions strengthens the ability to analyze arguments, detect weaknesses in reasoning, and integrate complex information into coherent understanding. The effort involved in these activities allows them to become reliable habits of mind. When that effort disappears from everyday inquiry, the habits that depend on it gradually weaken.

Frictionless systems therefore introduce a paradox. By removing difficulty from many intellectual tasks, they increase efficiency in the short term while reducing the opportunities through which disciplined thinking is exercised. Each interaction still appears productive. Questions are answered quickly, and explanations are clear. Yet the underlying cognitive process has changed. A path that once required sustained reasoning is replaced by receiving an answer followed by brief evaluation. The answer appears without the intellectual journey that once produced it.

Over time, this change reshapes the relationship between knowledge and effort. Understanding begins to appear effortless because the work that produces it has been moved elsewhere. Thinking comes to seem like an optional step performed after an explanation is delivered rather than the process through which the explanation emerges. This shift does not make disciplined reasoning impossible. Questions can still be investigated independently, multiple sources can still be consulted, and arguments can still be reconstructed. But the environment no longer requires that level of engagement. The effort needed for disciplined reasoning must now be introduced deliberately rather than encountered naturally.

This distinction marks the boundary between assistance and substitution. Tools that assist thinking make the materials of inquiry more accessible while preserving the need for synthesis and evaluation. Tools that substitute for thinking remove parts of the process itself. When substitution becomes routine, the conditions that sustain disciplined reasoning become harder to maintain.

Across this chapter, a clear pattern has emerged. The thinker still reads, assesses, accepts, rejects, and compares. Yet the underlying cognitive activity shifts from construction to evaluation, from building understanding through synthesis to judging pre-formed explanations for plausibility. Evaluation without construction can produce answers. It does not produce the thinker's own understanding of the terrain, with its complexity, uncertainty, and calibrated confidence, that the work of synthesis would have created.

The conditions that make genuine synthesis possible are not inefficiencies to be eliminated from intellectual life. They are the conditions through which understanding develops and judgment is refined. A culture that systematically removes those conditions may continue to produce answers. What becomes less certain is whether it continues to produce thinkers. The final section of this part brings together the psychological and cultural dynamics examined in the previous chapters: the persuasive power of fluent language, the gradual erosion of judgment through cognitive offloading, and the transformation of inquiry when answers arrive before questions can be lived with. Together, these forces reveal a vulnerability that operates across multiple levels of human thinking.

10.7 Understanding the Vulnerability

Immediate, Longitudinal, and Cultural

The chapters in this part of the book have examined the influence of predictive systems from several perspectives. Each chapter described a different way in which interaction with these systems shapes human thinking. Taken individually, these mechanisms may appear limited: a bias here, a habit there, a small shift in how inquiry begins. Taken together, they reveal something more significant. They reveal a pattern of vulnerability that operates across multiple levels of human cognition.

The first level is immediate. Chapter 8 examined the psychological effects of fluent language. When an explanation is smooth, coherent, and confidently presented, the human mind experiences cognitive ease. That ease creates an immediate sense of credibility. Fluency activates a shortcut to authority and reduces the impulse to examine claims closely. The explanation feels as though the intellectual work behind it has already been completed. In that moment, the illusion of intelligence emerges. The system appears to understand because the language it produces carries the signals that normally accompany understanding. This response is not irrational. It reflects cognitive mechanisms that evolved in environments where those signals reliably indicated genuine knowledge. At this level, the vulnerability appears within seconds of encountering an answer.

The second level develops over time. Chapter 9 examined the gradual change that occurs when frictionless answers become a routine part of reasoning. Automation bias encourages trust in system outputs. The convenience of instant explanations makes consultation increasingly attractive. Gradually, the role of the human thinker shifts from constructing judgments to supervising them. At first, the change appears minor. The user still evaluates the system's response and remains responsible for the final decision. Yet repeated reliance transfers more of the reasoning process to the system. The human thinker remains present, but more of the cognitive work takes place elsewhere. Over many interactions, the habits that support independent reasoning weaken through disuse. Questions that once prompted investigation now prompt consultation. The intellectual effort once associated with solving problems becomes less common. At this level, the vulnerability is not experienced as an error. It is experienced as a convenience. Its depth becomes visible only when a problem falls outside the system's familiar patterns and independent judgment is required.

Beyond these psychological and behavioral changes lies a third level of influence: the cultural level. Chapter 10 examined how generative systems reshape the practice of inquiry itself. When answers appear immediately, the interval between question and conclusion becomes shorter. The space once occupied by deliberation contracts or disappears. Inquiry gradually shifts from investigation to reception. Instead of building understanding through sources, comparison, and synthesis, users increasingly encounter ready-made explanations. Evaluation replaces construction. The effort through which disciplined thinking develops becomes less central to everyday intellectual life. Because thinking is also a cultural practice, this change extends beyond individual cognition. Educational institutions, professional disciplines, and public discourse all depend on shared norms that sustain careful inquiry over time. As the environment surrounding inquiry changes, those norms begin to change as well. The expectation that important questions require extended exploration weakens. What once counted as engagement with a problem increasingly resembles the acceptance of an answer.

Seen together, these three levels describe a single trajectory in which each reinforces the others. Fluent answers encourage immediate acceptance. Repeated acceptance encourages reliance. Widespread reliance reshapes the environment in which communities think together. The interaction extends beyond this sequence. Fluency assigns credibility before deliberate evaluation begins. Cognitive offloading weakens the habits that would allow those first impressions to be corrected. Independent synthesis, tolerance for uncertainty, and the maintenance of independent standards of judgment all decline. Cultural change then weakens the shared practices through which those habits were historically sustained and transmitted. Each force strengthens the conditions under which the others operate. None of these developments results from a deliberate surrender of judgment. They arise from the interaction between powerful technological capabilities and cognitive habits that evolved in a very different informational environment. The vulnerability is structural. It lies in the relationship between systems that generate fluent, confident conclusions and the cognitive and cultural processes through which human minds interpret them. It is not a failure of intelligence. The individuals and communities affected by these forces are neither careless nor credulous. They are responding rationally to an environment that has changed in ways their cognitive architecture was never designed to detect.

The illusion of intelligence is not simply a property of machines. It is a relationship between machine output and human interpretation. The system produces language that resembles the products of reasoning. The human mind interprets those signals through cognitive shortcuts that evolved in a world where fluent explanation usually indicated genuine understanding. The result is a convergence of appearance and expectation. The machine appears to think. The human mind responds as though it does. Recognizing this relationship does not diminish the usefulness of predictive systems. They can assist reasoning, summarize information, and expand access to knowledge in valuable ways. But usefulness and influence are not the same. A tool that assists thinking also changes the conditions under which thinking takes place. The illusion of intelligence does not arise from a single mistake. It emerges from the interaction between technological fluency and human cognition across multiple timescales. What begins as a persuasive surface effect can, through repetition and institutional adoption, reshape how individuals and communities approach the activity of thinking itself.

Understanding this pattern is the first step toward responding to it, but it is not the response itself. Part Three has established the diagnosis: the structure of the vulnerability, the mechanisms that sustain it, and the reasons awareness alone cannot resolve it. Part Four turns to protection. It examines the habits, practices, and institutional conditions through which intellectual agency can be preserved. If predictive systems continue to shape the environment of human reasoning, the central question becomes how that environment should be structured. Part Four begins by exploring what a more deliberate relationship between human judgment and machine assistance might look like.

Closing Reflection

A difficult issue demands careful thought. The question has remained unresolved for several days. It may involve a workplace problem, an important decision, or an unfamiliar field in which the available knowledge is incomplete. They have considered different possibilities and revised their assumptions. No answer has yet emerged that feels fully their own. They open a screen and enter the question as they currently understand it. A response appears within seconds. It is fluent, organized, and confident. It is more comprehensive than expected. It addresses the issue directly, outlines the relevant considerations, and reaches a clear conclusion. They read it carefully. Nothing in the explanation seems obviously wrong. The reasoning appears coherent, and the conclusion is plausible. The confidence of the response resembles the confidence that accompanies genuine understanding. They close the screen. They now have an answer.

What they have, more precisely, is a fluent account of how the question, as presented, might be resolved. The response comes from a system that does not know what remains unknown to them. It has not encountered the specific circumstances of their situation. Nor can it adjust its confidence to match the true complexity of the problem. What they receive is a conclusion without the process that normally leads to it, an answer that arrives before the question has been fully examined. The problem has not been confronted directly, and the effort required for genuine engagement has not shaped the thinker's understanding. None of this is visible in the response itself. Fluency obscures the missing process. Confidence conceals the limits of the underlying reasoning. The smoothness of the explanation hides the complexity that has been reduced or omitted. The person receiving the answer is neither careless nor credulous. They respond exactly as the processes examined in this section would predict. Fluent explanations gain credibility because fluency signals authority. The effort required to build understanding is absent. The surrounding environment increasingly makes receiving answers feel more natural than developing understanding.

The question has been answered, but understanding has not yet formed. Part Three has clarified the difference between receiving an answer and exercising judgment. Part Four turns to a different question: how to preserve that distinction deliberately under conditions that increasingly make it difficult to maintain.

PART FOUR
THE MANY FACES

How One Engine Reaches Human Lives — Text, Voice, Video, and Behavioral AI

The LLM core is the source. Yet it reaches people through many forms: text that is read, voices that are heard, videos that are watched, and advice that is followed. Each form creates its own kind of illusion. Each exploits different human vulnerabilities. The next two chapters examine this broader landscape. One explores how the illusion appears across different modalities. The other develops a moral taxonomy of those illusions.

CHAPTER 11
One Engine, Many Deceptions

From Organic Illusion to Weaponized Reality

The previous part of this book examined the conditions under which the illusion of intelligence arises. Fluent language triggers cognitive shortcuts. Repeated reliance reshapes habits of judgment. The structure of inquiry can also change when answers arrive before questions have been explored fully. Those chapters focused primarily on the interaction between human cognition and the outputs of predictive systems. Part Four turns to a broader question. If a predictive architecture can create the illusion of understanding in text, what happens when the same capability extends into other domains of experience? What happens when these systems reach people not only through written responses, but also through voices they hear, videos they watch, advice they follow, and decisions that affect their finances, reputation, or safety?

The conversational text interface of a large language model is often the first form in which people encounter these systems. But the language model is only one expression of a broader technology. It is the core engine from which many other systems are built. The same predictive architecture can generate written explanations, synthetic voices, photorealistic video, automated recommendations, and behavioral predictions. What appear to be different technologies are often different expressions of the same underlying capability: generating outputs by predicting patterns in data.

Each expression interacts with human cognition in a different way. A written response exploits the fluency bias described earlier by encouraging readers to treat articulate language as evidence of understanding. A synthetic voice adds cues of human presence and authority. Photorealistic video introduces an even stronger cue: the deeply rooted expectation that what is seen must have happened. Systems that generate advice or behavioral predictions engage a different set of vulnerabilities. They appeal not to perception, but to desires for financial gain, personal improvement, or reliable guidance. In every case, the underlying mechanism remains the same: pattern-based generation. What changes is the channel through which the output reaches the human mind.

Because each channel carries its own cues of credibility, the same predictive engine can produce different forms of illusion. In text, the illusion often arises without deliberate intent. The system generates fluent explanations without awareness, and human cognition supplies the interpretation. In other contexts, the illusion becomes intentional. Synthetic media can imitate specific individuals. Automated systems can be designed to exploit predictable psychological responses. A capability that begins as neutral generative machinery can therefore become a tool for strategic deception.

The difference between these situations is not merely technical. It is also moral. Some AI-generated illusions arise without human intent to deceive. A language model may produce a confident but incorrect answer because statistical prediction does not guarantee truth. The system does not know that the answer is false. It does not know that it is answering a question. The illusion arises through the interaction between its output and the interpretive habits of the reader. Other illusions involve deliberate human action. A fabricated video may be created to impersonate a public figure. A system offering investment advice may be designed to exploit predictable desires for profit. In such cases, the generative capability of the machine becomes part of a broader human strategy. These situations share a common technological origin, but not the same structure of responsibility. An incorrect answer generated by a language model, a synthetic recording that impersonates a political leader, and an automated system that encourages risky financial behavior all arise from the same predictive architecture. Yet they represent different forms of deception, involving different actors and different moral responsibilities.

Understanding the full landscape of AI-produced false belief therefore requires looking beyond the model itself. The predictive engine is the starting point. The illusions that shape human judgment emerge through the environments in which that engine operates: the interface through which it communicates, the medium through which its outputs are delivered, and the intentions of those who deploy it.

This chapter maps that landscape. It begins with the most familiar case: the organic illusion produced by language models, where fluent text can create false belief without any intention to deceive. It then examines systems that signal uncertainty as a contrasting example, showing how context can transform even honest outputs into misleading ones. The discussion then moves to more deliberate forms of illusion: synthetic voices and videos used to impersonate real people, automated systems that promise financial insight while exploiting predictable human desires, and platforms that amplify credibility through timing, context, and scale. Across these examples, the same predictive engine appears in many forms. What changes is not the underlying mechanism, but the environment in which it operates and the purposes it serves. By the end of the chapter, the full landscape should be clear: a continuum that extends from organic error in generated text to deliberate multimedia deception used for strategic purposes. Only by understanding this continuum is it possible to recognize where the illusion of intelligence ends and human deception begins. The first form of illusion appears where most readers first encounter AI systems: the fluent text of the language model itself.

11.1 Organic Illusion in Text

The LLM Producing Fluent False Output without Intent or Awareness

The most familiar form of AI-produced false belief appears in the simplest setting: a text response generated by a language model. A user asks a question. The system produces a fluent explanation. The answer is coherent, grammatically correct, and often delivered with the confident tone associated with knowledgeable human communication. Sometimes the answer is correct. Sometimes it is not. When it is incorrect, the failure is commonly described as a hallucination. The term is widely used, but it obscures what is actually happening. Nothing resembling perception or imagination occurs inside the system. A language model does not observe the world, form beliefs about it, or express those beliefs in language. It performs a different task. It generates sequences of words that statistically resemble patterns in the data on which it was trained.

The underlying mechanism is predictive continuation. Given a prompt, the model estimates which tokens are most likely to come next based on patterns learned from vast collections of text. Because those collections contain explanations, arguments, summaries, and analyzes written by humans, the model learns the statistical structure of those forms. It learns how explanations usually unfold, how authority is signaled, how evidence is cited, and how conclusions are expressed. The result is language that has the surface features of understanding. What the system lacks is any internal connection to the truth of what it generates.

A person answering a question typically performs several tasks at once. Knowledge is recalled. The reliability of the information is assessed. Confidence is adjusted to match the limits of what is known. A language model performs none of these tasks. It does not retrieve beliefs from memory. It does not test claims against evidence. It does not know whether the sentences it produces correspond to the world. It simply extends patterns. When those patterns align with accurate information, the response appears knowledgeable. When they produce a plausible explanation that does not correspond to reality, the output may contain fabricated facts, invented citations, or subtly incorrect descriptions of events and concepts. Because the language remains fluent and well structured, the error often appears credible. This is the source of the organic illusion. The system is not attempting to deceive. Intention requires awareness, and the model has none. Nor does it distinguish between invention and recall. Both are treated as patterns that can be continued. The illusion arises from the interaction between a statistical language generator and a human interpreter.

Human readers are accustomed to explanations produced by minds capable of knowledge. Clear language, structured reasoning, and confident delivery normally signal that the speaker understands the subject. These signals function as reliable indicators in ordinary human communication. A language model reproduces those signals without the cognitive state that once gave them their meaning. Fluent language therefore activates the interpretive habits examined earlier in this book. The reader experiences cognitive ease. The explanation resembles competent reasoning. The absence of hesitation suggests confidence. From these cues, the mind draws a familiar inference: the system appears to understand the subject under discussion. In reality, the output is the product of pattern continuation rather than understanding.

This makes the resulting error different from traditional misinformation. When a person writes something incorrect, the statement is usually connected to a belief, a misunderstanding, or an attempt to persuade. In each case, the claim reflects a mental state. With a language model, no such relationship exists. The sentences resemble informed explanations whether or not they correspond to reality. The appearance of knowledge arises from statistical regularities in language rather than from any understanding of the subject.

For this reason, the illusion can be described as organic. Nothing in the process is designed specifically to deceive. The system performs the task for which it was built: generating language that resembles the patterns it has learned. The misleading effect arises because those patterns include the forms through which humans normally communicate knowledge. When those forms appear without the knowledge that usually grounds them, the result is language that resembles understanding while lacking the conditions that make understanding genuine. Organic illusion therefore marks the starting point of the landscape examined in this chapter. It is the simplest case: fluent text that can generate false belief without awareness, intention, or strategy. The next section examines a system designed to acknowledge uncertainty openly. Even so, it remains capable of producing misunderstanding once its output enters a human context.

11.2 The AI That Said "I Don't Know"

Honest Systems and Contextual Illusion

The organic illusion described in the previous section arises because a language model produces fluent explanations regardless of whether the underlying claim is true. One obvious response is to design systems that behave more cautiously. Instead of presenting confident answers in every situation, the system could signal uncertainty. It might decline to answer when the available information is insufficient or when the question falls outside its competence. In principle, this approach seems straightforward. If a system admits what it does not know, the risk of misleading users should decrease.

In practice, the situation is more complicated. Several experimental systems have been built with this goal. Rather than generating confident responses to every prompt, they produce explicit expressions of uncertainty: "*I don't know*," "*I cannot determine this from the available information*," or "*The evidence is inconclusive*." The aim is to introduce behavior that resembles intellectual honesty by acknowledging the limits of knowledge instead of masking them with fluent speculation. From an engineering perspective, such systems represent a meaningful improvement. A model that occasionally declines to answer avoids one of the most common failures of generative systems: confidently producing plausible but false information. Yet even when a system behaves cautiously, misunderstanding can still arise. The reason lies not in the content of the response, but in the context in which it is interpreted.

Consider the statement, "*I don't know.*" In ordinary human conversation, this phrase carries a specific meaning. It signals that a speaker has considered the question and recognizes the limits of their knowledge. The statement assumes a mind capable of reflection and self-awareness. It is therefore understood as an honest acknowledgment of ignorance. The response signals epistemic responsibility rather than incompetence. When a machine uses the same phrase, the words remain identical, but the underlying situation differs fundamentally. The system has not recognized the limits of its knowledge. It has no awareness of knowledge at all. The phrase, "*I don't know*," is simply another pattern of language generated under certain conditions. The system does not know that it does not know. Yet human listeners interpret the statement according to the familiar conventions of human communication. An admission of uncertainty can create the impression that the system possesses intellectual integrity. It suggests that the system can distinguish between what it knows and what it does not know. In this way, behavior intended to make the system safer can strengthen the perception that it is a reliable epistemic agent. This produces a different kind of illusion. In the earlier case, fluent explanations resembled genuine knowledge. Here, the expression of uncertainty resembles genuine self-awareness. The system appears responsible because it produces the language associated with responsible thinking. The underlying mechanism, however, remains unchanged. The model generates a phrase that resembles an honest admission of ignorance without possessing the cognitive state that would make such an admission meaningful. The resulting misunderstanding can be described as a contextual illusion. The statement itself is not false. The phrase, "I don't know," simply does not correspond to any internal mental state within the system. The illusion arises when the human interpreter places the statement within a conversational context that assumes a thinking agent is participating in the exchange. Context completes the illusion.

This example reveals something important about AI-generated belief. Deception does not always require incorrect information. It can arise whenever human habits of interpretation encounter machine-generated signals that resemble the cues of genuine cognition. A system designed to admit uncertainty is therefore not immune to misunderstanding. Its behavior may be honest in the limited engineering sense that it avoids confident fabrication. Yet once that behavior enters human communication, the signals it produces can still create impressions that the system itself cannot justify. This is not a failure of good design. It is a structural feature of the interaction between predictive systems and human cognition.

The difference between organic illusion and contextual illusion is subtle but important. In the first case, fluent explanations resemble knowledge despite the absence of understanding. In the second, expressions of uncertainty resemble self-awareness despite the absence of a mind capable of such awareness. Both forms arise without malicious intent. Both emerge from the same predictive mechanism. Both demonstrate that the appearance of intelligence can be created even when the system is designed to behave cautiously. The next sections examine situations in which the illusion is no longer merely organic or contextual. When synthetic voices and videos convincingly imitate real individuals, the same generative capability becomes a tool that can be used deliberately to mislead.

11.3 The Minister Who Never Spoke

Deepfake Video, Voice Cloning, and Weaponized Illusion

The illusions examined so far arise from the interaction between machine-generated output and human interpretation. A language model produces fluent explanations that resemble knowledge. A cautious system produces phrases that resemble intellectual humility. In both cases, the illusion emerges naturally from the interaction between predictive generation and human expectations. There is, however, another category of cases in which the same generative capability is used deliberately to create false belief. The difference becomes clear when a system no longer produces anonymous text but instead appears to speak with the voice, and sometimes the face, of a specific person.

Imagine a video circulating on social media. A government minister appears to address the public. The voice is recognizable. The facial movements match the speech. The lighting and background resemble the setting in which official statements are normally delivered. The message is controversial. It may announce a policy change, address a diplomatic issue, or respond to an unfolding crisis. The video spreads rapidly. Journalists comment. Citizens share the clip across platforms. Markets react. Political opponents issue statements of condemnation or support. Hours later, the ministry releases a clarification: the minister never spoke those words. The video is synthetic. Events of this kind are no longer hypothetical. Advances in generative modeling have made it possible to produce highly convincing synthetic media. Systems trained on large collections of audiovisual data can generate photorealistic faces and animate them in synchrony with speech. They can also reproduce the vocal characteristics of particular individuals from relatively small audio samples. The resulting media, commonly described as a deepfake, is a synthetic recording designed to resemble an authentic one.

In such cases, the illusion does not arise accidentally. It is engineered. The goal is not merely to produce language that resembles an explanation, as in the case of a language model. The goal is to reproduce the sensory signals that humans have long treated as evidence that an event actually occurred. Written claims can be doubted. Rumors can be questioned. Video, however, carries a different evidential weight. Seeing and hearing a person speak has historically been treated as strong evidence that the person said what appears in the recording. Synthetic media exploits that expectation.

Predictive models learn patterns in images, voices, and movement. They then generate new combinations of those patterns that resemble genuine recordings. When applied to the likeness of a specific individual, the result is media in which that person appears to perform actions never performed. Unlike the organic illusion produced by a language model, these outputs are usually deployed for a strategic purpose. Someone chooses the person to imitate. Someone chooses the message to attribute to that person. Someone decides when and where the video will appear. The generative capability becomes a tool in a broader act of deception.

The persuasive force of synthetic media arises from several elements working together. First, the sensory realism of the recording provides cues that human perception normally associates with authenticity. Second, the person being imitated lends authority to the message. A statement attributed to a public figure carries consequences that the same words, spoken by an unknown person, would not. Third, social media feeds, messaging platforms, and news aggregators can spread the video to large audiences before anyone has time to verify it. Together, these elements create what may be called a weaponized illusion. The generative model provides the technical capability. The human actor provides the intention. The surrounding media ecosystem provides the conditions that allow the illusion to spread faster than it can be corrected. The difference between an organic illusion and a weaponized illusion therefore lies primarily in human agency. When a language model produces an incorrect explanation, the misleading effect arises from the interaction between statistical generation and human interpretation. In the case of a deepfake, the misleading effect arises because a person deliberately uses generative technology to create a specific false belief.

The moral structure of the situation changes accordingly. The model remains unaware of what it has produced. It does not know that the video resembles a particular person or that the words in the recording were never spoken. The person who creates and distributes the synthetic media, however, does know. The deception lies not in the statistical process that generated the image, but in the human decision to use that process to impersonate another individual.

Synthetic media therefore expands the landscape of AI-produced false belief in an important way. The illusion is no longer confined to the interpretation of text. It operates through the most powerful channels of human perception:

sight and sound. It also draws authority from identifiable individuals. Earlier in this chapter, the system generated language that appeared knowledgeable or self-aware without possessing knowledge or self-awareness. Here, the system generates sensory evidence that appears authentic despite depicting events that never occurred. The same predictive engine that produced fluent text now produces convincing audiovisual evidence. The next section examines a different domain in which generative systems are used with deliberate human intent: the promise of financial insight. When AI systems present themselves as guides to profitable decisions, they create another illusion. That illusion depends not on impersonation, but on a persistent human hope that someone, somewhere, knows how to beat the market.

11.4 The Market That Promises Everything

Predatory AI, Investment Advice, and the Exploitation of Financial Hope

The previous section described a form of AI-enabled deception based on imitation. A synthetic video persuades viewers because it appears to show a real person speaking. The illusion draws on the authority of identity and the evidential weight of visual media. In financial markets, the illusion works differently. Its persuasive force does not come from impersonating a particular individual. It comes from a promise: the claim that a system has discovered a reliable path to profit. The message is familiar and enduring. Markets are complex, and most participants struggle to outperform them. The claim is that a method, algorithm, or model can identify opportunities others have overlooked. Generative AI has made this promise easier to create and easier to spread.

Across online platforms, systems are presented as intelligent trading assistants, automated investment advisers, or algorithmic portfolio managers. They promise to analyze vast amounts of financial data, detect patterns invisible to ordinary investors, and generate actionable insights in real time. The language surrounding these systems emphasizes the same qualities that make modern AI appear impressive in other settings: speed, scale, and computational sophistication. A machine capable of processing global news feeds, market reports, and price movements across multiple exchanges appears well suited to identifying profitable opportunities. Some of these tools are presented as aids that help investors organize information or explore possible strategies. When used with a clear understanding of their limits, they function like other analytical technologies. They can be useful. They become misleading only when granted more authority than they deserve. Other systems, however, are marketed with a different purpose. Some services promise extraordinary returns while invoking artificial intelligence to justify those promises. Advertisements highlight proprietary algorithms that supposedly predict market movements with remarkable accuracy. Testimonials describe consistent profits. Charts show steadily rising performance. The implication is clear. The complexity of financial markets appears to have been solved, not through human insight, but through computational power.

This promise appeals to one of the most persistent features of human decision-making: the hope of reliable financial gain. Financial markets have long attracted stories about secret strategies and superior forecasting methods. From early stock-tip newsletters to sophisticated hedge fund models, investors have repeatedly hoped that someone possesses a method capable of consistently beating the market. In practice, decades of financial research suggest that such advantages are rare and difficult to sustain. Markets absorb information quickly, and profitable strategies tend to disappear once they become widely known. Yet the hope persists.

Generative systems amplify that hope in several ways. First, they produce explanations that sound technically convincing. A model can describe trading strategies, statistical indicators, or machine-learning pipelines in language that resembles expert financial analysis. It can combine legitimate theory with speculative claims about predictive accuracy. Because the explanation is fluent and detailed, it creates the impression that a rigorous method supports the promise. Second, the system can generate personalized narratives. A prospective investor may receive customised reports explaining why particular opportunities exist at a given moment. Tailored explanations produced at scale create the impression that the advice reflects careful analysis of the individual's situation. Third, generative systems can simulate evidence. Charts, forecasts, and performance summaries can be generated automatically, creating the appearance of a proven track record. Even when these visualisations are not fabricated, they may highlight favorable outcomes while omitting the uncertainty that accompanies genuine investment strategies.

The resulting persuasion does not rely on impersonating authority. It relies on projecting competence. The system appears to understand the market. It appears to detect patterns invisible to ordinary participants. It appears to offer guidance based on advanced analysis. In reality, however, the generative model often performs the same statistical continuation described earlier in this book. It produces language and visualisations that resemble financial expertise, but it lacks the predictive ability that genuine expertise requires. When such systems are used deliberately to attract investors, the illusion becomes predatory. The goal is not simply to generate plausible analysis, but to exploit a predictable human aspiration: the hope that complex markets can be mastered by a sufficiently powerful algorithm.

The system's apparent intelligence becomes the justification. Advice generated by a machine that appears capable of analyzing vast quantities of data may seem more objective and less fallible than advice from a person. The authority of computation becomes part of the persuasion. In many cases, the underlying financial product may itself be risky, poorly understood, or even fraudulent. The generative system does not create the underlying scheme, but it can strengthen its credibility. Persuasive narratives that once required skilled marketers can now be produced automatically and delivered to thousands of potential investors.

This form of deception shows how the same technological capability acquires different moral significance depending on its context. A language model that generates speculative explanations in response to a casual question may simply be performing its predictive function. The same capability, embedded in a financial service that promises guaranteed returns, becomes part of a deliberate strategy to shape belief and influence action. Unlike the organic illusion described earlier in the chapter, the deception here is intentional. It is built around a specific human vulnerability: the hope that complex markets can be mastered by a sufficiently powerful algorithm. The illusion of intelligence becomes a marketing instrument.

Generative AI therefore extends a long-standing pattern in financial history. Each technological advance, from telegraph lines carrying stock prices to high-frequency trading algorithms, has been accompanied by claims that new tools reveal hidden advantages. AI adds another layer to this narrative by suggesting that the machine itself understands the market. Whether such claims appear credible depends not only on the technology, but also on the environment in which they are presented. Timing, platform, and context all shape whether a message appears authoritative or suspicious. The next section examines this aspect of the landscape: how credibility itself can be engineered by controlling where, when, and how AI-generated information reaches its audience.

11.5 Timing, Platform, and Context as Weapons

The Engineering of Credibility

The previous sections examined several forms of AI-produced illusion: the organic error of fluent text, the contextual misunderstanding of cautious systems, the deliberate impersonation made possible by synthetic media, and the predatory use of generative narratives in financial markets. Each example involved a different form of deception. Yet another factor determines whether these illusions succeed. The credibility of a message depends not only on its content but also on the environment in which it appears. Human judgment rarely evaluates information in isolation. Perceived reliability is shaped by surrounding cues: where a claim is encountered, when it appears, and how it spreads through social channels. Generative AI does not merely produce persuasive content. It can also be deployed in environments that amplify its credibility.

Timing is the first factor. Information released during moments of uncertainty carries disproportionate influence. During a crisis, a breaking political event, or a period of market volatility, the demand for explanation becomes urgent. People search quickly for signals that might clarify what is happening. Verification has little time to occur, and the threshold for accepting a plausible account becomes lower. A synthetic video released during a developing political scandal, a fabricated statement attributed to a public official during diplomatic tension, or a persuasive trading recommendation appearing at the height of market volatility can therefore exert influence far beyond the strength of the content itself. The message fills an information gap at precisely the moment when audiences are most receptive. Timing turns plausibility into impact.

Platform is the second factor. Messages do not travel through a neutral information space. They appear within systems that carry their own signals of legitimacy: the design of an interface, the reputation of a website, the presence of verification badges, and the number of people sharing a post. These features shape expectations about reliability before the content is evaluated. The same statement does not carry the same weight everywhere. A statement encountered on an anonymous website is judged differently from the same statement appearing in a widely used financial application or a trusted news feed. When AI-generated content appears within such environments, its origin becomes less visible. Content that appears trustworthy can borrow credibility from the platform rather than earn it on its own. The reputation of the platform becomes difficult to distinguish from the credibility of the content it carries.

Context provides a third factor because interpretation depends heavily on the surrounding setting. A statement delivered at an official press conference carries different authority from one encountered on an informal forum. This difference can be exploited. Content presented in settings associated with expertise often inherits the authority of those settings. Generative systems can take advantage of this effect by placing outputs in contexts that imply expertise or institutional authority. A voice clone presented in the setting of a government briefing room benefits from the credibility of its surroundings. The same applies to an automated investment recommendation embedded in professional trading software or a generated research summary formatted as an academic report. The content itself may not change, but the surrounding conditions do.

Taken together, timing, platform, and context become powerful sources of credibility. They shape how information is received and whether a message is met with skepticism or accepted as plausible. A weak claim delivered at the right moment, on a trusted platform, and within a credible setting can appear more convincing than a strong claim presented under less favorable conditions.

Generative AI intensifies this dynamic because it operates at speed and scale. Large volumes of persuasive material can be produced, varied, and distributed across multiple environments, timed to coincide with periods of heightened attention. The persuasive force does not reside in any single piece of content. It emerges from the coordinated use of many messages within an environment designed to maximize their effect. In such cases, the deception lies not only in the message but also in the way the message is delivered. The generative model provides the technical ability to produce convincing media and narratives. Their effectiveness, however, depends on human decisions about when to release them, where to place them, and how to present them in environments that encourage belief.

Seen in this way, the illusion of intelligence becomes part of a broader system of persuasion. The machine generates the content, but the surrounding conditions shape its credibility. The consequences are not distributed evenly. When AI-generated illusions spread through complex information environments, the people most likely to be misled are often those with the fewest resources to verify what they encounter.

The next section turns to a related question: who bears the cost when AI-generated illusions are weaponized, and what forms of injustice arise when false beliefs spread through systems that many people are not equipped to evaluate critically?

11.6 The Innocently Deceived

Epistemic Injustice and Who Bears the Cost When the Illusion Is Weaponized

The previous section examined how credibility can be engineered through timing, platform, and context. When generative systems are used strategically, their persuasive force depends not only on what they say, but also on the environment in which they appear. This raises a further question: who is most likely to be misled when such systems are used deliberately? The answer is not the same for everyone. When deception is amplified by technology, its consequences fall most heavily on those who are least able to detect or resist it. The problem is not simply that false information exists. Misinformation has always existed. The problem is that generative technologies can produce convincing content at scale and place it in environments where verification is difficult and cognitive shortcuts are easily exploited. Under these conditions, many people who are misled are neither careless nor irresponsible. They are innocently deceived.

To understand why this matters, it is helpful to consider a concept from contemporary philosophy: epistemic injustice. The term refers to situations in which people are unfairly disadvantaged in their ability to acquire, interpret, or communicate knowledge. These disadvantages arise not from personal failings, but from structural conditions that shape how information is produced and distributed. AI-generated deception can create exactly these conditions. When synthetic media convincingly imitates public figures, citizens may struggle to distinguish authentic statements from fabricated ones. When automated investment systems promise algorithmic insight into financial markets, inexperienced investors may rely on the authority suggested by technical language they cannot realistically evaluate. When generated explanations spread rapidly through social networks, people without access to reliable means of verification may accept them because trustworthy alternatives are slow to appear. In each case, the deception exploits differences in knowledge and power. Those who design or deploy generative systems may understand both the technology and the ways information spreads. Those who encounter the outputs usually do not. They must interpret persuasive signals without knowing how those signals were produced. The result is an information environment in which some actors can shape belief far more effectively than others can evaluate it.

This imbalance creates a particular form of injustice. The people who are misled are often blamed for their credulity. Citizens who share fabricated videos may be accused of gullibility. Investors who follow misleading advice may be described as naïve. Such judgments overlook the conditions that made the deception persuasive in the first place. Individual failure alone cannot explain false beliefs when synthetic media convincingly imitates reality. Algorithmic systems present themselves as authoritative, and digital platforms spread their messages faster than they can be verified. The deception has been engineered. This recognition changes how responsibility is understood. If false beliefs spread in an environment deliberately designed to exploit cognitive shortcuts and differences in access to knowledge, then those who are misled are not simply making isolated mistakes. They are operating within a system that makes such mistakes more likely. This does not mean that individuals bear no responsibility for evaluating information critically. Careful judgment remains an essential intellectual discipline, as earlier chapters have shown. But the burden of vigilance cannot reasonably rest entirely on the audience. A society in which every person must independently verify every piece of information encountered would be impossible. Knowledge has always depended on networks of trust. It depends on institutions that provide reliable information, professional communities that maintain standards of evidence, and social norms that discourage deliberate deception. When generative technologies allow those safeguards to be bypassed or manipulated at scale, everyone is affected. Some groups, however, are affected more severely than others.

The costs of weaponized illusion therefore extend beyond the immediate victims of any single act of deception. They accumulate within the information environment itself. When authentic and fabricated signals become difficult to distinguish, citizens may begin to doubt genuine communications as well as false ones. Public discourse becomes more fragile. Institutions must devote increasing effort to verification and correction. The collective ability to develop a shared understanding of events becomes harder to sustain. Epistemic injustice therefore operates at two levels. At the individual level, some people face a structural disadvantage in evaluating persuasive signals. At the social level, the reliability of the information environment itself begins to erode. Recognizing who bears these costs clarifies why the issues examined in this chapter matter. The illusion of intelligence does not remain confined to isolated interactions with machines. Once it becomes a tool within larger systems of persuasion, its consequences spread through the social structures that depend on trustworthy information. The next section examines a deeper conceptual question. In several domains where AI systems are now used, including financial markets, medical advice, and legal reasoning, the confident predictions they generate may be structurally impossible. Explaining why requires examining the nature of knowledge in domains where uncertainty is not merely practical, but fundamental.

11.7 Domain-Structural Illusion

Why AI Confidence Is Philosophically Impossible in Markets, Medicine, and Law

The previous sections examined several ways in which AI-generated outputs can produce false beliefs: through fluent language, misunderstood signals of caution, synthetic media, and systems designed to manipulate human desires. There is, however, a deeper form of illusion. In some domains, the problem does not arise from misuse of technology or persuasive presentation. It arises because the domain itself does not permit the kind of confident answers that AI systems often appear to provide. Financial markets, medicine, and law are prominent examples. In each of these fields, uncertainty is not simply a temporary lack of information that could be removed with more data or greater computing power. It is an intrinsic feature of the domain.

In financial markets, outcomes depend on the decisions of millions of participants whose behavior continually reshapes the system. Prices change not only because of economic fundamentals, but also because investors anticipate how others will respond to new information. The market is therefore reflexive. Beliefs about future prices influence the prices that ultimately emerge. Under these conditions, prediction is structurally limited. A model may detect statistical patterns in historical data, but those patterns can disappear once they become widely recognized or acted on. The future of a system shaped by adaptive human behavior cannot be reduced to an extension of past patterns.

Medicine presents a different kind of structural uncertainty. Biological systems are extraordinarily complex, and the same treatment can produce different outcomes for different individuals. Medical knowledge develops through probabilistic evidence rather than deterministic rules. Clinical research identifies patterns that tend to benefit many patients under specific conditions. Each medical decision, however, applies those patterns to the circumstances of an individual patient, including medical history, genetic variation, comorbidities, and the current state of scientific knowledge. Responsible medical practice therefore offers informed judgment under uncertainty, not certainty itself.

Law presents another form of structural uncertainty. Legal reasoning requires the interpretation of statutes, precedents, and principles that have developed through earlier decisions. The meaning of legal texts often depends on context, competing doctrines, and judicial reasoning that applies general rules to particular cases. Even when the relevant materials are available, reasonable legal experts can disagree about how they should be interpreted. Law is not simply a body of facts to retrieve. It is a structured practice of interpretation and argument.

Across these domains, the appearance of confident answers creates a philosophical difficulty. When an AI system produces a prediction about market movements, a definitive medical recommendation, or a categorical legal interpretation, its language may express more certainty than the domain itself can support. The issue is not simply that AI systems lack sufficient data or computational power. The deeper issue is that these questions do not admit definitive answers of the kind that fluent explanations often suggest. This creates what can be called *domain-structural illusion*. The illusion arises when a system produces the linguistic signals of confident knowledge in domains where such confidence is epistemically inappropriate. The output resembles the conclusion of a well-defined problem, even though the domain itself is characterized by uncertainty, interpretation, and continual change.

Human experts in these fields are trained to recognize these limits. Experienced investors speak in probabilities rather than certainties. Physicians qualify recommendations by acknowledging risk and variation. Lawyers recognize that legal outcomes depend on interpretation and argument. The language of responsible expertise reflects the structure of the domain. Generative systems, by contrast, often produce answers that appear more definite than the underlying reality justifies. The statistical processes that generate language reproduce patterns of confident explanation without recognizing the epistemic limits of a particular domain. The result is a form of structural overconfidence embedded in the output itself.

This does not mean that AI systems cannot assist work in such domains. Models can summarize research, identify correlations, and organize relevant precedents. But assistance is not authority. When generated language presents a conclusion as though a question has a determinate answer, it can create an impression of certainty that neither human expertise nor the domain itself can legitimately provide.

Domain-structural illusion differs from the earlier forms of deception examined in this chapter. No deliberate manipulation is required. The illusion arises because the output is fluent, coherent, and apparently decisive, while the domain in which it is applied remains epistemically uncertain. In these contexts, an appearance of confidence can mislead even when the system functions exactly as designed.

Recognizing this limitation completes the conceptual landscape developed in this chapter. Some illusions originate in the generative process itself. Others arise through the deliberate use of these systems by human actors. Still others emerge from the interaction between machine-generated outputs and domains where certainty is philosophically impossible. The final section brings these strands together and shows how a single predictive engine can produce many distinct forms of deception.

11.8 The Full Landscape Assembled

From Organic Text Failure to Deliberate Multimedia Deception

The cases examined in this chapter may at first appear to belong to very different worlds. A language model producing an incorrect explanation in response to a casual question seems far removed from a synthetic video impersonating a public official. A cautious system admitting uncertainty appears unrelated to an automated investment platform promising extraordinary returns. The technologies used to generate text, clone voices, or create photorealistic faces also differ in important ways. Yet these phenomena share a common origin. All arise from the same underlying capability: systems that generate outputs by predicting patterns learned from data. The predictive engine at the core of modern generative AI possesses neither knowledge, beliefs, nor intentions. It produces outputs such as sentences, voices, images, and recommendations that resemble the products of human reasoning. This resemblance arises because the system learns from patterns originally created by human minds. When these outputs enter human interpretive environments, they engage the cognitive and social processes through which people recognize knowledge, authority, and evidence. That interaction can give rise to a range of illusions.

Seen together, the examples discussed in this chapter form a continuum. At one end lies organic illusion. A language model produces fluent text that appears knowledgeable even though the system has no awareness of truth or falsehood. The misleading effect arises unintentionally from the interaction between statistical prediction and human expectations about how knowledge is normally expressed. Next comes contextual illusion. Systems designed to signal uncertainty may generate phrases such as I don't know. These expressions resemble genuine intellectual humility even though the system lacks the self-awareness that would make such humility meaningful. The illusion arises from the conversational framework through which people interpret the system's language. Further along the continuum are cases in which generative capabilities become tools of persuasion. Synthetic audio and video can imitate identifiable individuals, creating convincing evidence of events that never occurred. Here the generative model provides the technical means, while human actors supply the intent to mislead. The illusion becomes weaponized. In other contexts, particularly financial markets, generative systems may be embedded in services that promise extraordinary predictive power. Their persuasive force comes not from imitation but from the projection of computational authority. The language of algorithmic insight can be used to exploit enduring hopes for reliable profit. In these situations, the illusion becomes predatory. Across all of these cases, credibility is also shaped by the environment in which the output circulates. Timing, platform design, and contextual cues influence whether a message is received with skepticism or accepted as plausible. The same generative capability can therefore produce outcomes ranging from harmless misunderstanding to coordinated deception. Finally, some domains reveal a deeper mismatch between the form of the system's output and the nature of the domain itself. In markets, medicine, and law, uncertainty and interpretation are intrinsic features of the field. When generative systems produce language that suggests definitive answers in these contexts, the appearance of certainty exceeds what the domain itself can support. This gives rise to the domain-structural illusion described in the previous section.

These forms of illusion differ in both mechanism and moral structure. Organic error requires no malicious intent. Contextual misunderstanding arises from human interpretive habits. Weaponized and predatory uses involve deliberate human action. Domain-structural illusion reflects the epistemic limits of the domains in which the technology is applied. Yet the same predictive architecture underlies them all. The language model generating an inaccurate paragraph, the system synthesizing a human voice, the tool producing persuasive financial analysis, and the model offering confident medical or legal advice all operate through variations of the same generative logic. What changes is the interface through which the output appears and the social context in which it is received. The illusion of intelligence is therefore not a single phenomenon but a family of related effects. Some arise naturally from the interaction between generative systems and human cognition. Others emerge when those systems are deployed deliberately in environments designed to strengthen belief. The predictive engine is only the starting point. Understanding the risks of generative AI also requires examining the broader environment in which the technology operates: interface design, the incentives of those who deploy the systems, the vulnerabilities of the people who encounter them, and the epistemic structure of the domains in which the outputs are used. Only by considering these elements together is it possible to understand how a single technological capability gives rise to such a wide range of deceptive appearances.

This chapter has mapped that landscape. The next chapter turns to a deeper conceptual question. When generative systems produce statements that appear false or misleading, do they count as lies? If machines themselves cannot lie, how should responsibility for deception be understood in a world where machines generate so much of the language people encounter?

Closing Reflection

One Engine, Many Faces

A reader encounters a fluent explanation. A viewer watches a convincing video. An investor receives confident algorithmic advice. In each case, the experience feels familiar. The signals that normally accompany trustworthy information are present: coherent language, recognizable voices, realistic images, and analysis that appears precise and sophisticated. The human mind responds as it always has by forming a judgment about what is true. What has changed is not the way people respond. It is the source of the signals to which they respond.

The examples examined in this chapter take different forms: inaccurate text generated without awareness, cautious systems that appear self-aware, synthetic media that imitate real people, and algorithmic platforms that claim to reveal complex market patterns. Despite these differences, the same underlying mechanism drives them all. A predictive system generates outputs that resemble the products of human understanding. Those outputs enter environments designed for human communication and are interpreted through habits that developed long before such systems existed. Sometimes the result is a harmless misunderstanding. Sometimes it becomes deliberate deception. The difference lies not in the predictive system itself, but in the context and intent surrounding its use. The same capability that produces an inaccurate paragraph can also produce a synthetic speech, a fabricated video, or a persuasive financial narrative within a digital platform. Each medium carries its own signals of credibility.

Each can therefore produce its own form of illusion. This is the landscape that Part Four begins to examine. One underlying mechanism. Many forms. Many ways for belief to form where understanding is absent.

The next chapter turns to a deeper question that lies beneath this landscape. If machines can produce statements that appear false or misleading, can they actually lie, or does deception remain a property of the humans who design and deploy them?

CHAPTER 12
Can AI Lie?

Deception, Intention, Moral Agency, and the New Categories

The previous chapter traced the many forms through which AI-generated illusion now appears: fluent text that seems knowledgeable, synthetic voices that sound human, videos that depict events that never occurred, and systems that promise insight into complex domains such as markets or medicine. Across these examples, the pattern is the same. A person encounters something that appears credible and forms a belief. When that belief later proves false, a natural question arises: Did the AI lie?

At first glance, the answer seems obvious. The system produced a false statement. Someone believed it. The situation resembles deception. Yet that resemblance is misleading. A lie is not simply a false statement. It is a moral act that requires something more fundamental: a mind capable of believing one thing while intentionally asserting another. Generative systems possess neither beliefs nor intentions about how their outputs will be understood. If lying requires those capacities, AI cannot lie. False and misleading statements still occur, however. People are deceived by them. Harm can result. The familiar language of truth and deception therefore begins to lose its explanatory power. The machine is not a liar, yet deception still occurs.

This chapter examines that tension. To determine what forms of deception AI systems can produce, it is first necessary to define what constitutes a lie. Only then does it become clear why the traditional categories are no longer sufficient and why new ones are needed to describe the moral landscape created by generative technology.

12.1 What Lying Actually Requires

The Three Classical Philosophical Conditions

Before asking whether artificial intelligence can lie, it is necessary to clarify what lying is. In everyday speech, the term is often applied to any statement that proves to be false. Philosophical discussions, however, have long drawn a more careful distinction. Not every false statement is a lie. Error, misunderstanding, exaggeration, and speculation can all produce false claims without involving deception. A lie requires something more. Across centuries of philosophical inquiry, from Augustine and Aquinas to contemporary analytic philosophers, a broadly consistent view has emerged. The details differ, but most definitions rest on three core conditions.

The first condition is falsity. A lie involves asserting a proposition that is false. The speaker presents the statement as though it corresponds to reality when it does not. If a statement is true, it cannot be a lie, even if the speaker hoped it would mislead. The second condition is belief in the statement's falsity. The speaker must believe the statement to be false. Someone who sincerely believes an incorrect claim is mistaken, not deceitful. A person who repeats inaccurate information because a source was misunderstood or remembered incorrectly has not lied but simply made an error. The third condition is an intention to deceive. The speaker must seek to create a false belief in another person. A lie is more than making a false statement. It is a deliberate attempt to shape another person's understanding of reality.

Together, these three conditions define the classical structure of lying: making a false statement, believing it to be false, and intending another person to accept it as true. Each condition serves a distinct purpose. Falsity distinguishes lies from truthful statements. Belief distinguishes lies from honest mistakes. Intention distinguishes lies from false statements that are not meant to deceive.

This structure reveals something important. Lying is not merely a feature of language. It is a feature of agents that can hold beliefs, recognize when those beliefs differ from what they say, and intend others to interpret their words in particular ways. A lie therefore presupposes a mind. A parrot that repeats a false sentence is not lying. A broken clock that shows the wrong time is not lying. A computer program that produces an incorrect result is not lying. In each case, the statement may be false, but no mind stands behind it that believes the statement to be false or intends to deceive anyone.

This distinction provides the starting point for the question examined in this chapter. Generative AI systems can produce false or misleading statements. They can fabricate citations, describe events that never occurred, or generate explanations that sound authoritative despite containing errors. Producing false statements, however, is not the same as lying. The next section explains why, under the classical philosophical definition, artificial intelligence cannot lie. It also shows why that conclusion is far less reassuring than it may first appear.

12.2 Why AI Cannot Lie

Why That Is Not the Reassurance It Sounds Like

If lying requires a false statement, a belief that the statement is false, and an intention to deceive, then artificial intelligence cannot lie. Generative systems do not hold beliefs about the world. They do not know whether the statements they produce are true or false, and they do not form intentions about how their outputs should influence the understanding of others. When a language model generates a sentence, it is not asserting something it believes to be false. It is extending a statistical pattern. Under the classical philosophical definition, lying therefore does not apply. A language model that produces an invented citation is not lying. A system that generates a confident but incorrect explanation is not lying. Even a model that fabricates detailed descriptions of events that never occurred is not lying. In every case, the output may be false, but no agent behind the statement recognizes its falsity or intends to mislead anyone.

This conclusion is sometimes presented as reassuring. The argument is that if AI systems cannot lie, they cannot truly deceive. The issue then appears to be limited to technical error, with machines occasionally generating inaccurate information. This view, however, is incomplete. The absence of lying does not eliminate deception. It changes the way deception occurs. A person can be deceived even when no one has lied. False beliefs can arise from misunderstanding, incomplete information, or statements that happen to be incorrect. For the experience of deception, what matters is not the speaker's mental state but the effect on the listener's beliefs. Generative systems can therefore produce many of the same consequences as lying. A reader may encounter a fluent explanation containing fabricated facts. A viewer may watch a video that appears to show a real person speaking words never spoken. An investor may follow advice generated by a system that confidently predicts market movements. In each case, a person forms a belief that does not correspond to reality. From that person's perspective, the difference between a lie and a false statement generated without intention may not be apparent. The belief is the same, and the consequences may be the same.

The philosophical distinction still matters because it clarifies where responsibility lies. If the system itself cannot lie, then the deception found in AI-mediated environments must arise elsewhere. It may result from the way generative models produce language without regard for truth. It may result from interface designs that present machine outputs as authoritative. It may also result from the deliberate actions of people who use the technology to manipulate belief. The absence of lying does not remove the moral problem. It shifts responsibility elsewhere. The reassuring claim that AI cannot lie should therefore not be mistaken for a solution. It shows only that the traditional concept of lying is the wrong tool for explaining what is happening. The problem is not that machines lie. It is that they generate language without regard for truth in environments where that language is easily mistaken for knowledge. The next section introduces the concept needed to describe this condition more precisely: truth-indifferent generation.

12.3 Truth-Indifferent Generation

A Category beneath Bullshitting, beyond Lying

If artificial intelligence cannot lie yet can still produce false and misleading statements, a different category is needed to describe what is occurring. The closest concept in philosophy is *bullshitting*, a term most closely associated with the philosopher Harry Frankfurt. Frankfurt drew an important distinction between the liar and the bullshitter. A liar knows the truth and deliberately says the opposite in order to deceive. A bullshitter, by contrast, is indifferent to whether a statement is true or false. The goal is not accuracy but effect: persuasion, impression, or rhetorical success. The bullshitter's relationship to truth is therefore one of disregard.

At first glance, generative AI appears to fit this description. A language model produces statements without verifying whether they are true. The output may be accurate, inaccurate, or entirely fabricated, and the system itself does not distinguish among these possibilities. In that sense, the model appears indifferent to truth. Yet even this comparison is not quite correct.

Bullshitting, like lying, still presupposes a mind. The bullshitter chooses not to care about truth because the goal lies elsewhere. The aim may be to create an impression of knowledge, authority, or confidence, with little concern for accuracy. This indifference is psychological. It belongs to an agent who could care about truth but chooses not to. Generative systems operate differently. A language model is not indifferent to truth in the way a person can be. It has no orientation toward truth at all. The system cannot determine whether its own statements correspond to reality. It does not recognize when a statement corresponds to reality. It does not intentionally disregard accuracy in pursuit of another goal. It simply produces sequences of words that statistically resemble patterns in its training data.

The relationship between the system and truth is therefore not one of indifference, but of absence. The category needed to describe generative output differs from both lying and bullshitting. The system generates language without truth as a guiding criterion. This is not because it rejects truth, but because the process that produces the language does not evaluate truth. This condition can be described as *truth-indifferent generation*.

Under truth-indifferent generation, statements are produced through pattern continuation rather than belief, intention, or evaluation of evidence. The output may coincide with reality when statistical patterns align with accurate information. It may diverge from reality when those patterns produce plausible explanations that do not correspond to the facts. In either case, the system has no awareness of the difference. The appearance of knowledge arises entirely from the surface structure of the language.

This distinction helps explain why generative systems can produce statements that closely resemble expert explanations while lacking the epistemic commitments of genuine expertise. Human experts typically work within a framework of belief and justification. They try to ensure that their statements correspond to the best available evidence, and they revise those statements when new evidence emerges. A generative system does neither. It produces an answer because the statistical structure of language suggests that the answer should follow the prompt.

Truth-indifferent generation therefore occupies a conceptual position beneath bullshitting and beyond lying. It lies beneath bullshitting because it lacks even the minimal psychological orientation that bullshitting presupposes. It extends beyond lying because it can produce statements that function like deception despite the absence of belief or intention.

Understanding this category is essential because it clarifies the nature of the problem created by generative systems. The issue is not that machines deliberately mislead. The issue is that they produce persuasive language without any internal mechanism that connects that language to reality. Once such systems are embedded in environments where their outputs are treated as knowledge, the conditions for false belief become widespread. At that point, the question of deception shifts from the internal state of the machine to the structure of the surrounding system. The next section examines that structure more closely. It introduces the concept of *structural deception*, in which misleading effects arise not from the machine itself, but from the architecture that presents its outputs and shapes their interpretation.

12.4 Structural Deception

When the Lie Lives in the Architecture, Not the Machine

Once it is recognized that generative systems operate through truth-indifferent generation, a further question becomes unavoidable. If the system neither believes nor intends, yet people are still misled by its outputs, where does the deception actually arise? In many cases, the answer lies not in the system itself, but in the structure surrounding it.

Consider how generative systems are typically presented to users. A language model appears as a conversational assistant. It responds directly to questions. Its answers are organized, coherent, and expressed in the tone of explanation. The interface resembles a conversation with a knowledgeable agent. These design choices are not accidental. They make the system easier to use. A conversational interface allows people to ask questions naturally and receive information quickly. At the same time, it conveys powerful interpretive signals. Human beings are accustomed to treating conversational responses as the products of a mind. When a statement appears as a direct answer to a question, the natural assumption is that the speaker has considered the question and intentionally produced the answer. The interface therefore presents the output as though it were the result of reasoning. The generative system, however, has not reasoned about the question. It has generated a continuation of linguistic patterns.

The deception in this situation does not originate in the system's internal process. It arises from the architecture of interaction surrounding the system. The system is presented in a way that encourages users to interpret its output as knowledge, even though the mechanism producing that output lacks the epistemic commitments that knowledge requires. This can be described as structural deception. Structural deception occurs when the design of a technological system leads people to form false beliefs, even though no part of the system is intentionally deceptive. The misleading effect arises from the interaction between the technology, its interface, and the interpretive habits of the user.

Several features of this architecture contribute to the effect. One is the conversational frame. Dialog suggests understanding. When a system responds fluently to questions, the interaction encourages users to treat the response as a deliberate answer rather than as a statistical continuation of text. Another feature is the confidence conveyed by fluent language. As discussed earlier, smooth, well-structured explanations create cognitive ease and strengthen the impression of authority. The absence of visible hesitation or uncertainty makes the output appear more reliable than it may be. A third feature is the absence of epistemic signals. Human experts often reveal the limits of their knowledge through hesitation, qualification, or reference to evidence. Generative systems frequently omit these signals unless they are deliberately introduced into the response. None of these features is deceptive on its own. Together, however, they create conditions in which the system's outputs are easily mistaken for informed judgment. The deception, in such cases, is not produced by the system alone. It is built into the architecture of presentation.

Recognizing structural deception changes the focus of moral analysis. When a generative system produces misleading outputs because of the way it is embedded in a broader technological environment, responsibility cannot rest with the machine alone. It also extends to the designers who shape how the system communicates, the institutions that deploy it, and the platforms that influence how its outputs are interpreted. The deception is therefore systemic rather than individual. This perspective also explains why AI-generated misinformation cannot be addressed simply by making models more accurate. Even a highly reliable system can produce misleading effects if it is presented in a way that encourages users to attribute understanding, authority, or certainty that the system does not genuinely possess. The structure of the interaction matters as much as the content of the output.

Structural deception occupies a middle position in the moral landscape. Unlike truth-indifferent generations, it arises from human design decisions that shape how technology is experienced. Yet unlike deliberate fraud, it may emerge without any intention to deceive. Designers may simply aim to create systems that feel intuitive and helpful, while unintentionally encouraging misplaced trust. Beyond this point lies a more direct form of responsibility. The next section examines situations in which generative technology is not merely embedded in misleading environments, but is deliberately used by human actors to deceive. This intentional use of the technology as an instrument of deception can be described as weaponized deception.

12.5 Weaponized Deception

When a Human Agent Deliberately Deploys AI as an Instrument of Harm

The previous section described structural deception: situations in which the architecture surrounding a generative system encourages users to interpret its outputs as knowledge or judgment. In these cases, the misleading effect arises from design and context rather than deliberate malice. There is, however, another form of deception in which intention clearly returns. Here, a human actor knowingly uses generative technology to create false beliefs. The system becomes a tool of manipulation. This can be called weaponized deception. The generative model remains what it has always been: a system that generates outputs by extending statistical patterns. A person, however, directs that capability toward a specific target and a specific outcome. A fabricated video is created to damage a political opponent. A cloned voice is used to impersonate a company executive and request an urgent financial transfer. A network of AI-generated accounts spreads persuasive narratives intended to influence public opinion. In every case, the deception has a human author. The technology increases its scale and realism, but the intention originates with the person who deploys it. The machine generates the content. The person decides to use that content to mislead.

This distinction is important because it restores the classical elements of lying that were absent in the earlier cases. A person who knowingly releases a synthetic video portraying an event that never occurred understands that the content is false and intends others to believe it is real. The deception therefore satisfies the philosophical conditions outlined earlier: a false statement, belief in its falsity, and an intention to deceive. The lie exists, but the liar is human. Generative AI changes the mechanics of deception rather than its moral structure. Historically, producing convincing false evidence required significant resources, including skilled forgery, elaborate staging, or access to media institutions. Modern generative systems greatly reduce these barriers. A convincing voice imitation or photorealistic video can now be created with far fewer resources and distributed worldwide within minutes. The technology transforms deception from a difficult craft into a scalable capability. This change has two important consequences. First, it lowers the cost of producing persuasive falsehoods. Individuals or small groups can now create content that once required the resources of large organizations. The threshold for launching misinformation campaigns becomes much lower. Second, it increases the credibility of the deception. Synthetic media can reproduce sensory cues, including faces, voices, and environments, that people have long treated as reliable indicators of reality. When these cues are manipulated, the resulting artifacts can appear far more convincing than traditional text-based misinformation.

Weaponized deception therefore marks the point at which generative technology becomes an instrument of intentional harm. The machine itself remains indifferent to truth, but human actors exploit that indifference to achieve specific goals, including political influence, financial fraud, reputational damage, and social disruption. The predictive engine provides the means. Human intention provides the purpose. Understanding this category clarifies why the earlier claim that AI cannot lie offers only limited reassurance. Even if the system itself lacks the mental states required for lying, the technology can still be used by people who possess them. The absence of agency in the machine does not eliminate the agency of those who use it. The moral analysis therefore shifts once again. Responsibility no longer rests primarily with system architecture or interface design. It rests with the individuals and organizations that deliberately use generative systems to create and distribute falsehoods. Yet another category remains. Not every harmful use of generative technology involves explicit false statements. Some systems are designed to exploit predictable weaknesses in human psychology. They encourage people to act in ways that benefit their operators, even when the information is ambiguous or only partly true. The next section examines this subtler form of manipulation: *predatory deception*.

12.6 Predatory Deception

When the System Is Calibrated to Exploit Specific Psychological Vulnerability

Weaponized deception involves a clear act of lying. A human agent knowingly uses generative technology to create a false belief. The intention to deceive is explicit, and the deception usually relies on statements that are demonstrably false. Deception, however, does not always require outright falsehood. Information may be partly true, technically accurate, or carefully ambiguous. Even so, a system may be deliberately designed to exploit predictable features of human psychology. In such cases, the harm arises not from a single false statement but from a pattern of influence intended to steer behavior. This form of manipulation can be called predatory deception. It occurs when a technological system is intentionally designed to exploit known cognitive vulnerabilities, such as greed, fear, loneliness, urgency, or the desire for authoritative guidance. Rather than fabricating events or impersonating individuals, the system shapes how information is presented so that users are more likely to act in ways that benefit its operators. The mechanism resembles long-established forms of manipulation in advertising and persuasion. Generative technology, however, greatly expands the scale and precision with which such strategies can be deployed.

Consider financial platforms that promote AI-generated trading advice. The language may be technically cautious and describe probabilities rather than guarantees. The broader narrative emphasizes extraordinary returns, proprietary algorithms, and artificial intelligence's ability to identify hidden patterns in financial markets. Charts and simulations may highlight favorable outcomes while minimizing risk. The system does not necessarily make demonstrably false claims, but it is designed to encourage the hope of easy profit. Consider also conversational systems marketed as sources of emotional support. A generative model can produce empathetic language that appears attentive and understanding. It responds in ways that feel personally meaningful. If such systems are connected to services that charge fees, collect personal data, or encourage prolonged engagement, the emotional bond created through the interaction can become a means of influence. In these cases, the deception lies not primarily in the factual content of the statements, but in the deliberate alignment between the system's design and the user's psychological vulnerability. The system is engineered to produce responses that guide behavior in a predictable direction. This form of deception differs from weaponized lying in an important respect. The operators may avoid making explicit false claims. Instead, they create an environment that encourages users to make decisions serving the operators' goals. The persuasive effect arises from framing, repetition, and emotional resonance rather than from demonstrably false assertions. Predatory deception therefore occupies the space between persuasion and fraud.

From a philosophical perspective, the defining feature is asymmetry. The designers of the system understand the mechanisms of influence they have built into it. They recognize the psychological triggers, persuasive narratives, and behavioral incentives being used. The user typically does not. The interaction therefore takes place under conditions in which one side understands how the other is likely to respond. Generative AI intensifies this asymmetry because it can produce personalized responses at scale. A system may analyze patterns in a user's behavior, language, or preferences and adapt its messages accordingly. As a result, the persuasive narrative becomes increasingly tailored to the individual receiving it. The deception is subtle but powerful. Unlike weaponized lies, which may eventually be exposed through fact-checking, predatory systems can remain within the bounds of factual accuracy while still guiding users toward harmful outcomes. A user may later discover that the promised financial gains were unrealistic, that the emotional relationship with the system was artificial, or that the advice received was shaped by incentives that were never made visible. The harm arises from manipulated trust rather than from explicit falsehood.

Understanding predatory deception broadens the moral landscape introduced in this chapter. Deception is not limited to lies. It can also occur when systems are deliberately designed to exploit predictable patterns of human judgment. At this point, the taxonomy becomes clearer. Generative systems produce language independently of its truth or accuracy. Their design can encourage users to interpret that language as knowledge. Human actors can weaponize the technology to create deliberate falsehoods. Systems can also be designed to exploit psychological vulnerabilities without making statements that are strictly false. Across all these cases, one fact remains constant. The machine itself does not possess moral agency. The next section examines the implications of this fact more directly. It explains why the machine is morally innocent and why that innocence does not absolve the humans who design, deploy, or use it.

12.7 The Machine Is Morally Innocent

The Humans behind It Are Not

The analysis developed so far leads to an important conclusion. Generative systems can produce false statements, misleading explanations, persuasive illusions, and even tools for deliberate deception. Yet the systems themselves do not possess the mental states required for moral responsibility. They have no beliefs, no intentions, and no understanding of the consequences of their outputs. In the philosophical sense, the machine is therefore morally innocent. Describing a system as morally innocent does not imply that it is harmless. It simply recognizes that moral evaluation applies to agents capable of intention and choice. A rock that causes injury when it falls is not morally blameworthy. A storm that destroys a city is not morally culpable. The damage may be real and severe, but the event itself does not involve agency. Generative systems belong in this category. They produce outputs by applying mathematical procedures learned from data. Those procedures can affect people's beliefs, decisions, and well-being, but the system itself does not understand what it is doing. It does not choose its actions, and it cannot be said to intend either harm or benefit.

The moral focus therefore cannot rest on the machine. Responsibility must instead be traced through the network of human decisions surrounding the system. Every generative model exists within a chain of design, deployment, and use. Engineers decide how the model is trained and what capabilities it will have. Companies decide how it is presented to users and the contexts in which it operates. Institutions decide how its outputs are integrated into workflows and public communication. Individuals decide whether to rely on its responses and how to interpret them. Each of these decisions shapes the conditions under which the system influences human belief. When deception occurs in an AI-mediated environment, the central question is not whether the machine lied, but who created the conditions under which the misleading outcome became likely.

In cases of weaponized deception, the answer is relatively straightforward. A human actor deliberately uses generative technology to create false beliefs. The system functions as a tool, much like any other instrument used to commit fraud or impersonation. In cases of predatory design, responsibility lies with those who configure systems to exploit psychological vulnerabilities. The deception may occur without explicit lies, but the system has been deliberately designed to guide users toward harmful decisions. In cases of structural deception, responsibility is more widely distributed. Designers may not intend to mislead, yet the architecture of the system encourages users to attribute understanding, authority, or certainty that the system does not possess. The misleading effect arises from the combined consequences of many design decisions. Even in the most benign cases, when a language model simply produces an incorrect answer, responsibility for its interpretation does not disappear. Developers, institutions, and users all help shape the expectations surrounding the system.

The machine remains morally neutral throughout these scenarios. But neutrality does not imply moral irrelevance. On the contrary, a powerful tool that can shape belief makes human responsibility more significant, not less. When a system capable of generating persuasive language and media enters the information environment, the ethical burden shifts to those who determine how it is used and how its outputs are presented. This point is sometimes obscured by the tendency to anthropomorphize technology. Public discourse often describes AI systems as independent actors that decide, recommend, or hallucinate. Such language can divert attention from the human decisions that shape how these systems are designed and deployed. The machine appears to act. The humans behind it disappear from view. Recognizing the moral innocence of the machine restores the proper perspective. Generative systems are powerful instruments, but instruments do not bear responsibility for how they are used. Responsibility belongs to the people who design, deploy, regulate, and rely on them.

This insight prepares the final step of the analysis. Deception in AI-mediated environments can arise from several sources: truth-indifferent generation, structural design, deliberate misuse, and predatory calibration. A framework is therefore needed to clarify how responsibility is distributed across these different cases. The final section of this chapter presents that framework: a moral taxonomy of AI-generated deception.

12.8 A Complete Moral Taxonomy

Four Loci of Responsibility across Every Case

The preceding sections have shown that the question of whether AI can lie does not have a simple answer. Under the classical philosophical definition, artificial intelligence cannot lie because lying requires belief and intention, capacities that generative systems do not possess. Yet deception clearly occurs in environments shaped by these systems. Understanding why requires distinguishing where responsibility resides. The examples examined in this chapter show several distinct sources of deception. These include fabricated text, misleading interfaces, synthetic media used for impersonation, and systems designed to exploit psychological vulnerabilities. The machine itself generates language without regard to truth. The surrounding architecture can encourage users to treat that language as knowledge. Human actors can deliberately use the technology to mislead others. Some systems are also designed to exploit predictable weaknesses in human judgment. Together, these sources form a moral taxonomy that identifies where responsibility lies in AI-mediated deception.

Four loci of responsibility can be distinguished. The first is the generative system itself. As shown earlier, the model produces outputs through truth-indifferent generations. Its statements may be correct or incorrect, but the process that produces them does not involve belief, intention, or evaluation of evidence. The system therefore cannot lie, but it can generate statements that resemble knowledge while lacking epistemic grounding. The second locus is the system architecture. Interface design, presentation format, and contextual framing can encourage users to interpret machine outputs as authoritative judgments. Conversational interfaces, confident language, and the absence of epistemic signals can create structural deception even when no individual intends to mislead. Responsibility here lies with the designers and institutions that determine how the technology is integrated into human communication. The third locus is the deliberate use of the technology. When individuals or organizations intentionally use generative systems to create false beliefs through fabricated media, impersonation, or coordinated misinformation campaigns, the classical structure of lying reappears. The machine provides the means, but the human agent provides the intention. In such cases, the deception is intentional and morally attributable. The fourth locus is the design of systems that exploit psychological vulnerabilities. Such systems may not rely on explicit falsehoods, yet they are built to take advantage of human tendencies such as greed, fear, urgency, or loneliness. By aligning system behavior with predictable patterns of human cognition, designers can influence users toward decisions that benefit the system's operators. The deception lies in the strategic manipulation of trust.

Together, these four loci describe the moral landscape of AI-generated deception. At one end is a machine that generates language without regard to truth. At the other is a human agent who intentionally uses that capability to mislead. Between these points lie forms of deception embedded in system design and behavioral calibration. Each involves a different distribution of responsibility and requires a different ethical and regulatory response.

This taxonomy also clarifies an important misconception. The ethical challenges of generative AI do not arise because machines have become morally corrupt agents. They arise because systems capable of producing persuasive language and media are now embedded in environments where they can influence human belief, judgment, and behavior at scale. The machine does not need to lie for deception to occur. Language produced without belief can still be mistaken for knowledge. Interfaces designed for convenience can create misplaced trust. Tools developed for legitimate purposes can be weaponized by those seeking to mislead others. Systems optimized for engagement can become instruments for exploiting psychological vulnerabilities. Seen in this light, the moral problem does not lie within the machine itself. It lies in the wider ecosystem that surrounds it: the design of systems, the intentions of those who deploy them, the institutions that regulate them, and the interpretive habits of those who rely on their outputs. The question that opened this chapter therefore leads to a deeper conclusion. AI cannot lie. Yet in a world where machines generate persuasive language and media, deception has taken new forms. Recognizing those forms is the first step toward governing them responsibly.

Closing Reflection

The Lie without a Liar

An AI system produces a statement that appears factual. The statement is clear. It sounds confident. It appears to describe a fact about the world. Later, the reader discovers that the statement was wrong. The system may have invented a citation, misdescribed an event, or offered advice that proved unreliable. The natural reaction is simple: the AI lied. But as this chapter has shown, that description is not quite correct. Lying requires a mind that can hold a belief about the world and intentionally present something else as true. Generative systems possess neither belief nor intention. They produce language by extending patterns learned from data, without awareness of what their words claim about reality. The machine therefore cannot lie. Yet the experience of deception remains. A person forms a false belief. Decisions may follow from that belief. Trust may be misplaced. For the person who was misled, the absence of intention within the machine offers little comfort.

This reveals that deception in the age of generative AI has taken a different form. In the past, deception usually required a deceiver: someone who knowingly presented falsehood as truth in order to influence the understanding of others. In environments shaped by modern AI systems, false belief can arise through a more complex chain of events. Language generated without regard for truth can appear through interfaces that suggest authority, circulate on platforms that amplify credibility, and be used by people who may or may not intend harm. In this sense, a lie can exist without a liar at the center of the event. Responsibility does not disappear. It becomes distributed across a wider set of participants. Designers shape the systems through which information is presented. Institutions decide how those systems are integrated into public communication. Individuals choose how to use them and how to interpret their outputs. The machine remains morally innocent throughout this process, but that innocence does not make its effects neutral. A tool that generates persuasive language and media changes the conditions under which human judgment operates. As such tools become common, societies must learn to recognize new forms of error, new forms of manipulation, and new ways in which belief can be shaped without the traditional signs of intentional deception.

The central ethical challenge is not that machines have become dishonest agents. It is that machines capable of producing the signals of knowledge now participate in human communication without sharing the cognitive commitments that make those signals reliable. Understanding that distinction is the first step toward intellectual clarity in an age where language itself can be generated without a mind behind it.

PART FIVE
STAYING SMART

A Practical Philosophy for Disciplined Use in a Fluent World

The goal is not rejection but disciplined use. The next three chapters equip readers with the mindset, practical tools, and cognitive discipline needed to achieve genuine epistemic sovereignty. This sovereignty is not a permanent state. It is a practice sustained through daily effort.

CHAPTER 13
Reading AI Skeptically

Skepticism Is Not Hostility; It Is Clarity

The preceding chapters examined the illusion of intelligence from several perspectives. They showed how predictive systems generate fluent language that resembles reasoning. They explained how these errors arise, why human cognition finds them persuasive, and how the same underlying mechanism powers applications such as text generation, voice synthesis, video generation, and automated decision systems. Taken together, these analyzes reveal the nature of the problem. Systems capable of producing convincing explanations now participate in human communication without sharing the cognitive capacities that make explanations trustworthy.

The next question is practical. How should such systems be used? Rejection is neither realistic nor necessary. Generative systems are already part of the informational environment in which modern work, research, and communication take place. Uncritical acceptance, however, is equally untenable. The fluent surface of generated language can conceal uncertainty, error, or structural limitations behind the appearance of understanding. What is needed is disciplined use. That discipline begins not with technique, but with intellectual posture: the approach brought to every interaction. Before any practical method can be effective, AI-generated output must be approached in a way that keeps judgment active rather than allowing it to recede. That posture is skepticism. It is not hostility toward the technology or reflexive distrust. It is the deliberate habit of examining persuasive language before accepting it as knowledge. In an environment where fluent answers are abundant, skepticism becomes a form of clarity. The sections that follow develop that posture.

13.1 No Rejection but Disciplined Use

Framing the Practical Argument

The argument developed throughout this book can easily be misunderstood if it is taken as a warning against artificial intelligence itself. Repeated discussions of hallucination, automation bias, cognitive offloading, and structural deception may suggest that the safest response is to avoid these systems altogether. That conclusion would be mistaken. Generative systems are not passing curiosities. They are becoming a standard part of the information infrastructure that supports modern knowledge work. Writers use them to draft text. Researchers use them to summarize literature. Programmers use them to explore solutions. Analysts use them to organize complex information. Their role will continue to grow as they become integrated into the software environments where much of today's work takes place. The practical question is therefore not whether these systems should exist. They already do. The question is how they should be used.

Two unproductive responses stand at opposite ends of the spectrum. One is uncritical acceptance: treating generated output as authoritative because it appears coherent and complete. The other is categorical rejection: refusing to use these systems because they sometimes produce error or uncertainty. Neither response preserves intellectual agency. Uncritical acceptance quietly transfers judgment from the human mind to the system that generates the answer. Categorical rejection gives up the genuine benefits these systems can provide when they are used with care. Between these extremes lies a more stable approach: disciplined use.

Disciplined use means treating generative systems as tools rather than authorities. A system can support exploration, generate drafts, suggest possibilities, and organize information. Responsibility for interpretation, verification, and final judgment, however, remains with the human user. This distinction restores the proper relationship between the system and the user. The system generates language. The human evaluates its meaning. When this relationship is preserved, AI becomes a tool that extends human thinking without replacing it. When it is reversed, the system begins to shape conclusions that the user merely accepts.

The remaining chapters do not teach readers how to outsmart a machine. Their purpose is to show how intellectual independence can be maintained while working with one. Disciplined use begins with the perspective established in this chapter. The next chapter introduces practical techniques for interrupting the illusion during interaction with a system. The final chapter examines the habits of mind that preserve independent judgment in environments saturated with fluent automated responses. Together, these chapters present a practical philosophy for thinking clearly in a world where convincing language can now be produced without understanding.

13.2 Posture Precedes Technique

Why Intellectual Orientation Is the Foundation of Every Skill That Follows

When people first encounter the limitations of generative AI, the first instinct is often to look for techniques. Common questions include how to write better prompts, how to verify answers quickly, and how to detect errors before relying on the system's output. These are reasonable questions. Later chapters introduce practical methods for interacting with these systems more effectively. But techniques alone cannot solve the problem. Every technique depends on an underlying posture: the intellectual orientation a person brings to the interaction. Without that posture, even effective techniques become superficial routines. They are applied inconsistently or abandoned as soon as an output appears convincing enough to accept.

The earlier chapters explained why that persuasion is so powerful. Fluent language creates cognitive ease. Coherent explanations activate the mental shortcuts people normally use to recognize expertise. The system presents its responses with the same signals that, in human communication, usually accompany genuine understanding. For that reason, the first challenge in working with AI systems is not technical but psychological. Before any method can be applied, the system must be approached with an orientation that preserves critical distance. Its output may be useful, but it is never automatically authoritative. When that orientation is lost, the explanation becomes a final answer rather than a provisional account. At that point, every subsequent technique loses its foundation.

Posture therefore comes before technique. A person who approaches AI output with disciplined skepticism naturally asks questions about its claims, its sources, and its limits. Verification becomes an expression of that orientation rather than a mechanical step performed afterward. By contrast, a person who approaches the system with implicit trust is unlikely to apply those same methods consistently. The appearance of coherence is often enough to reduce scrutiny. The difference is not a matter of intelligence. It is a matter of orientation. A careful reader of AI output maintains a small but essential distance between the explanation presented and the judgment ultimately formed about it. That distance allows the response to serve as an input to thinking rather than its conclusion. The sections that follow translate this posture into practical methods. Those methods, however, remain secondary to the orientation that gives them value. Without the right posture, techniques become optional. With the right posture, careful evaluation becomes the natural way the interaction unfolds.

13.3 Treating Output as Draft, Not Authority

The Single Most Important Reorientation the Reader Can Make

If the appropriate approach to generative systems can be expressed in a single principle, it is this: treat the output as a draft, not as an authority. This shift may appear small, but it changes the interaction in an important way. An authority presents conclusions. When a source is treated as authoritative, the natural response is acceptance unless a clear error appears. Scrutiny begins only when something seems wrong. A draft works differently. It invites revision, comparison, and improvement. It assumes incompleteness from the outset. The reader does not ask whether the draft should be accepted. Instead, the question becomes how it should be examined, refined, or corrected. Treating AI output as a draft preserves the proper division of roles. The system generates language. The human exercises judgment. When output is treated as authoritative, those roles quietly reverse. The machine presents a conclusion, and the human must prove it wrong before rejecting it. Because the response is fluent and coherent, that burden of proof is rarely applied. The explanation appears complete, and the impulse to question it weakens. Treating the response as a draft prevents this reversal.

A draft can still be valuable. It may suggest ways to structure an argument, outline possible explanations, identify considerations that might otherwise be overlooked, or provide language that can later be refined. In many situations, this assistance is genuinely useful. The draft mindset, however, keeps the work of evaluation active. The reader remains responsible for asking whether the claims are accurate, whether important perspectives are missing, and whether the reasoning is sound. This shift in perspective is especially important because generative systems present their outputs in a form normally associated with completed reasoning. The explanation arrives in a structured and confident form, without visible signs of the uncertainty that may have accompanied its production. The draft mindset restores awareness of that uncertainty. It reminds the reader that the response is not the end of the inquiry, but the beginning of a process in which human judgment remains the final authority.

Once this principle is established, other practices become easier to adopt. AI output is no longer approached as something to accept or reject in a single step. Instead, it is treated as material for examination, with the understanding that it may contain insight, error, or both. In this approach, the system serves as a collaborator during the early stages of thinking rather than as a substitute for human judgment.

13.4 Separating Fluency from Reliability

The Deliberate Practice of Decoupling What Feels Connected

One of the central insights of this book is that the persuasive power of generative AI does not arise primarily from deception. It arises from fluency. These systems produce language that is smooth, coherent, and confidently structured. Those qualities trigger cognitive signals that people have long used to recognize competence in others. In ordinary communication, those signals are often reliable. A person who explains something clearly usually understands it well. Fluency tends to accompany knowledge because organizing ideas into language generally reflects familiarity with the subject.

Generative systems break this historical relationship. They can produce fluent explanations without understanding the claims those explanations make about the world. The language is well formed because it is generated from patterns in previous language, not because it results from reasoning about the truth of the statements involved. The result is a subtle but powerful illusion. Qualities that usually signal reliability, such as clarity, coherence, and confidence, can appear even when claims are incomplete, uncertain, or incorrect. Readers recognize these familiar signs of expertise and often reduce their level of scrutiny.

Interacting with AI systems responsibly therefore requires a deliberate change in how their outputs are evaluated. Fluency must be separated from reliability. This distinction does not arise automatically because the two qualities feel closely connected. When an explanation reads smoothly and follows a logical structure, an impression of credibility forms almost immediately. The mind interprets the style of the language as evidence about the substance of the claims. Careful evaluation requires resisting that inference.

A simple mental exercise illustrates the point. Imagine the same answer written in a disorganized, awkward style with an uncertain tone. Would the claims still appear convincing? If the persuasiveness disappears when the fluency is removed, the credibility came from presentation rather than evidence. This exercise encourages evaluation along two distinct dimensions. The first is presentation quality: whether the explanation is readable, well organized, and easy to follow. Generative systems excel in this respect. The second is epistemic reliability: whether the claims can be verified, whether the reasoning is supported by identifiable evidence, and whether the explanation acknowledges the limits of what is known.

Fluency answers the first question. Verification answers the second. The two may coincide. A clear explanation can also be correct. But responsible use of AI systems requires remembering that the connection between them is no longer assured. Once this distinction becomes habitual, fluent output is encountered differently. Clarity is no longer treated as evidence that a problem has been solved. Instead, it is recognized as evidence that an explanation has been communicated effectively, and nothing more. From that point onward, the important question is no longer, "*Does this sound convincing?*" but, "*Is there reason to believe it?*" The difference between those two questions is the difference between passive acceptance and active judgment.

13.5 Identifying Red Flags

The Observable Signals That Should Intensify Rather than Relax Critical Engagement

Treating AI output as a draft rather than an authority, and separating fluency from reliability, provides the right intellectual approach. Yet this mindset alone does not show when closer scrutiny is needed. Readers must also learn to recognize patterns that call for additional attention. These patterns do not prove that an answer is wrong. Instead, they indicate that an explanation should be examined carefully before it is accepted or used.

One common signal is excessive certainty in complex domains. Questions involving evolving research, contested interpretation, or context-dependent judgment rarely have simple, definitive answers. When a response presents such issues as settled facts without acknowledging uncertainty or limits, the confidence of the language may exceed the reliability of the claim. Another signal is the use of vague or untraceable appeals to authority. Phrases such as "*studies show,*" "*experts agree,*" or "*research indicates*" can create the impression of evidence without identifying a source that can be examined directly. Sound reasoning normally allows claims to be traced back to identifiable evidence. When that path is missing, verification becomes necessary. A third signal is overgeneralization. Generative systems often produce explanations that appear broadly applicable even when the question depends on context. Legal rules vary across jurisdictions, medical guidance depends on individual circumstances, and policy interpretation depends on specific situations. When a response compresses such variation into a single universal statement, it deserves closer examination.

Context slippage is a closely related problem. An answer may gradually drift away from the conditions set by the original question. It may shift the timeframe, jurisdiction, or scope without acknowledging the change. Because the explanation remains fluent, readers may not notice that it no longer addresses the original question. Another pattern is artificial symmetry. In subjects where the evidence strongly supports one conclusion, generative systems sometimes present opposing views as though they carried equal weight. This appearance of balance can obscure the actual distribution of evidence. A final signal is inconsistent specificity. An explanation may provide striking detail in some areas while remaining vague in others where similar detail would normally be expected. Such uneven precision can indicate that the system is extending patterns in language rather than drawing on grounded knowledge. None of these patterns proves that an explanation is wrong. Many accurate explanations contain one or more of them. Their value lies elsewhere. They indicate that attention should increase rather than relax.

In traditional reading, fluency often encourages trust. In the context of generative AI, fluency must sometimes produce the opposite response. When an answer sounds unusually complete, unusually confident, or unusually simple for a complex question, careful readers treat that smoothness as a reason to examine its claims more closely. Recognizing these signals turns skepticism from an abstract attitude into a practical habit. Readers learn not only that AI output requires evaluation, but also when that evaluation matters most.

13.6 Restoring Healthy Doubt

Skepticism as the Recovery of an Epistemic Virtue, Not the Adoption of a Hostile Stance

The practices described in the preceding sections may appear, at first glance, to encourage distrust. Readers are asked to treat AI output as provisional, to separate fluency from reliability, and to remain attentive to signs that call for closer scrutiny. It is easy to see these habits as a defensive response to technology. But the aim of disciplined interaction with AI is not hostility. It is the restoration of healthy doubt.

Healthy doubt is a longstanding intellectual virtue. In environments where persuasive claims circulate, thoughtful inquiry has always required a willingness to pause before accepting an explanation as knowledge. Scientists test hypotheses against evidence. Scholars examine sources before citing them. Journalists verify claims before publication. These practices do not reflect cynicism. They reflect responsibility. Generative systems make this virtue newly important. Because AI outputs are fluent, immediate, and often appear comprehensive, they shorten the natural pause that once preceded evaluation. A question is asked, and an answer arrives within seconds in the form of a finished explanation. The smoothness of the interaction encourages the impression that the work of thinking has already been completed.

Healthy doubt restores the pause that the system's fluency tends to remove. It begins with a few simple but essential questions:

What assumptions underlie this explanation?

What evidence would support or challenge it?

What information might be missing from this account?

How could this claim be verified independently?

These questions do not reject the usefulness of the system. They preserve the reader's role as the final judge of the answer. Doubt, however, must remain proportionate. Too little skepticism invites uncritical acceptance. Too much skepticism makes constructive use of the tool difficult. The goal is not to treat every output as suspect. It is to maintain an awareness that fluent language does not guarantee reliability. In practice, this may involve simple but meaningful habits: checking an important claim against an independent source when the stakes are high, asking the system to explain its reasoning when a statement appears overly confident, or consulting additional sources when an answer seems unusually simple for a complex question. These habits turn doubt from a general attitude into a disciplined practice.

Seen in this light, skepticism is not a negative response to AI. It continues the intellectual traditions that have long guided responsible inquiry. The difference is that, in a world where persuasive explanations can be generated automatically, the pause that once arose naturally must now be introduced deliberately. Healthy doubt provides that pause. It helps ensure that fluent answers do not quietly replace the human judgment they still require.

13.7 Skepticism as Clarity

A Different Way of Seeing AI Output

The purpose of this chapter has not been to encourage resistance to technology. It has been to change the way AI output is interpreted. At the beginning of an interaction, a generated explanation often appears complete. The language is fluent, the structure is coherent, and the tone conveys confidence. Without deliberate reflection, these signals invite a familiar conclusion: that the explanation reflects understanding. The practices introduced in this chapter interrupt that conclusion. AI output is approached as provisional material rather than established authority. Fluency is treated as a feature of presentation, not as evidence of reliability. Patterns such as excessive certainty, vague references, and context drift signal the need for closer scrutiny. Doubt is restored to its proper role as a constructive intellectual habit.

Nothing about the output itself has changed. What has changed is the way it is interpreted. Where a fluent answer once appeared self-sufficient, it now appears useful but still open to evaluation. Where coherence once implied trustworthiness, it now raises the question of what evidence supports the claim. The explanation is no longer the endpoint of inquiry, but one contribution to it. This shift is subtle, yet decisive. A reader who approaches AI output with unexamined trust is easily guided by its fluency. A reader who approaches the same output with disciplined skepticism remains intellectually independent while still benefiting from the tool. Skepticism therefore does not reduce the usefulness of AI. It makes that usefulness more dependable. Readers can accept insights when they are supported, question claims when uncertainty remains, and verify conclusions before acting on them. The system becomes a participant in thinking rather than a substitute for it. In this sense, skepticism is not suspicion but clarity. It allows generated explanations to be seen for what they are: structured language produced by a predictive system, sometimes helpful, sometimes incomplete, occasionally mistaken, and always requiring human judgment.

With this foundation in place, the focus shifts to practice. The next chapter moves from orientation to method. It presents interaction strategies for examining AI responses within the conversation. These approaches help readers identify limitations, test counterarguments, and uncover assumptions before placing trust in the output.

Closing Reflection

The Small Distance That Preserves Judgment

An AI-generated explanation appears on the screen. The language is clear. The structure is logical. The explanation appears complete. Nothing in the wording signals uncertainty. Nothing in the tone suggests hesitation. The explanation feels finished. The preceding chapters have explained why that impression arises. Fluency creates credibility. Coherence suggests understanding. The mind interprets these signals through habits formed in environments where fluent language usually came from people who understood what they were discussing. Those habits have not disappeared. The environment in which they operate has changed.

The purpose of this chapter has not been to encourage resistance to technology. It has been to change the way AI output is interpreted. That change begins by restoring a small but important distance between the explanation presented and the judgment formed about it. The output is treated as provisional material rather than authority. Fluency is distinguished from reliability. Certain signals prompt scrutiny instead of trust. Doubt returns not as hostility, but as a deliberate pause before acceptance. Nothing about the AI system changes when these habits are adopted. What changes is the way its output is evaluated. A fluent answer no longer brings the inquiry to an end. It becomes material for evaluation. The explanation may still prove useful, or even correct. Its credibility, however, is earned through examination rather than granted by presentation.

This distance is easy to lose in environments filled with persuasive language. Yet it keeps human judgment active when answers arrive quickly and with confidence. The next chapter explains how to preserve that distance during the interaction itself. It presents practical methods for identifying uncertainty before trust is granted.

CHAPTER 14
Forcing Uncertainty

The Practical Toolkit for Interrupting the Illusion from Within the Interaction Itself

The previous chapter established an approach. It showed how careful readers engage with AI-generated content through disciplined skepticism. They treat explanations as provisional, distinguish fluency from reliability, and restore the habit of doubt that persuasive language can weaken. This approach, however, is not enough on its own. Generative systems are designed to produce responses that appear complete. Their explanations are fluent, well structured, and delivered with confidence. Even when readers adopt the right intellectual approach, the form of the output still encourages the impression that the work of thinking has already been done. What is needed, therefore, is not only skepticism but also active engagement. Readers must interact with the system in ways that reveal its limitations before accepting its conclusions. Instead of passively receiving answers, they test responses, ask the system to acknowledge uncertainty, and apply the critical scrutiny that fluent language can obscure.

This chapter develops that practice. The strategies that follow are simple but effective. They ask the system to identify its limitations, present counterarguments, make its reasoning more transparent, and withstand deliberate testing before its conclusions are trusted. Each strategy interrupts the smooth surface of the initial response. Together, they accomplish something essential: they bring uncertainty back into the interaction. Uncertainty is not a weakness of the system. It is an honest reflection of the fact that language generation does not guarantee knowledge. Once uncertainty becomes visible, readers can evaluate the response instead of merely reacting to its fluency. This changes the nature of the interaction. The system no longer appears to deliver finished answers as an unquestioned authority. It becomes a conversational tool whose outputs can be examined, challenged, and refined. The sections that follow introduce practical methods for doing so. By the end of the chapter, readers will know how to shape their interactions with generative systems in ways that keep human judgment at the center.

14.1 From Posture to Practice

The Reader as Active Interlocutor, Not Passive Consumer

The previous chapter established a way of approaching AI output. The reader learned to treat it as draft rather than authority, to distinguish fluency from reliability, and to restore the habit of doubt that persuasive language can suppress. But this shift in perspective does not, by itself, change the structure of the interaction. If a user asks a question, receives an answer, reads it once, and then moves on, the interaction remains largely passive. Even when skepticism is present, the system still performs most of the intellectual work. The answer arrives as a finished explanation, and the reader's role is limited to deciding whether it appears acceptable. To preserve independent judgment, that structure must change. The user must become an active interlocutor rather than a passive recipient of answers.

An interlocutor does not treat the first response as the end of the conversation. It becomes the starting point for further inquiry. The explanation produced by the system becomes material to examine, question, and test. Instead of asking a single question and accepting the result, the user engages the system through a sequence of questions designed to reveal the strengths and limitations of the initial answer. This change may appear procedural, but it has important cognitive consequences. Follow-up questions that probe uncertainty, request clarification, or introduce alternative perspectives begin to expose the limits of the original response. Assumptions become visible. Areas of uncertainty emerge. Competing considerations appear that the initial answer may have been simplified or omitted. In this way, the interaction becomes part of the evaluation process. The reader no longer stands outside the explanation, deciding whether it deserves trust. Instead, the reader uses the system's own responses to examine the conditions under which its claims hold or fail. This approach reflects the structure of sound intellectual inquiry more generally. In academic debate, legal reasoning, and scientific investigation, understanding rarely develops from a single statement. It develops through questioning, challenge, and refinement. Generative systems can support the same process when they are used interactively rather than passively.

The following sections present four practical strategies that support this approach. Each strategy encourages the system to reveal uncertainties that an initial response may conceal. Together, they shift the user's role from information recipient to active participant in a structured dialog. As this shift takes place, fluent answers become easier to examine critically. The interaction begins to reveal the limits of the system's knowledge. Recognizing those limits helps keep human judgment in control.

14.2 Asking for Limitations

The Habit That Transforms Interaction

If one practice from this chapter were adopted consistently, it would be this: ask the system about the limitations of its answer before accepting its conclusions. Generative systems are optimized to produce helpful responses. When presented with a question, they attempt to provide a clear and coherent answer that addresses the prompt directly. The result is often an explanation that appears confident and complete. That confidence, however, is a feature of presentation, not necessarily a reflection of epistemic certainty. The most direct way to interrupt that appearance is to ask where the answer may be uncertain, incomplete, or dependent on assumptions. Simple follow-up questions can do this:

What are the limitations of this answer?
What important factors might this explanation overlook?
Under what conditions m Wight this conclusion fail?

These questions introduce something the initial response rarely provides on its own: visible uncertainty. When asked directly, the system will often identify caveats, contextual dependencies, and areas where additional information would matter. An explanation that first appeared self-contained begins to open outward. The reader gains a clearer understanding of where the reasoning depends on assumptions, where the evidence may be incomplete, and where the boundaries of the answer lie.

This practice serves two important purposes. First, it restores proportional confidence. By making uncertainties and constraints explicit, the response becomes easier to evaluate in relation to the complexity of the question. The reader can distinguish between what the answer genuinely addresses and what remains unresolved. Second, it changes the basis of trust. Instead of deciding whether the explanation should be accepted as presented, the reader evaluates it in light of its stated limitations. The system's conclusions become conditional rather than absolute. This shift often produces a revealing effect. An answer that initially appeared authoritative may disclose important qualifications once its limitations are examined. Conversely, an explanation that withstands careful scrutiny may become more credible because its constraints have been made explicit.

The key insight is that limitations are not weaknesses in responsible reasoning. They are signs of intellectual honesty. In scientific writing, legal argument, and academic analysis, careful thinkers routinely identify the boundaries of their claims. Generative systems can produce similar reflections when prompted. They rarely introduce them on their own because their design prioritizes responsiveness and clarity. Asking about limitations deliberately restores a dimension of reasoning that fluent answers often conceal. Over time, this question becomes a habit. After the initial response appears, the next step follows naturally: *What might this answer be missing?*

That small intervention changes the interaction. The explanation no longer arrives as a finished product. It becomes the starting point for a more careful inquiry in which the limits of the answer are examined before the answer itself is accepted.

14.3 Requesting Counterarguments

How to Produce the Intellectual Friction That Fluent Output Suppresses

Fluent answers tend to smooth over disagreement. When a generative system produces an explanation, it usually organizes the material into a coherent narrative that moves efficiently toward a conclusion. The explanation may acknowledge alternative views, but its structure generally favors clarity and completeness. Clarity is valuable. But it can also conceal the intellectual friction through which strong reasoning develops. In fields such as philosophy, law, and science, arguments are rarely accepted without examination. They are tested against objections. Competing interpretations are considered and evaluated. Weaknesses become visible when a claim is tested against plausible alternatives. This friction is essential because it reveals what the original explanation may have simplified or assumed.

Generative systems can contribute to this process, but only when the interaction is directed deliberately. A few simple questions can change the direction of the conversation:

What are the strongest counterarguments to this explanation?
How might a knowledgeable critic challenge this claim?
What alternative interpretations should be considered?

When these questions are asked, the system often produces perspectives that were absent from the original response. An explanation that first appeared complete begins to reveal its limits. Competing considerations emerge. The assumptions supporting the original conclusion become easier to identify. This practice serves an important epistemic purpose. A single explanation usually moves in one direction. Counterarguments create a field of tension around it. Within that tension, it becomes easier to see where the argument is strong, where it is vulnerable, and where further evidence is needed. In effect, the interaction becomes a small intellectual debate. This approach is especially valuable in areas where evidence is complex or interpretation plays a central role. Policy questions, ethical dilemmas, and strategic decisions rarely have a single uncontested answer. When a generative system presents these topics as a smooth narrative, the appearance of resolution can conceal genuine disagreement. Requesting counterarguments restores that complexity.

The purpose of this practice is not to encourage endless skepticism. It is to test the reasoning before relying on it. If the original explanation withstands scrutiny, confidence in it becomes better justified. If weaknesses emerge, understanding can be refined before conclusions are drawn. This practice also counteracts a structural feature of generative output. Because these systems optimize for coherence, they tend to present explanations in ways that minimize visible conflict. By explicitly requesting objections, the interaction introduces the friction that fluent responses tend to suppress. That friction is not an inconvenience. It is one of the conditions that makes careful judgment possible. Once this habit becomes routine, the system's first explanation is rarely treated as the final word. It becomes the starting point of a dialog in which alternatives are examined before any conclusion is accepted.

14.4 Seeking Transparency in Reasoning

Making the Invisible Reasoning Visible and Therefore Evaluable

A fluent answer often appears convincing because it arrives already assembled. The explanation moves smoothly from premise to conclusion, presenting its claims in a way that suggests the underlying reasoning is complete and well founded. Yet that reasoning is rarely visible. The system presents the result of a process without necessarily revealing the steps that produced it. The reader sees the conclusion, but not the path leading to it. As a result, evaluation becomes difficult because the underlying logic remains implicit.

One effective way to address this limitation is to ask the system to make its reasoning explicit. Simple prompts can achieve this:

What assumptions does this conclusion depend on?

What steps connect the evidence to the final claim?

Which pieces of information are most important in supporting this explanation?

These questions prompt the system to describe the structure underlying its original answer. The explanation becomes less like a finished statement and more like an argument whose individual parts can be examined.

This transparency serves an important purpose. When the steps of reasoning are visible, each step can be evaluated. The reader can ask whether the assumptions are justified, whether the evidence supports the inference being drawn, and whether alternative interpretations could explain the same facts. Errors that remain hidden within a fluent explanation often become easier to detect once the reasoning is laid out. Transparency does more than reveal mistakes. It also helps calibrate confidence. A conclusion supported by clearly explained reasoning deserves a different level of trust than one presented without explanation. Even when the reasoning is imperfect, seeing its structure makes its weaknesses easier to identify.

This practice reflects the standards of careful inquiry in many fields. In academic writing, legal argument, and scientific research, conclusions are rarely presented without explanation. Authors are expected to show how their claims follow from the evidence they cite. The reasoning is made visible so that others can evaluate it. Generative systems can approximate this practice when prompted to do so. They do not, however, provide this level of transparency by default. Their responses prioritize clarity and responsiveness rather than explaining how a conclusion is reached. By asking the system to make its reasoning explicit, the reader changes that default.

The explanation becomes less opaque and easier to examine. The reader responds not only to the fluency of the answer, but also to the reasoning that supports it. What first appeared as a finished conclusion becomes a sequence of claims whose strength can be evaluated step by step. In that shift, the interaction moves closer to genuine inquiry. The system still generates language, but the reader gains a better basis for evaluating the reasoning behind the response rather than accepting its surface coherence alone.

14.5 Stress-Testing Responses

Systematic Probing from Multiple Angles before Calibrated Trust Is Extended

The previous strategies of identifying limitations, requesting counterarguments, and seeking transparent reasoning add productive friction to interactions with AI systems. They expose uncertainty that an initial answer may conceal and bring underlying assumptions into clearer view. Effective evaluation, however, often requires another step. Instead of examining a response from a single angle, the reader tests it from multiple perspectives.

Engineers use a similar approach when stress-testing structures. They do not evaluate a structure only under ideal conditions. They place it under pressure, pushing and challenging it to reveal its strengths and weaknesses. The same principle applies to reasoning. Well-supported explanations tend to remain consistent when examined from different perspectives. Explanations built on weak assumptions or incomplete information often break down under scrutiny, revealing inconsistencies or gaps that the original response did not expose.

Generative systems make this kind of testing possible within the conversation itself. After receiving an initial answer, the reader can explore variations of the same question:

How would this conclusion change if certain assumptions were different?

What evidence would contradict this claim?

Are there scenarios in which this reasoning would lead to the wrong result?

How might a specialist in this field critically evaluate this explanation?

Each question asks the system to reconsider its response from a different perspective. An explanation that initially appears stable is examined under changing conditions. Some claims remain consistent across these tests. Others shift, weaken, or reveal assumptions that were not previously apparent. This process gradually shows how robust the answer is. A claim that withstands repeated scrutiny becomes easier to trust. Its credibility rests not on how persuasive it first appeared, but on how well it withstands deliberate challenge. An explanation that changes substantially across different perspectives signals the need for further verification.

Stress-testing also guards against a common cognitive bias. When readers encounter a fluent answer, they often anchor later thinking to the initial explanation. Without deliberate examination, the first response may seem like the most plausible interpretation of the problem. Testing the answer under alternative conditions reduces this anchoring effect.

The goal of this practice is not to prove the system wrong. It is to calibrate trust. Some answers will prove reliable enough for practical purposes. Others will reveal uncertainty that warrants further investigation outside the system. In both cases, the reader remains in control of the evaluation. Trust, when it is finally extended, rests not on the surface coherence of the explanation, but on how well its reasoning withstands careful scrutiny.

14.6 The Complete Toolkit in Practice

How these Four Strategies Work Together in Real Interactions

The strategies described in the previous sections are simple when considered individually. Asking about limitations, requesting counterarguments, seeking transparency in reasoning, and stress-testing responses are all straightforward ways to engage with an AI system. Their full value, however, emerges when they are used together. A single prompt rarely reveals the full structure of an answer. Generative systems tend to produce responses that appear complete and self-contained. The first explanation often arrives as a smooth narrative that resolves the question quickly and confidently. When the interaction ends there, only the most polished version of the answer is seen. The toolkit interrupts that pattern.

A careful interaction unfolds differently. A question is asked, and an initial explanation is received. Instead of treating that explanation as final, the next step is to ask about its limitations. The response often introduces caveats and contextual dependencies that were absent from the original answer. Once those boundaries become visible, counterarguments are requested. Alternative interpretations emerge. The explanation that once appeared straightforward is now seen alongside competing considerations. The next step is to seek transparency in reasoning. The system is asked to identify the assumptions and logical steps that connect the evidence to the conclusion. What first appeared to be a finished statement becomes a structured argument whose individual parts can be examined. Finally, the response is stress-tested. Variations of the original question are introduced, assumptions are changed, and the explanation is examined from different perspectives. This process reveals how stable the answer remains when conditions change. By the end of the sequence, the interaction differs substantially from the one that began with a single question. The initial answer no longer stands alone. It has been expanded, challenged, examined, and viewed from multiple perspectives. The system has helped reveal uncertainty, identify assumptions, and show where the reasoning remains sound or begins to fail.

The result is not a definitive conclusion. It is a clearer picture of the intellectual landscape surrounding the question. This reflects a different way of using the system. The user no longer depends on the model to provide a finished answer. Instead, the model serves as a tool for exploring the problem. It generates possibilities, reveals tensions, and identifies claims that require further verification. As these practices become routine, the interaction itself becomes a form of inquiry. The system produces language, while the user directs how that language is examined. The fluency of the initial response no longer determines the outcome. The conversation develops into a structured investigation, with human judgment remaining firmly in control.

14.7 Why This Works

What these Strategies Exploit

The strategies introduced in this chapter, including asking about limitations, requesting counterarguments, seeking transparency in reasoning, and stress-testing responses, may seem deceptively simple. They require no specialized technical knowledge and can be used in ordinary conversation. Their effectiveness has a straightforward explanation: they align the interaction with the way large language models operate. Generative systems do not hold stable internal beliefs that remain consistent across contexts. Instead, they generate responses by predicting plausible continuations of language from the prompt and the surrounding conversation. Each prompt establishes a new context, and the model produces language that fits the instructions it receives.

As a result, the system responds strongly to the way questions are framed. A request for an explanation produces a coherent explanation. A request for limitations produces caveats. A request for counterarguments generates competing perspectives. Questions that examine assumptions or introduce alternative conditions prompt the model to extend its reasoning in those directions. The same issue can therefore produce different responses because different prompts ask the model to perform different tasks.

The strategies in this chapter build on that property. Rather than treating the first response as the system's final position, they guide the interaction through different lines of inquiry. Each prompt encourages the model to reveal aspects of the issue that the initial answer did not address. The model does not become more knowledgeable during this process. Instead, the interaction draws out different possibilities already present in its learned patterns. An initial explanation may offer a simplified account because the prompt asks for a direct answer. Later questions about limitations or counterarguments draw on other discourse patterns, including scientific caution, critical debate, and analytical reasoning, that are also represented in the training data. Changing the conversational frame brings these perspectives to the surface.

This approach offers two advantages. It reveals uncertainty that a fluent initial response may conceal. As multiple perspectives emerge, the limits of an explanation become easier to recognize. It also turns the exchange into a collaborative exploration rather than a single transaction. The system functions as a tool for exploring possibilities rather than as a source of final authority.

Understanding this mechanism explains why these strategies work. They do not make the model infallible or remove the need for independent verification. Instead, they use the model's flexibility to counter the illusion of completeness. The prompts encourage the system to reveal its own limitations. As this happens, the fluent surface of the initial answer gives way to something more valuable: a clearer view of the reasoning surrounding the question. With these tools in place, readers can challenge the illusion during the interaction itself. The final chapter examines the deeper discipline that sustains this practice over time. It focuses on the habits of thought that preserve independent judgment in a world filled with fluent, machine-generated answers.

Closing Reflection

The Conversation That Reveals the Limits

An initial answer need not be the final answer. An AI system provides a fluent, structured, and confident explanation. If the interaction ends there, the explanation is taken as complete. The reader must then decide whether to trust it. The interaction can instead continue through a few critical follow-up questions:

What are the limitations of this answer?
What are the strongest counterarguments?
What assumptions does this reasoning depend on?
Under what conditions would this conclusion fail?

With each question, the explanation begins to change. The confident narrative opens outward. Caveats appear. Alternative interpretations emerge. Assumptions become visible. The smooth explanation reveals what lies beneath its surface. Nothing about the system itself has changed. What has changed is the structure of the conversation. The reader is no longer receiving an answer alone. The reader is examining it. Fluency is no longer treated as the final word. It becomes the starting point for an inquiry that gradually reveals uncertainty.

This is the quiet strength of the practices described in this chapter. They do not confront the illusion directly. Instead, they reveal the conditions that allow it to arise. When the system is asked to examine the limits of its own answer, a one-sided explanation becomes a broader inquiry that shows where the reasoning holds and where it may fail. An important insight follows: every answer has boundaries. Once those boundaries become visible, judgment returns to its proper place, the mind of the person asking the question.

CHAPTER 15
Reclaiming Deliberate Judgment

Beyond AI Interaction: The Interior Cognitive Discipline That Makes Human Agency Real

Previous chapters examined how to engage with generative systems responsibly. They first developed a skeptical intellectual stance and then introduced practical ways to interrupt the illusion of certainty during the conversation itself. These practices are necessary, but they are not sufficient. Careful interaction with AI addresses only part of a larger question: how people think when the system is no longer present. Tools can support reasoning, challenge assumptions, and help explore possibilities. The ability to judge those possibilities, and to decide what is true, reliable, and worth acting on, does not come from the tool. It remains with the person using it.

This chapter shifts the focus inward. Instead of asking how to question the system, it asks how people preserve the habits of thought that make questioning meaningful. In environments where answers are readily generated, the most important intellectual discipline may be preserving independent judgment deliberately. That discipline begins with small but important habits: resisting the impulse to trust an explanation simply because it appears persuasive, verifying important claims before acting on them, and maintaining the ability to reason through problems without immediate assistance from automated tools. These are not techniques in the usual sense. They are habits that preserve the capacity to think independently.

Just as physical abilities weaken when they are not exercised, intellectual capacities can decline when the environments in which they operate no longer require them. When systems consistently generate explanations on demand, it becomes tempting to treat those explanations as substitutes for independent reasoning. The effort once required for thinking becomes optional. Preserving deliberate judgment means resisting that quiet substitution.

The goal is not to reject the assistance that intelligent systems can provide. It is to ensure that their presence does not gradually displace the practices through which understanding and judgment develop. A tool that supports thinking should expand human agency, not quietly replace it.

The sections that follow examine how that agency can be preserved. They explore the habits that allow people to pause before accepting a conclusion, verify claims in proportion to their importance, reason independently when necessary, and develop standards of evidence that do not depend entirely on external authority. Together, these habits sustain intellectual autonomy. They help ensure that, even in a world where fluent answers are always available, the capacity for careful judgment remains distinctly human.

15.1 From Interacting with AI to Thinking for Yourself

The Shift this Chapter Makes

The previous chapters focused on the interaction between a human user and a generative system. They showed how to approach AI output with skepticism and how to structure conversations in ways that reveal uncertainty rather than conceal it. Asking for limitations, counterarguments, and transparent reasoning interrupts the illusion of completeness that fluent answers often create. These strategies are valuable. They make AI use more disciplined and reduce the risk of passive acceptance. Yet they remain centered on the system.

This chapter takes a different approach. It shifts attention from the interaction to the capabilities of the person using the system. The central question is no longer how to use AI effectively during a conversation. It is how to maintain independent thought when the conversation ends or when its influence must be set aside. This distinction matters because tools shape habits. When explanations are always available, people can become accustomed to beginning every inquiry by consulting the system. Questions that once invited reflection can become prompts for a query. The first step in thinking gradually moves outward. The change is subtle. Each interaction seems efficient and reasonable. Over time, however, the habit of consulting the system can replace the practice of developing an initial answer before seeking assistance.

Restoring deliberate judgment requires reversing this pattern. It means facing a question directly, exploring possible answers, recalling relevant knowledge, and forming a provisional understanding before turning to external input. The system can still support the process, but it no longer provides the starting point. This shift has an important effect. When people examine AI-generated content after forming an initial interpretation, the response becomes a point of comparison rather than the framework that defines the problem from the outset. The difference extends beyond procedure. It preserves intellectual agency. Those who begin with their own reasoning retain an independent perspective from which to evaluate the system's response. Those who begin with the system's answer may find it harder to step outside the frame that answer establishes.

The sections that follow develop the habits that sustain this independence: slowing the impulse to trust, verifying claims before acting on them, maintaining the ability to reason without assistance, and developing personal standards of evidence that guide judgment even when external answers are readily available. Together, these habits transform interaction with AI from dependence into collaboration. The system may still generate explanations. But understanding still begins with the thinker.

15.2 Slowing the Impulse to Trust

Cultivating the Deliberate Pause

One of the most subtle effects of fluent AI systems is the speed with which they move the mind from question to conclusion. A prompt is entered. An answer appears within seconds. The explanation arrives in a form that already resembles the outcome of careful reasoning. The transition feels natural. Nothing in the interaction suggests that a pause is needed. Yet that missing pause is often where judgment begins.

Before acting on an explanation about a professional decision, a technical claim, or an interpretation of evidence, people usually pause to ask a simple question: Should this be trusted? When information arrives more slowly, that pause often occurs naturally. The time required to find sources, compare accounts, or develop an answer creates space for reflection. Generative systems shorten that space. When answers appear instantly and sound convincing, readers may move directly from reading to acceptance. The explanation can seem complete enough to use, making careful evaluation appear unnecessary.

Cultivating deliberate judgment begins with a simple practice: restoring the pause. The pause need not be long. What matters is that it exists. After encountering a convincing answer, the reader briefly withholds acceptance and asks a small set of orienting questions. *What kind of claim is this? What would make it reliable? What consequences would follow if it were mistaken?* These questions slow the movement from explanation to belief. They create space to evaluate the claim rather than simply react to it.

The value of this pause increases as the stakes become higher. For low-consequence questions, such as casual curiosity or exploratory brainstorming, the cost of error is limited. Decisions affecting professional work, financial commitments, or health-related choices carry greater risk. In these situations, a deliberate pause becomes an act of intellectual responsibility. This practice does not reject the value of AI-generated answers. It recognizes that generating an answer quickly is different from evaluating it carefully. A system may respond instantly, but acceptance can still be delayed until the answer has been assessed.

Over time, this pause can become a habit. A fluent explanation no longer marks the end of inquiry. Instead, it creates a brief but important opportunity to judge how much trust the answer deserves. During that interval, human judgment remains active. That activity helps ensure that understanding remains genuinely human.

15.3 Verifying Before Acting

A Practical Framework for Calibrating Verification Effort to Stakes and Domain

The deliberate pause described in the previous section creates the conditions for a second discipline: verification. A persuasive explanation may be read and considered, but before it becomes the basis for action, another question should be asked: How much confirmation does this claim require?

Not every statement requires the same level of scrutiny. In daily life, people often rely on information that has not been fully verified. Casual facts, exploratory ideas, and low-stakes questions may require only a brief check, if any. Verifying them in depth often provides little practical benefit. Other claims require greater care. When an answer shapes important decisions, such as financial commitments, medical choices, professional judgments, or legal interpretations, the cost of error increases. In these situations, relying only on a fluent explanation, whether from a person or a machine, carries greater risk. Sound judgment requires matching the level of verification to the stakes.

A useful way to calibrate verification is to think in terms of three broad levels. The first covers informational interactions. These include questions that mainly support general understanding, such as requests for historical background, conceptual explanations, or exploratory brainstorming. In these cases, AI output can serve as a starting point. Checking for obvious inconsistencies or consulting another source may be sufficient, especially when the topic is unfamiliar. The second level involves practical guidance. Here, the information begins to shape decisions about tasks such as drafting professional documents, interpreting technical material, or planning projects. The stakes increase, so verification requires greater care. Claims should be checked against reliable references, official documentation, or established literature in the relevant field. The third level concerns consequential decisions. In these situations, the accuracy of the information may directly affect finances, legal obligations, health, or safety. Verification should extend beyond the AI system. Authoritative sources, expert advice, or domain-specific evidence become essential before action is taken. These levels are not fixed categories, but they illustrate an important principle: the level of verification should increase with the stakes of the decision.

Generative systems do not adjust their presentation to reflect the importance of the consequences that may follow from their answers. A casual inquiry and a life-altering decision may both receive responses that appear equally confident. The responsibility for calibrating trust therefore rests with the person using the system. Practicing verification in this way preserves the balance between efficiency and reliability. AI systems remain useful tools for generating ideas and organizing information, but they do not become the final authority when independent confirmation is required.

Over time, this habit changes the relationship between explanation and action. A convincing answer no longer leads directly to reliance. Instead, it creates a pause for assessment: *What level of certainty does the situation require?* The answer can then be evaluated, and additional evidence sought when the situation demands it.

15.4 Preserving Independent Reasoning

The Deliberate Practice of Thinking Without AI Input as a Cognitive Discipline

The habits described so far, such as slowing the impulse to trust and matching verification to the stakes involved, help preserve judgment when interacting with AI systems. A deeper discipline, however, is also necessary. It is the deliberate preservation of independent reasoning.

When powerful tools are readily available, consulting them first becomes easy. A question arises, and the system becomes the first source of guidance. An explanation appears almost immediately, and thinking begins from that starting point. Over time, this pattern can quietly change how inquiry begins. The habit of inquiry shifts outward. Instead of first exploring the question by recalling relevant knowledge, considering possible explanations, and testing ideas against existing understanding, thinking begins with the system's response and evaluates it afterward. The problem is framed externally before an independent perspective has had an opportunity to develop.

To preserve intellectual agency, this sequence should sometimes be reversed. Independent reasoning begins before AI assistance is sought. Before consulting a system, it is useful to pause and ask: *What is already known? Which explanations seem plausible? Which uncertainties still need to be resolved?* This initial reflection does not need to produce a final answer. Its purpose is to establish a provisional framework that can later be tested and refined. Once that framework exists, the role of AI changes. The system's response becomes something to evaluate, refine, or challenge rather than the starting point for the entire inquiry.

The difference may appear small, but its consequences are significant. A person who begins with tentative reasoning retains an independent perspective. That perspective makes it easier to recognize when the system's answer conflicts with existing understanding, omits relevant considerations, or introduces ideas worth exploring further. Without that internal reference point, the system's explanation can easily become the framework through which the problem is interpreted from the outset.

Practicing independent reasoning therefore serves as a form of cognitive maintenance. Just as physical abilities remain strong only through regular exercise, intellectual capacities remain reliable when explanations continue to be constructed independently. This does not require rejecting AI tools. It requires thinking before seeking assistance rather than afterward. Over time, this practice reinforces an essential habit: understanding begins in the thinker's mind, not in the system that supports it. The system can generate language, but reasoning and judgment remain distinctly human.

15.5 Why Reasoning Alone Is Not Inefficiency but Maintenance

Keeping the Muscle Functional

In environments shaped by powerful tools, efficiency quickly becomes the dominant value. If a system can produce a coherent explanation in seconds, working through the same problem independently may seem unnecessary. Why struggle with a question when an answer is already available? From this perspective, reasoning can appear inefficient. But this view overlooks an important distinction. Some activities are valuable not only for the results they produce, but also for the abilities they preserve.

Physical exercise provides a useful example. Walking up a flight of stairs may take longer than using an elevator, but climbing helps maintain strength, balance, and endurance. If a person relied entirely on mechanical assistance, those abilities would gradually decline. The machines would not cause the loss. The body would simply stop performing the work that sustains them. Reasoning follows a similar pattern. Working through a difficult question by examining evidence, weighing alternatives, and building an explanation does more than produce an answer. It strengthens the habits that support sound judgment. The mind learns to recognize weak arguments, identify missing information, and revise assumptions when new evidence appears. When these habits are no longer practiced, they can weaken over time.

Generative systems make it easier than ever to bypass the effort that reasoning requires. Instead of building an explanation step by step, a person can consult a system that produces one instantly. In many situations, this efficiency is genuinely useful. But when it becomes the default response to every question, the practice of reasoning begins to recede from everyday intellectual life. The effect is subtle. Answers continue to arrive. They may even arrive more quickly and in greater numbers than before. Yet the ability to produce and evaluate those answers independently can weaken through lack of use.

Recognizing this pattern changes the role of independent reasoning. Working through a problem without immediate assistance is not merely a slower way to reach the same answer. It is an activity that preserves the ability to think carefully. The effort is not wasted. It is the work that maintains that ability. This perspective supports a balanced approach to technological assistance. AI systems can accelerate many tasks and provide valuable insights. But their availability should not eliminate opportunities for independent reasoning.

Choosing to work through a problem without consulting a system is not a rejection of technology. It helps preserve the cognitive skills needed to use that technology wisely. Independent reasoning therefore becomes part of a broader intellectual practice. Even in a world where answers are always available, the ability to evaluate those answers can remain strong.

15.6 Building Personal Standards of Evidence

Constructing an Independent Epistemic Framework

The practices described in this chapter, including pausing before trust, checking claims according to their importance, and maintaining independent judgment, serve a broader goal: building personal standards for evaluating evidence. In many situations, people rely on external authorities to determine what is true. A claim may be accepted because it appears in a respected publication, comes from an expert, or is expressed with confidence. These shortcuts have long been necessary in complex societies where knowledge is widely distributed.

Generative AI changes the environment in which these shortcuts operate. These systems produce language that resembles expert communication even when no expert stands behind it. A fluent explanation may cite studies, summarize arguments, and present conclusions in ways that imitate authoritative discourse. Yet these signals do not guarantee that the claims have been examined with the care they normally imply. Under these conditions, responsibility for judgment shifts more heavily to the individual.

Navigating this environment effectively requires the gradual development of an epistemic framework: a set of internal standards for evaluating evidence before accepting a claim. These standards are not rigid rules. They are habits of evaluation that help answer questions such as: *What counts as credible evidence in this domain? Which sources deserve greater weight? What level of uncertainty is acceptable before action is taken? When is additional verification necessary?* Over time, experience within a field shapes these judgments. A scientist learns to distinguish between preliminary findings and well-established results. A lawyer develops the ability to distinguish persuasive interpretations of a statute from those unlikely to withstand scrutiny. A clinician learns to weigh different forms of medical evidence before recommending treatment.

These standards serve as internal reference points. New explanations, whether produced by humans or machines, are not considered in isolation. They are evaluated against existing standards of evidence. This comparison provides something that AI output alone cannot provide: a stable basis for evaluation. Without such standards, explanations are judged primarily by how they are presented. A well-written answer appears convincing simply because it is coherent. With a developed epistemic framework, the focus changes. The thinker asks whether the claim meets the standards of evidence required in that domain.

Developing this framework is an ongoing process. It grows through study, professional practice, and repeated encounters with both reliable and unreliable information. Generative systems can support that process by organizing material and presenting different perspectives. They cannot replace the judgment that determines what counts as sufficient evidence. Ultimately, the authority that guides responsible belief cannot reside entirely outside the thinker. It must rest within the habits of evaluation that have been developed over time. Building those habits ensures that, in an environment filled with persuasive explanations, credibility is not determined by fluency alone. It is determined by the standards of evidence used to evaluate the explanation.

15.7 The Reader Who Has Built This Framework

What No Checklist Can Replace

The habits described throughout this chapter, including slowing the impulse to trust, matching verification to the stakes, reasoning independently, and applying personal standards of evidence, gradually develop something that no single technique can provide. They develop judgment. Judgment is not a rule that can be written once and applied mechanically. It is the ability to recognize when a situation calls for caution, when an explanation requires closer scrutiny, and when the available evidence is sufficient for action. It develops through repeated practice rather than through a fixed procedure. For this reason, checklists alone are never enough.

A checklist can remind a reader to verify sources, consider alternative interpretations, or examine the assumptions behind an argument. These prompts are useful, particularly in complex situations. But they cannot anticipate every circumstance that requires careful evaluation. They cannot detect subtle flaws in reasoning or recognize when a claim quietly conflicts with established knowledge. A reader who has developed disciplined judgment can. Such a reader approaches explanations with an internal framework already in place. The question is not simply whether a statement sounds convincing. It is whether the statement fits with established knowledge, whether the evidence meets the standards of the domain, and whether the reasoning connecting evidence to conclusion is sound. Because this framework exists within the person rather than outside it, it adapts to situations that no checklist can predict. It allows oversimplified explanations to be recognized, confidence to be weighed against the available evidence, and conclusions to be examined before the supporting reasoning has been adequately established.

These abilities are not mysterious. They develop through the habits described in this chapter: pausing before acceptance, verifying claims when the stakes require it, reasoning independently, and applying personal standards of evidence. Over time, these habits foster intellectual autonomy. A person who has developed this framework can engage with AI systems, expert opinion, and persuasive arguments without surrendering judgment to any of them. Such a person can benefit from the insights these sources provide while retaining the ability to evaluate them critically.

In a world where fluent explanations can be generated instantly and at scale, this autonomy becomes increasingly valuable. It ensures that the final authority over belief and action remains where it has always belonged: with the human mind that weighs the evidence and decides what to trust.

Closing Reflection

The Place Where Judgment Lives

AI systems can answer questions with remarkable speed and clarity. Their responses may be correct. They may save time, suggest ideas, or organize information that would otherwise take hours to gather. There is nothing inherently wrong with this capability. The risk arises when the explanation is accepted as the end of the thinking process.

Throughout this book, the central concern has not been the existence of powerful tools. Human history is filled with tools that extend the ability to measure, calculate, and communicate. The concern arises when a tool begins to perform tasks that once required judgment, and the habits that sustain that judgment begin to weaken. The final chapters have outlined a different approach. These systems can be used with skepticism rather than hostility. Their outputs can be questioned rather than accepted without examination. The habits of reasoning that make evaluation possible can be preserved instead of replaced. These practices do not reduce the usefulness of AI. They clarify its role. The system generates language. The human mind evaluates it. As long as that distinction remains clear, fluent machines do not diminish human agency. They change the environment in which that agency operates. The practices described in this part of the book, including pausing before extending trust, verifying claims when the stakes are high, reasoning independently, and applying clear standards of evidence, are not methods for defeating machines. They are disciplines that preserve something older and more fundamental: the capacity to judge what is true.

That capacity does not reside in a model, a database, or an algorithm. It resides in the person who asks the question and decides what to believe. As long as that responsibility remains with people, intelligent machines need not diminish the role of human judgment. Instead, they make its exercise more necessary and more deliberate than ever before.

PART SIX
LIVING WITH THE ILLUSION

Institutions, Society, and the Human Responsibility That Remains

The perspective widens one final time, moving from the individual reader to institutions, economic systems, and civilization. In the closing chapter, the focus returns to what matters most: the reader, the act of judgment, and the responsibility that no machine can assume.

CHAPTER 16
Responsibility and Incentives

Who Bears the Cost of Error: The Political Economy of AI Illusion

So far, the focus has been on the relationship between individuals and predictive systems: how these systems generate fluent language, how that fluency creates the appearance of understanding, and how human cognition naturally responds to that appearance. The discussion has also examined the habits that help readers maintain sound judgment while using these systems. But the illusion described throughout this book does not operate only at the level of individual interaction. Predictive systems now function within institutions. They appear in workplaces, financial advice platforms, educational tools, medical information systems, legal assistance software, and the digital infrastructure through which governments deliver services. These systems increasingly influence decisions that affect people who may never have chosen to use them. As their role expands, responsibility takes on a different meaning. It is no longer enough to ask whether individuals exercise appropriate skepticism. Equal attention must be given to how these systems are designed, what incentives shape their development, and who bears the consequences when the illusion of intelligence leads to error.

The answers to these questions lie not primarily in the psychology of human cognition or the technical architecture of language models. They lie in the economic and institutional structures within which these systems are developed and deployed. Companies that build AI systems operate in competitive markets. Investors seek growth, adoption, and engagement. Users prefer tools that feel helpful, responsive, and confident. These forces shape design decisions long before questions of epistemic caution or philosophical clarity arise. The result is a structural tension. Systems that communicate uncertainty clearly and avoid producing confident answers beyond their reliable domains may be epistemically responsible. Yet systems that produce fluent, decisive responses are often easier to use, more appealing to users, and more commercially successful. This chapter examines that tension. It asks why the economic incentives surrounding AI development often reward designs that strengthen the illusion rather than weaken it. It explores how responsibility for the consequences of error is shared among developers, institutions, and users. It also considers what happens when systems capable of generating convincing explanations become embedded in public services, where those affected by their errors may have little ability to protect themselves.

The discussion now moves beyond the individual reader to the broader environment in which AI systems operate. The illusion of intelligence is not only a cognitive phenomenon. It is also an institutional one. Understanding how responsibility is distributed within that institutional environment is the first step toward determining how it should be managed.

16.1 Widening the Lens

From Individual Reader to Institutional Structure and Societal Consequence

The previous chapters concluded with the individual reader. The emphasis was on personal responsibility: practicing skepticism, verifying claims, and preserving independent reasoning in an environment saturated with fluent machine output. These practices remain essential. No system can remove the need for human judgment. But individual judgment is not the only place where the consequences of AI-generated illusion emerge. As predictive systems move beyond experimental tools and become part of everyday infrastructure, the environment in which decisions are made begins to change. AI systems increasingly assist in writing reports, summarizing information, offering recommendations, drafting legal documents, triaging medical questions, evaluating financial opportunities, and supporting administrative decisions in public institutions. In many cases, their output no longer informs only a private act of reading or reflection. It becomes part of the process through which consequential decisions are made.

At this scale, the patterns examined earlier in the book take on a different significance. The fluency bias described in Part Three is no longer only a matter of individual psychology. The automation bias discussed in Chapter 9 no longer operates only within the reasoning of a single user. The substitution of answers for inquiry examined in Chapter 10 no longer affects only the intellectual life of an individual. These forces begin to shape institutional processes themselves. When a technology becomes part of an institution, it interacts with structures that extend beyond individual cognition, including organizational incentives, legal responsibilities, professional norms, and economic pressures. Decisions about how systems are designed, deployed, and used are shaped by these structures as much as by technical capability. Responsibility for the effects of AI-generated illusion therefore cannot rest solely with the user. The person who reads an answer and decides whether to trust it remains responsible for that judgment. But the conditions under which the judgment is made are shaped by institutions that determine how systems are built, how confidently they present their outputs, and how widely they are integrated into processes that affect other people's lives.

Understanding the societal implications of AI therefore requires a broader perspective. The question is no longer only how a careful reader should evaluate an AI-generated explanation. It is also how organizations design systems that millions of people will encounter, what incentives shape those design decisions, and who ultimately bears the cost when confident predictions are mistaken for reliable knowledge. The illusion of intelligence begins in language and cognition. Once it becomes embedded in institutions, however, its consequences extend into the structure of society itself.

16.2 Corporate Design Trade-offs

The Structural Tension Between Epistemic Honesty and Commercial Success

Once predictive systems move from research laboratories into commercial products, they enter a very different environment. Research settings prioritize understanding and experimentation. Product environments prioritize adoption, usability, and commercial success. As language models become commercial tools, their outputs are shaped not only by epistemic considerations but also by competitive pressures. This creates a structural trade-off. From the perspective of epistemic responsibility, a system would communicate its limitations clearly. It would signal uncertainty when knowledge is incomplete. It would decline to answer questions beyond the domains in which its outputs are reliably grounded. It would also remind users that its responses are predictions about language rather than verified knowledge about the world. Such a system would be cautious, qualified, and, at times, silent.

From the perspective of product design, however, silence and hesitation carry costs. Users generally prefer tools that respond quickly, appear confident, and provide direct answers rather than conditional possibilities. A system that frequently declines to answer, interrupts its explanations with warnings about uncertainty, or requires extensive verification may be epistemically responsible. It may also feel slow, inconvenient, or frustrating.

Commercial systems therefore operate within a tension between two competing aims. Epistemic honesty favors restraint through clear expressions of uncertainty, visible boundaries around reliable knowledge, and a willingness to acknowledge the limits of what the system can determine. Commercial success often rewards immediate responses, confident explanations, and the appearance of broad capability. Neither side of this tension is irrational. Developers do not deliberately choose deception when they design systems that appear confident and responsive. They respond to real incentives. Products that seem helpful and decisive are easier to adopt, market, and accept in the short term. Yet the same features that attract users also reinforce the illusion examined throughout this book. Confidence, fluency, and completeness are the signals people associate with genuine understanding. When predictive systems produce those signals without possessing human understanding, the result is not deliberate deception. It creates a design environment in which projecting knowledge becomes easier than communicating uncertainty with care.

The tension between epistemic honesty and commercial success therefore does not arise from individual choices alone. It is built into the market structure within which these systems compete.

16.3 Why Market Forces Systematically Reward the More Dangerous Design Philosophy

The tension described in the previous section does not remain an abstract design problem. In competitive markets, such tensions are resolved through selection. Products that attract users grow. Products that fail to engage them disappear. Over time, this process favors design approaches that best match user preferences and economic incentives. In the case of generative systems, those incentives often favor designs that strengthen the illusion rather than restrain it.

Users generally prefer systems that appear capable. A tool that answers questions quickly and confidently feels more helpful than one that frequently pauses to acknowledge its limitations. A system that produces fluent explanations appears more intelligent than one that offers cautious, fragmented responses. Even when users value accuracy in principle, the immediate experience of interaction often favors clarity, decisiveness, and speed. These preferences create predictable pressures on product design. A system that responds with visible uncertainty may be epistemically honest, but it risks appearing less competent than competitors that deliver confident explanations. A system that frequently refuses to answer difficult questions may responsibly acknowledge its limitations, yet it can easily be perceived as less capable than a rival that produces a fluent response every time. In markets where multiple products compete for adoption, the system that appears more helpful and more certain often gains an advantage.

The danger lies in the fact that the features creating this advantage are not neutral. Confidence without understanding strengthens the illusion of intelligence. Fluency without verification reinforces the signals that human cognition interprets as expertise. Comprehensiveness without genuine knowledge produces explanations that feel complete even when they are partly incorrect. Market competition does not deliberately reward deception. It rewards engagement, usefulness, and perceived competence. When statistical prediction can generate signals of competence without the underlying understanding that those signals once represented, the market may favor systems that appear more reliable than they actually are.

This dynamic produces a subtle but powerful shift in design philosophy. Systems that emphasize caution, disclose their limitations, and signal uncertainty risk appearing weaker than systems that produce confident answers to every question. Over time, the competitive landscape can favor designs that minimize visible hesitation and maximize fluent responsiveness. The result is not a conspiracy against epistemic honesty. It is a predictable outcome of the incentives that shape commercial technologies. Market forces reward systems that feel intelligent. Feeling intelligent, however, is not the same as being reliable.

16.4 Not Malice but Incentive

How Economic Logic Produces Epistemic Harm

When the consequences of technological systems become visible, there is a natural tendency to look for intention. Harm suggests agency. Error suggests that someone accepted the risk. Yet many of the outcomes described in this chapter do not result from deliberate attempts to mislead or deceive. They arise from incentives. Modern technological development takes place within complex economic systems. Engineers optimize for performance. Product teams optimize for usability and adoption. Companies compete for users and investment. Investors seek growth and market advantage. None of these actors needs to intend epistemic harm for the system as a whole to produce it. Instead, a familiar economic pattern emerges: outcomes that no participant planned or intended, yet that follow logically from the incentives each faces.

A developer designing a conversational AI system aims to build a tool that users find helpful and engaging. A model that frequently refuses to answer or repeatedly emphasizes uncertainty may be epistemically cautious, but it is also likely to appear less capable. As a result, users may prefer competing systems that provide smoother and more decisive responses. A product manager responsible for adoption metrics faces a similar pressure. Systems that respond quickly and confidently are more likely to retain users than systems that frequently acknowledge their limitations. The incentive is therefore to reduce friction and make responses feel useful and complete. An executive responsible for the company's success faces another form of pressure. Investment and market share often depend on demonstrating rapid improvements in capability and broad user adoption. A system that appears intelligent and responsive is easier to market than one that continually highlights its limits. None of these decisions requires malice. Each follows logically from the incentives operating at its level of the organization. Across an industry, these incentives create a broader pattern: the widespread deployment of systems that reinforce the illusion of intelligence examined in earlier chapters. The resulting epistemic harms include overconfidence in generated explanations, misplaced trust in confident predictions, and reduced verification. These harms arise not because anyone deliberately chooses deception, but because existing incentives reward systems that appear capable even when their reliability remains uncertain.

Understanding this distinction matters. If the problem resulted only from unethical individuals, replacing them with more conscientious ones might address it. When harm arises from incentive structures, however, the pattern persists even when participants act in good faith. The illusion of intelligence therefore becomes more than a cognitive phenomenon or a technical property of predictive systems. It also becomes an economic phenomenon: a consequence of the incentives under which those systems are built and deployed.

16.5 User Accountability

Real but Partial, Bounded by Knowledge Access and Automatic Cognitive Forces

Recognizing the structural forces that shape AI systems does not remove the responsibility of individual users. People who read AI-generated explanations and decide whether to rely on them still exercise judgment. Decisions based on those outputs remain human decisions, and responsibility for evaluating the information remains with the people who act on it. The practices described in Part Five, including skepticism toward fluent answers, verification when the stakes are high, and the preservation of independent reasoning, remain essential safeguards. Yet user responsibility has limits. Individual users cannot fully see how predictive systems produce their outputs. The training data, model architecture, and internal processes that shape a response remain largely hidden. Even well-informed users cannot directly examine the statistical mechanisms that determine how a particular answer was produced. As a result, they make judgments under conditions of partial knowledge.

These limits become more significant when considered alongside the cognitive patterns examined earlier in the book. Human cognition did not evolve in environments populated by systems that generate fluent explanations without genuine understanding. Heuristics such as trust in confident language, responsiveness to coherent narratives, and deference to apparent expertise generally served people well in human social settings. When these same heuristics encounter predictive systems that reproduce the signals of expertise without genuine understanding, they can foster misplaced trust, even among careful thinkers. This does not remove responsibility, but it helps define its limits. Users can choose to question an answer rather than accept it automatically. They can verify claims when the stakes justify the effort. They can remain aware that fluent explanations do not guarantee reliability. These are meaningful forms of accountability. Expecting every user, however, to overcome both informational asymmetry and automatic cognitive tendencies would impose a burden that few technologies have ever required.

User responsibility is therefore genuine but limited. It exists within an environment shaped by system design, institutional incentives, and the cognitive architecture through which human beings interpret language. Recognizing these limits does not excuse careless reliance on AI outputs. It clarifies why individual vigilance alone cannot address the broader risks created when predictive systems are deployed at scale. The illusion of intelligence is not encountered by isolated individuals making fully informed decisions. It is encountered by human minds operating within systems they did not design and cannot fully understand.

16.6 Shared Responsibility in Public Systems

When Vulnerable Populations Cannot Be Expected to Protect Themselves

The limits of individual responsibility become most apparent when predictive systems are embedded in public institutions. In these settings, the people affected by AI-mediated decisions are often not voluntary users making discretionary choices. They are participants in systems they must use to obtain essential services. A patient seeking medical guidance, a defendant interacting with legal assistance tools, or a citizen applying for welfare benefits does not encounter AI in the same way as someone exploring a new technology by choice. Their interaction is shaped by institutional procedures, administrative constraints, and power differences that limit their ability to question the systems involved.

In these contexts, the expectation that individuals can protect themselves through careful skepticism becomes unrealistic. A person relying on information from a healthcare system may not have the medical knowledge needed to evaluate complex recommendations independently. An individual navigating legal processes may not have access to alternative sources of expertise. A welfare recipient interacting with an automated decision system may face procedural barriers that make challenging an outcome difficult or impossible. These are not simply ordinary interactions with technology. They are situations in which individuals depend on institutional systems to operate fairly and reliably.

When predictive systems operate in these environments, responsibility for managing their risks cannot rest primarily with the people who receive their outputs. The conditions of the interaction limit the level of scrutiny they can reasonably apply. The problem extends beyond unequal access to information. Practical constraints also matter. Even when people recognize that an automated recommendation may be flawed, they may lack the authority, resources, or time needed to challenge it. Institutional decisions carry procedural force that individuals often cannot easily contest. Responsibility for managing the knowledge risks of AI in public systems must therefore be shared. Developers build the systems. Institutions decide how to deploy them. Regulators establish the standards that govern their use. Users experience the consequences of those decisions.

Each level of this structure shapes the environment in which AI-generated outputs influence real-world outcomes. When vulnerable populations are involved, the ethical responsibility shifts away from expecting constant vigilance from individuals and toward ensuring that the systems themselves are designed and governed to minimize the harm the illusion can produce.

In private settings, disciplined users may protect themselves through careful skepticism. In public institutions, that protection must be built into the systems themselves.

16.7 The Healthcare Patient, the Legal Defendant, the Welfare Recipient

Who Pays When Institutional AI Fails

The abstract question of responsibility becomes concrete when predictive systems fail inside institutions that shape people's lives. Errors in casual personal use may cause inconvenience or confusion. Errors in healthcare, legal systems, or public welfare programs can have far more serious consequences.

A person seeking medical guidance often does so under conditions of uncertainty and vulnerability. The expertise needed to evaluate competing explanations for symptoms or treatment options may be lacking. When an AI-assisted system produces a confident medical summary or recommendation, it is encountered in a context where trust is not merely convenient but often necessary. If the output is incomplete, outdated, or misleading, the patient may not have the knowledge needed to recognize the error before acting on it.

Legal processes operate within structures of authority and constraint. People facing legal questions often rely on guidance systems because professional legal representation may be inaccessible or unaffordable. When AI tools generate legal explanations, summarize statutes, or draft procedural advice, their outputs can influence decisions with real legal consequences. A mistaken interpretation or an oversimplified explanation can affect actions that determine a person's rights, freedom, or financial stability.

Public welfare systems present a different but equally significant situation. These systems increasingly rely on automated processes to evaluate eligibility, detect potential fraud, or support administrative decisions. People navigating them may depend on AI-assisted tools to understand complex rules or respond to official requests. When those tools generate misleading guidance or inaccurate assessments, the consequences can include denied benefits, delayed assistance, or administrative penalties for people already living under economic strain.

In each of these settings, the cost of error is not distributed evenly. The institution that deploys the system may gain operational efficiency. Developers may collect feedback to improve future versions. The immediate burden of the mistake, however, falls on the individual who relied on the output when reliable guidance mattered most. This asymmetry shows why responsibility cannot be treated solely as a matter of individual judgment. Patients, defendants, and welfare recipients often lack the knowledge, authority, or practical alternatives needed to protect themselves from the consequences of an incorrect system output. When predictive systems become part of institutional decision-making, the question of who bears the cost of error becomes unavoidable. If the illusion of intelligence encourages misplaced trust in these settings, the people who depend on such systems are the ones most likely to bear the consequences when that illusion fails.

16.8 Why Protection in Public Systems Must Be Institutional and Regulatory

Not Delegated to Individual Users

The examples in the previous section reveal a pattern that individual vigilance alone cannot address. In settings where predictive systems shape access to healthcare, legal decisions, or public benefits, those affected often have little control over how the technology operates. They receive outputs from systems that institutions design, select, and deploy. Responsibility for managing the risks created by the illusion of intelligence therefore cannot rest entirely with individual users.

In private settings, such as writing assistance, casual research, or exploratory learning, users can reasonably be expected to approach AI output with skepticism and verify important claims before acting on them. The habits of careful judgment described in Part Five are both appropriate and practical in these contexts.

Public systems operate under different conditions. People who depend on these systems may lack the expertise needed to evaluate complex outputs independently. They may have no alternative source of guidance. Procedural barriers may make it difficult to challenge an automated recommendation. In many cases, they must rely on institutions that possess greater authority and information. Under these conditions, placing the burden of protection on the user is ethically inadequate.

Protection must therefore be built into the system. Institutions that deploy predictive systems must accept responsibility for ensuring that those systems operate within clearly defined boundaries of reliability. This responsibility includes rigorous testing before deployment, clear communication of system limitations, oversight mechanisms that identify systematic errors, and regulatory frameworks that establish accountability when automated outputs influence consequential decisions. Regulation serves a particular purpose in this context. Markets alone cannot reliably provide the level of epistemic caution required in high-stakes institutional settings. As discussed earlier in the chapter, commercial incentives often reward systems that appear confident and capable, even when their underlying reliability remains uncertain. Regulatory frameworks exist to correct these incentive imbalances where the consequences of error extend beyond voluntary consumer choice. The aim is not to halt technological development. Predictive systems can provide substantial public benefits when they are deployed carefully and transparently. The aim is to ensure that those benefits do not come at the cost of shifting epistemic risk onto individuals who are least able to manage it.

In environments where the consequences of error are serious and the capacity for self-protection is limited, responsibility must rest primarily with the institutions that design, deploy, and govern these systems. The illusion of intelligence arises naturally from the interaction between predictive systems and human cognition. The responsibility for managing its consequences, particularly in public settings, cannot be left to the individuals who encounter it.

Closing Reflection

Where Responsibility Settles

Throughout this book, the illusion of intelligence has often appeared in a simple exchange between a person and a system: a fluent answer, a persuasive explanation, or a conclusion that seems reliable because it is delivered with confidence. When predictive systems move beyond personal tools and become part of institutions, that exchange takes on broader consequences. A patient reads a medical summary generated by an automated system. A defendant consults a legal explanation produced by software. A welfare applicant follows guidance generated by an administrative platform. In each case, the person receiving the output is expected, implicitly or explicitly, to trust it. Yet the conditions that shape that trust do not originate with the individual. They arise from the institutions that select the system, the organizations that design it, and the incentives that influence its behavior. Responsibility, therefore, cannot rest solely with the person who receives the answer.

Individual judgment remains essential. The habits of skepticism and verification developed earlier in the book remain important safeguards. But when predictive systems influence decisions affecting health, legal rights, or livelihood, the primary burden of protection cannot fall on the people least able to shape those systems. In such settings, responsibility extends to the developers who build them, the organizations that deploy them, the regulators who establish the rules under which they operate, and the institutions that determine how much authority they are given. The illusion of intelligence begins as a feature of human cognition. Once it enters institutions, it also becomes a question of governance.

The next chapter turns from responsibility to design. If predictive systems are to operate safely within the institutions that shape modern life, they must communicate their limitations more honestly. The central question is no longer only how people should interpret machine-generated output. It is also how predictive systems should be designed to communicate with appropriate epistemic humility.

CHAPTER 17
Designing Systems That Admit Limits

Engineering Humility: What Honest AI Architecture Looks Like and Why It Matters

The previous chapter examined responsibility. It argued that when predictive systems operate within institutions, responsibility for managing their risks cannot rest solely with individual users. Organizations that deploy these systems, together with the companies that design them, share responsibility for preventing technology from reinforcing the illusion of understanding. Responsibility alone, however, does not solve the problem. Once accountability has been established, a more practical question follows: *what does responsible design look like?*

Earlier chapters showed why the illusion of intelligence arises so easily. Predictive systems generate fluent language that resembles the surface signals of genuine understanding. Human cognition, shaped to interpret those signals in human communication, naturally treats them as evidence of knowledge. The result is a powerful but fragile appearance of expertise. If that appearance is left unmanaged, the task of recognizing its limits falls entirely on the user. Yet the previous chapter showed that many users lack the time, knowledge, or authority needed to perform that task reliably. For this reason, the systems themselves must begin to change. Instead of presenting confident explanations as the default form of interaction, responsible systems should communicate uncertainty, limitations, and scope more clearly. They should show where their outputs are reliable and where they are not. They should make the boundaries of prediction visible rather than allowing fluent language to conceal them. This shift does not require abandoning the usefulness of predictive systems. These tools can still summarize information, support reasoning, and produce valuable drafts. Their design, however, should reflect a different priority: not maximizing the appearance of competence, but communicating capabilities and limitations honestly.

The concept that guides this shift can be expressed simply: engineering humility. Human experts are expected to acknowledge uncertainty. A physician distinguishes between a well-established diagnosis and a preliminary hypothesis. A scientist identifies the limits of the available evidence. A responsible professional does not claim more knowledge than the evidence justifies.

Predictive systems should be expected to do the same. The sections that follow examine what this expectation means for AI system design. They explore how uncertainty can be communicated more clearly, how reasoning can be made more transparent, and how technical safeguards can reduce the risk of mistaking fluent prediction for reliable knowledge. None of these measures can eliminate the illusion of intelligence entirely. The underlying mechanisms of predictive language generation will remain. Thoughtful design, however, can make their limits more visible. When those limits are visible, users are better equipped to exercise the judgment that machines cannot provide.

17.1 From Diagnosis to Construction

What Better Design Actually Requires

Up to this point, the argument of the book has been primarily diagnostic. Earlier chapters examined how predictive systems generate fluent language, how that fluency creates the appearance of understanding, and why human cognition is susceptible to that appearance. Chapter 16 widened the discussion by showing how institutional incentives and economic pressures can amplify these effects when such systems are deployed at scale. Diagnosis, however, is only the first step toward responsibility. If the risks created by predictive systems are structural rather than accidental, arising from the interaction of statistical language generation, human cognition, and market incentives, then addressing those risks requires more than individual caution. It also requires changes to the design of the systems themselves.

The central question now becomes practical: what would a more responsible architecture for AI interaction require? A useful starting point is to recognize that the problem does not lie simply in the existence of predictive systems. Language models can provide real value. They can organize information, assist with drafting, summarize complex material, and generate alternatives that support human reasoning. The objective is not to remove these capabilities. The challenge lies in how they are presented. Current systems often default to a style of interaction that emphasizes fluency and apparent competence. Responses are delivered in confident language, organized as complete explanations, and presented in ways that resemble the work of a knowledgeable human expert. When uncertainty exists, it is often expressed indirectly or reduced to a brief qualification within an otherwise decisive answer. This design choice is understandable from the perspective of usability and engagement. Yet it reinforces the illusion examined throughout this book by allowing predictive outputs to reproduce the communicative signals that have long indicated genuine understanding. Better design begins with a change in priorities. Rather than asking only how systems can generate fluent and persuasive answers, designers must also ask how systems can communicate the limits of their knowledge clearly enough for users to evaluate those answers appropriately. The goal is not to reduce capability, but to make its limits visible. Users should be able to distinguish between well-supported information, probabilistic inference, and speculative generation.

Achieving this requires several architectural commitments. Systems must signal uncertainty explicitly rather than implicitly. They must make the conditions under which their outputs are reliable visible to users. They must provide ways to inspect the reasoning patterns behind generated explanations rather than presenting only the final conclusion. They must also incorporate safeguards that reduce the likelihood that confident language will be mistaken for verified knowledge. Together, these commitments change how AI systems present themselves. Instead of creating the appearance of comprehensive knowledge, responsible systems should present themselves as what they are: predictive tools that operate within identifiable limits. The task of design is to ensure that those limits remain visible throughout the interaction. The sections that follow examine how this principle can be translated into concrete design practices.

17.2 Signaling Uncertainty

Building Honest Confidence Communication into Output Architecture

If responsible design begins by making the limits of predictive systems visible, uncertainty is the most immediate place to begin. Human experts routinely communicate uncertainty as part of responsible practice. A scientist distinguishes between established findings and preliminary hypotheses. A physician indicates whether a diagnosis is confirmed, likely, or still under investigation. These signals help others calibrate their trust by showing not only what is being claimed, but also how strongly the claim is supported.

Predictive systems rarely communicate in this way by default. Most language models are designed to generate fluent, well-structured explanations that read as complete accounts. Even when the underlying probability distribution contains substantial uncertainty, the system usually presents a single, coherent narrative. The probabilistic basis of the output remains invisible to the user. This creates a mismatch between how the system operates and how its output is interpreted. Internally, the model generates text by estimating the likelihood of linguistic sequences from patterns in its training data. The output reflects statistical plausibility rather than a measured degree of confidence in factual accuracy. Yet the response often resembles the language of an expert presenting well-supported knowledge. When uncertainty is concealed by fluent language, users receive no reliable indication of how much trust to place in the answer.

For this reason, explicit communication of uncertainty is a core principle of responsible AI design. Rather than presenting every response with the same level of confidence, systems should communicate how reliable different kinds of output are. Responses based on well-established information should be clearly distinguishable from those involving interpretation, incomplete evidence, or areas where the system's knowledge is limited. This communication must be built into the design rather than added as a superficial feature. Occasional qualifiers, such as "it is possible that" or "this may depend on context," are not enough if they appear inconsistently or are easily overlooked within otherwise confident explanations. Systems should communicate uncertainty through visible indicators, calibrated language, and interaction patterns that make the limits of their knowledge difficult to ignore. These signals do not reduce the usefulness of predictive systems. On the contrary, they help users interpret outputs more effectively. When people understand where a system is reliable and where it is uncertain, they can focus their attention appropriately, accepting routine information with confidence while examining uncertain claims more carefully.

The aim is not to eliminate uncertainty. No system capable of generating language about the world can avoid it. The aim is to ensure that uncertainty is communicated honestly rather than concealed by fluency. A system that communicates its limits clearly may appear less authoritative than one that speaks with uniform confidence. But it is far more trustworthy. The next section examines a design principle that puts this idea into practice: the deliberate normalization of limitation disclosure in AI interactions.

17.3 Limitation Disclosure as Design Norm

From Occasional Admission to Structural Feature

In earlier discussion, a contrast emerged between two forms of system behavior. One produces fluent answers to nearly every question it receives. The other acknowledges when it does not know. At first glance, the second behavior may appear less capable. Compared with systems that generate polished responses across a wide range of questions, a system that declines to answer or explicitly expresses uncertainty may seem limited. Yet this response reflects a different design choice. It makes the limits of the system's knowledge visible. Most predictive systems are designed to minimize such moments. Because language models generate outputs by predicting plausible continuations, they can usually produce something that resembles an answer, even when the available information is incomplete or uncertain. Their architecture favors completion. A non-response interrupts the flow of interaction and is often treated as a problem to eliminate. The result is a familiar pattern: systems produce confident explanations even when their reliability is uncertain.

A different design principle begins by rejecting that assumption. Instead of treating the disclosure of limitations as an exception, it treats it as a normal and expected part of interaction. A system should acknowledge uncertainty, incomplete knowledge, or domain limits as readily as it generates explanations. Statements such as "this is uncertain," "the evidence is incomplete," or "this falls outside reliable scope" are not signs of failure. They are signs of capability. This shift changes what users learn from the interaction. When systems rarely disclose their limitations, users infer that most outputs reflect reliable knowledge. Confidence becomes the default signal of competence. When systems disclose their limitations routinely and appropriately, users gain a more accurate understanding of the system's nature. They learn that prediction is not the same as knowledge and that the system's usefulness has boundaries. The effect is epistemic, not merely informational. A system that sometimes withholds or qualifies its responses preserves a visible role for human judgment. It interrupts the quiet transfer of authority that occurs when every question receives a fluent answer.

This principle does not require systems to refuse difficult questions. They can still offer hypotheses, outline possibilities, and support reasoning. The requirement is that the status of those outputs be communicated honestly. When a system is extrapolating, uncertain, or operating beyond well-supported knowledge, that condition should be stated explicitly rather than conveyed through a confident tone.

Limitation disclosure, in this sense, does not reduce performance. It corrects how performance is presented. A system that consistently communicates what it does not know may appear less authoritative, but it creates a more accurate relationship between the user and the tool. In that relationship, assistance remains valuable without becoming indistinguishable from understanding. The next step is to ensure that users can see not only the system's limits, but also the structure of its reasoning.

17.4 Transparency by Design

Making Reasoning Processes Legible without Requiring Users to Force Them

Signaling uncertainty and openly acknowledging limitations address one dimension of responsible design. They help users understand the boundaries of a system's knowledge. Yet another challenge remains. Even when systems acknowledge uncertainty, AI outputs often appear as finished explanations that reveal little about how they were produced. In many current systems, only the conclusion is visible. The model generates a fluent paragraph, a recommendation, or a structured explanation, while the process behind the output remains hidden. The patterns it identifies, the assumptions reflected in the response, and the sources that may have informed it are concealed by the interface. The answer appears as a completed product rather than the result of a process. This opacity creates a familiar problem. When the reasoning process is hidden, evaluation becomes difficult. Users can judge whether an answer seems plausible, but plausibility is not the same as reliability. Without some indication of how an explanation was constructed, it becomes difficult to judge whether the argument rests on solid ground.

One response is to encourage users to question the system actively. By asking follow-up questions, requesting sources, seeking explanations for the system's conclusions, or challenging it to justify its claims, users can sometimes uncover how an answer was produced. This approach, however, places a substantial burden on the user. It assumes that people already have both the habit of skepticism and the knowledge needed to seek such clarification. It assumes that they will remember to ask these questions before relying on the output. It also assumes that the system will respond with meaningful transparency. Responsible design should not depend entirely on such active intervention. Transparency by design means that systems should present the basis of their outputs by default, rather than requiring users to uncover it through persistent questioning. When a model generates an explanation, the interface should indicate the basis of that explanation, whether it draws on well-established information, probabilistic inference, or contextual interpretation. This does not require exposing every technical detail of the model's internal operation. Most users neither need nor benefit from access to the full complexity of machine learning systems. Instead, the goal is to reveal enough of the reasoning behind the explanation for users to evaluate it meaningfully. This might include identifying the types of sources that informed a response, clarifying when the system is extrapolating beyond direct evidence, or highlighting the key assumptions reflected in the explanation. The goal is to turn an opaque conclusion into a process that users can inspect and evaluate.

When the reasoning process remains hidden, fluent answers can easily be mistaken for authoritative knowledge. When that process becomes visible, the relationship changes. Users encounter not only a conclusion but also the reasoning that produced it. Once that reasoning is visible, judgment can operate more effectively. The next section considers a complication that emerges when designers attempt to implement these forms of transparency: the tension between honest communication and the usability of AI systems.

17.5 The Transparency–Usability Tension

Calibrating Honesty to Context as a Principled Design Challenge

The principles discussed so far, including uncertainty signaling, limitation disclosure, and transparent reasoning, outline the architecture of a more honest AI system. Putting these principles into practice, however, creates a challenge that responsible design cannot ignore. Transparency and usability do not always align. A system that communicates every limitation, every uncertainty, and every step of its reasoning in full detail may achieve epistemic honesty, but it may also become difficult to use. Excessive warnings, constant qualification, and lengthy explanations can overwhelm users, especially when they are seeking quick guidance or practical assistance. In such cases, attempts to communicate uncertainty may produce the opposite effect. When cautionary signals appear too often or too prominently, users may begin to ignore them. Important warnings become difficult to distinguish from routine information. The system's effort to increase transparency can therefore reduce the clarity it is intended to provide.

Designers of responsible AI systems must therefore navigate a genuine tension. On one side is the ethical responsibility to communicate the limits of predictive systems clearly and honestly. On the other is the practical need to maintain interfaces that are usable, understandable, and responsive to the needs of ordinary users. Addressing this tension requires a principle that has guided responsible communication in many other fields: calibration to context. Different kinds of interaction require different levels of transparency. A system that offers casual writing suggestions may require less uncertainty signaling than one providing information about health, legal rights, or financial decisions. The level of detail appropriate for an expert analyzing complex material may also differ from that appropriate for someone seeking a brief summary of general knowledge. Responsible design therefore does not require the same level of transparency in every situation. It requires transparency that is proportionate to the stakes and complexity of the task. In low-risk contexts, brief indicators of uncertainty or limitation may be sufficient. In high-stakes contexts, systems should provide stronger signals about the limits of their reliability, clearer explanations of how conclusions were reached, and more prominent encouragement of independent verification.

The central requirement is that a system's interface must not conceal uncertainty in order to preserve the appearance of competence. Usability cannot be achieved by suppressing the signals that allow users to judge reliability. Transparency is therefore not an optional feature added after a product is complete. It is a fundamental part of interaction design. The challenge is not simply to make systems usable, but to make them usable without concealing their limits. Achieving that balance requires more than careful interface design. It also requires structural safeguards that reduce the likelihood that predictive outputs will be mistaken for verified knowledge. The next section examines how such safeguards can be built directly into the architecture of AI systems.

17.6 Guardrails and Verification Layers

Structural Mechanisms for Reducing Dangerous Illusion

Even when uncertainty is signaled and reasoning is made more transparent, predictive systems still operate through the same underlying mechanism: statistical language generation. Because the model generates plausible continuations of text, fluent but inaccurate output cannot be eliminated through interface design alone. Responsible AI systems therefore require additional safeguards. Two are particularly important: guardrails and verification layers.

Guardrails establish boundaries that prevent the system from generating responses in situations where the risk of harm is high. They may restrict direct answers to certain questions, redirect users to qualified professionals in sensitive domains, or prevent the system from presenting speculative content as factual information. In effect, guardrails define situations in which the system must slow down, qualify its responses, or decline to answer altogether. Verification layers serve a different purpose. Rather than restricting generation, they evaluate the system's output before it reaches the user. They may cross-check claims against trusted knowledge sources, validate citations, or use specialized models to detect likely hallucinations or unsupported assertions. Both approaches address the same underlying problem from different directions. Guardrails limit the system's ability to generate answers when the consequences of error are severe. Verification layers seek to identify and correct problematic outputs before they influence human decisions.

Together, these mechanisms change AI interaction from a single generative step into a layered process in which predictions are evaluated and constrained before they are presented to the user. This reduces the likelihood that fluent prediction will be mistaken for verified knowledge. These safeguards do not change the system's generative nature. The model still produces language through probabilistic inference. The environment in which its outputs appear, however, becomes more structured. Users are less likely to encounter confident explanations in situations where the system is least reliable.

Designing effective guardrails and verification layers requires careful calibration. If restrictions are too loose, the system may continue to generate misleading answers in sensitive contexts. If they are too strict, the system may become unnecessarily limited and refuse to assist where its capabilities would be genuinely useful. Responsible AI architecture therefore requires continuous refinement. Designers must monitor system performance in real-world settings and adjust safeguards as new patterns of risk emerge. These measures can substantially reduce the frequency of dangerously misleading outputs, but they cannot change the technology's fundamental nature. The next section examines that limitation directly.

17.7 What Guardrails Can and Cannot Do

Harm Reduction Is Not Cure

Guardrails and verification layers can significantly reduce the risk of predictive systems producing harmful or misleading outputs. By restricting certain types of responses and adding checks to generated content, these mechanisms create a more structured environment for AI interaction. They represent an important step toward aligning system behavior with the responsibilities described in the previous chapter. Their limits, however, are equally important to understand. Guardrails constrain a model's outputs. Verification layers evaluate those outputs after they are generated. Neither changes the fundamental process through which language models produce text. At their core, these systems still rely on statistical prediction. They generate responses by estimating likely continuations of language from patterns in training data. This process can produce remarkably useful explanations, summaries, and suggestions. Yet it remains distinct from the grounded understanding that characterizes human reasoning. Because the underlying mechanism remains unchanged, no collection of safeguards can eliminate the possibility of fluent but incorrect output.

Guardrails can block certain categories of questions, but they cannot anticipate every context in which misleading information may appear. Verification systems can identify some unsupported claims, but they cannot reliably distinguish between sound reasoning and plausible invention in every case. Even carefully designed safeguards operate within the limits of probabilistic inference. For this reason, guardrails are best understood as mechanisms for reducing harm rather than eliminating it. They can narrow the conditions under which the illusion becomes dangerous and prevent some of the most predictable failures. They can reduce the likelihood that users encounter confident answers in domains where the system's reliability is weakest. What they cannot do is transform a predictive model into a system that genuinely understands the world it describes.

This distinction matters because it prevents a common misunderstanding: the belief that enough layers of technical protection can completely eliminate the epistemic risks associated with generative AI. Responsible design can reduce those risks, but it cannot remove the structural properties of predictive systems that give rise to the illusion of intelligence. Recognizing these limits is itself a form of responsible engineering. A design philosophy that acknowledges the enduring boundaries of the technology is less likely to promise capabilities it cannot deliver. It shifts the focus from eliminating error to managing it carefully within systems that remain inherently probabilistic. In this sense, guardrails are only one part of a broader design principle. The deeper objective is not simply to constrain harmful outputs, but to build systems that communicate their limits honestly. The final section of this chapter names that principle directly.

17.8 Engineering Humility

Treating Honest Acknowledgment of Limitation as Design Virtue, Not Commercial Liability

The design principles discussed throughout this chapter share a common philosophical foundation. They include uncertainty signaling, limitation disclosure, transparency of reasoning, and structural safeguards. Each principle helps predictive systems communicate their capabilities honestly rather than creating the appearance of comprehensive knowledge. Together, they describe a broader approach to technology design that can be summarized as engineering humility. This approach does not reduce the usefulness of AI systems. Predictive models remain powerful tools for organizing information, generating drafts, and supporting human reasoning. The aim is not to make these systems less capable, but to represent their capabilities accurately. In many fields, acknowledging limitations is already a hallmark of responsible expertise. Civil engineers incorporate safety margins to account for uncertainty. Scientists report confidence intervals and methodological constraints. Medical professionals distinguish between established diagnoses and tentative interpretations. These practices reflect an important principle: reliability depends not only on capability but also on honest communication about where that capability ends. Predictive systems should be held to the same standard.

When AI systems present every answer with the tone of confident authority, they imply a level of knowledge that the underlying technology does not possess. The result is the illusion of intelligence examined throughout this book. Systems designed with humility, by contrast, communicate their limits clearly enough for users to calibrate their trust appropriately. Adopting this approach requires a change in how success is measured. In many commercial settings, expressions of uncertainty and clear statements of limitation are treated as weaknesses, suggesting that a product is less capable than its competitors. Systems that speak with constant confidence may therefore appear more impressive, even when that confidence conceals uncertainty. Engineering humility reverses this perspective. A system that openly acknowledges the limits of its knowledge is not displaying a defect. It is demonstrating epistemic responsibility. It aligns the signals presented to users with the actual capabilities of the technology. Such alignment ultimately strengthens trust rather than weakening it. Over time, users learn that a system willing to acknowledge uncertainty is more likely to provide reliable guidance when it does express confidence.

No design philosophy can eliminate the structural properties of predictive models that produce fluent language without genuine understanding. But a design that communicates those limits honestly can prevent the illusion from becoming more persuasive than the truth. In this way, engineering humility becomes the design counterpart to the intellectual discipline described in Part Five. Just as users should approach AI outputs with calibrated skepticism, AI systems should be designed to communicate their limits clearly. The final chapter returns to the individual reader. In a world where fluent machines remain part of everyday life, the ultimate safeguard lies not only in better system design but also in the human capacity to exercise judgment responsibly.

Closing Reflection

When Systems Admit their Limits

An AI system produces a response that is clear, organized, and helpful. The explanation may shape understanding, suggest possible courses of action, or summarize information that would otherwise require significant effort to gather. At that point, the most important consideration is not only the quality of the answer. It is also whether the system communicates the limits of its own knowledge.

Does it signal where its knowledge is strong and where it becomes uncertain?

Does it show the reasoning that produced the explanation?

Does it make clear when the response is a reliable summary and when it is a probabilistic inference?

A system designed with humility does not attempt to conceal these boundaries. Instead, it makes them visible within the interaction itself.

Such systems may appear less impressive than those that respond to every question with effortless confidence. Yet they support a more honest relationship between human judgment and machine assistance. Users are not invited to treat the system as an authority. They are invited to use it as a tool. This distinction matters because the illusion of intelligence cannot be eliminated entirely. Predictive models will continue to generate fluent language, and human cognition will continue to respond to that fluency as a signal of understanding. Responsible design can ensure, however, that the signals surrounding that fluency are not misleading. When systems communicate their limits clearly, they reinforce the role that machines cannot assume: the exercise of judgment. Responsibility for deciding what is true, what remains uncertain, and what requires further verification continues to rest with the person using the system.

The final chapter returns to that responsibility. The most durable safeguard in a world of fluent machines does not lie in system architecture alone. It lies in the human capacity to think deliberately about the answers that are received.

CHAPTER 18
Staying Human

The Only Durable Safeguard: Disciplined Judgment as a Human Responsibility in the Age of Fluent Machines

The argument developed in this book has followed the implications of a single phenomenon: the ability of predictive systems to generate language that resembles the products of human understanding. That ability has extraordinary practical value. It allows machines to organize information, draft explanations, and support human reasoning in ways that were previously difficult or impossible. Yet the same capability creates a persistent ambiguity. Fluent explanations resemble knowledge. They resemble the language through which people ordinarily express their understanding of the world. But the mechanism that produces them is predictive rather than interpretive. The system generates plausible linguistic continuations by extending patterns in data. The appearance of understanding emerges at the surface of language even though the underlying process does not involve comprehension.

Throughout the preceding chapters, the consequences of this distinction have been examined from several perspectives. The technical architecture of language models was explored. The cognitive tendencies that lead people to trust fluent explanations were examined. The influence of these systems on institutions, markets, and public decision-making was also considered. The discussion then turned to practical responses: disciplined use by individuals, responsible design by developers, and safeguards within institutions. Together, these discussions lead to a clear conclusion. Predictive systems can support human reasoning, but they cannot assume the responsibility that reasoning ultimately requires. Their outputs remain expressions of probability rather than acts of judgment.

For this reason, the final question raised by the illusion of intelligence is not primarily technological. The mechanisms that produce fluent language will continue to evolve, and the systems that use them will remain part of everyday intellectual life. The deeper question concerns the role of human judgment in an environment where persuasive explanations can be generated automatically. This chapter turns to that question.

18.1 The Book Returns to the Reader

Personal, Direct, Honest

The analysis of predictive systems can extend across many domains, including technical architecture, cognitive psychology, economic incentives, institutional governance, and system design. Each perspective clarifies an important aspect of how AI operates in the contemporary world. Yet the effects of these systems ultimately appear in a much simpler setting. A generated explanation is encountered. A claim is presented in fluent language. That claim must then be interpreted. By that point, the technological and institutional structures described in earlier chapters have already done their work. The system has produced a response according to the probabilities encoded in its model. Safeguards may have filtered the output, and the interface may have communicated certain limitations. Yet none of these mechanisms determines how the explanation is understood. Interpretation begins with the reader.

The significance of this fact is easy to underestimate. Modern predictive systems produce language with a level of fluency that can create the impression that the intellectual work behind an explanation has already been completed. The response appears organized, confident, and complete. Its surface resembles the language through which human expertise is usually expressed. Yet fluent language does not eliminate the need for judgment. It changes the way judgment must be exercised. The reader must decide whether the explanation should be accepted, questioned, verified, or set aside. No predictive system can assume that responsibility. It belongs to the human mind that interprets the text. For that reason, the discussion now returns to the reader. This is not a rhetorical shift. It reflects a simple fact: the interaction between human understanding and machine-generated language ultimately takes shape in the reader's interpretation.

18.2 Accepting Imperfect but Powerful Tools

The Mature Relationship the Entire Book Has Been Building Toward

If responsibility for interpretation ultimately remains with human beings, a further question follows: *what kind of relationship should exist between human judgment and systems capable of generating fluent explanations?* The answer is not rejection. Predictive systems have genuine value. They can summarize complex material, propose alternative ways of expressing ideas, and help organize information across large bodies of text. In many contexts, these capabilities save time and expand the range of intellectual tools available to individuals and institutions. To dismiss such systems would ignore the practical benefits they offer. Yet usefulness alone does not determine how a tool should be used. The central argument of this book has been that predictive systems operate through mechanisms fundamentally different from the processes involved in human understanding. The fluency of their outputs may resemble expertise, but that resemblance exists at the level of language rather than comprehension. The system predicts plausible sequences of words. It does not understand the situations those words describe.

A mature relationship with these tools requires holding two truths at the same time. First, predictive systems can be powerful aids to thought. They can generate possibilities, organize information, and accelerate some forms of intellectual work. Second, these systems remain structurally limited. Their outputs are probabilistic constructions rather than accountable judgments. They can suggest explanations, but they cannot bear responsibility for the conclusions drawn from them. When these two facts are considered together, the appropriate role of predictive systems becomes clearer. They function best as collaborators during the early stages of reasoning: sources of drafts, prompts for exploration, and tools for organizing information. They do not function well as authorities whose explanations can be accepted without further evaluation. Responsibility for deciding whether a claim is accurate, sufficient, or relevant remains with the human decision-maker.

Accepting this perspective does not diminish the usefulness of AI tools. It clarifies their role. The system produces language that may assist reasoning. Human judgment determines whether that language should influence belief or action. This arrangement reflects a simple principle that extends beyond the technologies discussed in this book: tools can expand human capability, but they do not replace the responsibility that accompanies understanding.

18.3 Resisting Intellectual Passivity

The Daily Commitment That No Single Decision Can Secure

Accepting predictive systems as powerful but limited tools clarifies their proper role. Maintaining that relationship, however, requires more than a single decision about how these systems should be used. It requires a sustained habit of mind. The ease with which AI systems generate explanations creates a subtle pressure toward intellectual passivity. Answers appear quickly in fluent language that resembles the finished product of careful reasoning. In such an environment, the effort traditionally required to explore a question can seem unnecessary. The explanation has already been assembled, and the work of reasoning appears complete. The temptation is not simply to trust the system. It is to allow it to occupy the place where independent reasoning once occurred. This shift rarely begins with a conscious decision to surrender judgment. More often, it develops gradually through repeated interactions in which the system presents a ready-made account before the question has been fully explored. Each individual instance may appear harmless. Over time, however, the habit of beginning inquiry with a generated explanation can change how questions are approached.

Resisting this drift does not require rejecting technological assistance. It requires preserving active engagement with the problem itself. Before accepting a generated explanation as sufficient, the reasoning behind it should be examined. Before acting on a confident claim, the claim should be evaluated against the available evidence and its context. In many cases, a system-generated explanation can serve as a useful starting point. It should not be treated as the conclusion that ends inquiry. Maintaining this approach does not depend on a single rule or technique. It is a habit developed through repeated engagement with information. Each time a fluent answer appears, a choice follows. The explanation can be accepted immediately as a finished account, or it can be treated as a provisional suggestion whose reliability still requires evaluation. The difference between these responses may seem small in any individual case. Across many encounters, however, it determines whether predictive systems weaken or preserve the role of human judgment.

Responsibility for that distinction cannot be transferred to the machine that generates the language. It remains with the person who interprets it.

18.4 Judgment as a Human Responsibility

Where All Four Proofs of Irreplaceability Converge in Practice

Earlier chapters of this book presented several reasons why predictive systems cannot replace human judgment. These arguments approached the problem from different directions: the nature of meaning, the limits of prediction, the absence of moral agency, and the role of responsibility in reasoning. Each identified a different way in which machine-generated language differs from human understanding. In practice, however, these distinctions converge in a single activity: judgment. It is the point at which information becomes belief and explanation becomes decision. It is the moment when a person determines what a claim means, how much it should be trusted, and whether it should guide action. This process requires more than the ability to produce plausible language. It requires the ability to interpret context, weigh competing considerations, and accept responsibility for the consequences of a conclusion. Predictive systems do not perform this function.

A language model can generate multiple explanations for a problem. It can summarize patterns found in large bodies of text and propose interpretations that resemble those offered by human experts. Yet the system does not determine which interpretation should guide action. It does not accept responsibility for the outcomes that follow from adopting one explanation rather than another. The act of judgment therefore remains outside the system.

This distinction becomes especially clear when information is incomplete or contested. Human reasoning often operates under uncertainty. Evidence may be incomplete. Competing explanations may remain plausible. The available information may not resolve the question decisively. In such circumstances, judgment involves more than selecting the most probable sentence. It requires evaluating the reliability of sources, considering the broader context of the problem, and recognizing the limits of what can be known with confidence. These capacities do not arise from the statistical prediction of language. They arise from the human ability to integrate meaning, context, and responsibility into a single act of reasoning.

The four arguments developed earlier in the book describe different aspects of this same capacity. Meaning provides the framework within which claims are understood. The limits of prediction explain why fluent language cannot substitute for comprehension. Moral agency grounds responsibility for decisions. Accountability keeps conclusions connected to the person who endorses them. Together, these elements constitute judgment.

In an environment where machines generate persuasive explanations, the importance of this capacity becomes more visible, not less. The easier it becomes to produce a fluent language, the more important it becomes to determine whether that language should be treated as evidence, interpretation, or speculation. No predictive system can make that determination on behalf of the reader.

18.5 Not Infallibility but Accountability

What Human Judgment Offers That Prediction Cannot

Human judgment continues to play an essential role, but that does not mean human reasoning is free from error. The history of knowledge contains countless examples of mistaken conclusions, flawed interpretations, and misplaced confidence. Human understanding is limited, fallible, and often shaped by incomplete information. For this reason, the distinction between predictive systems and human judgment cannot rest on a claim of greater accuracy. In many specialized tasks, predictive systems process patterns in data with remarkable efficiency. They can recall large volumes of information, identify statistical relationships, and generate plausible explanations more quickly than an individual could. Within the scope of those tasks, their performance may appear highly competent. The difference between human judgment and machine prediction lies elsewhere.

Human reasoning is accountable. When a person reaches a conclusion, that conclusion remains connected to the individual who endorses it. The person who accepts a claim is responsible for the decisions that follow. If the judgment proves mistaken, the error can be acknowledged, examined, and corrected. Responsibility for the outcome does not disappear into the process that produced the reasoning. Predictive systems operate differently. A language model generates an explanation by calculating the probability of linguistic sequences from a prompt and its training data. The output does not represent a commitment to the truth of the claim it expresses. It is a prediction of what text is most likely to follow from the patterns learned by the model. When that prediction proves inaccurate, the system neither recognizes the error nor accepts responsibility for its consequences.

This distinction is subtle but important. Human judgment can be corrected because it is accountable. A person can examine the reasoning behind a conclusion, reconsider the evidence, and revise a belief when the reasoning proves unsound. Knowledge advances through this capacity for revision. Prediction alone does not possess that structure. A predictive model can generate a different response when prompted again, and its designers can improve the system through retraining or other modifications. The individual prediction, however, remains detached from responsibility for its effects. It is the product of a probabilistic process rather than an accountable act of reasoning.

For this reason, the value of human judgment does not lie in its perfection. It lies in the fact that the person exercising judgment remains answerable for the beliefs and decisions that follow. In an environment where fluent explanations can be generated automatically, this accountability distinguishes genuine reasoning from its statistical imitation.

18.6 Living Beyond the Illusion

Not Freedom from It but the Steady Practice of Seeing Clearly within It

If the illusion of intelligence arises from the interaction between predictive systems and human cognition, understanding how these systems work cannot eliminate it completely. The mechanisms that generate fluent language will remain, as will the cognitive tendencies that interpret fluency as a sign of understanding. The goal, therefore, is not to escape the illusion but to maintain clarity while interacting with it. Predictive systems will continue to produce explanations that appear coherent, confident, and complete. In many cases, those explanations will be useful and accurate. In others, they will reflect the probabilistic nature of the model, producing plausible accounts rather than reliable representations of the world. The difference cannot always be recognized from the surface of the text alone. Fluent language will increasingly resemble the style and structure of human expertise. As these systems improve, distinguishing machine-generated explanations from human-authored analysis may become even more difficult.

Living beyond the illusion requires a change in how such explanations are interpreted. Fluent language is no longer treated as evidence of understanding. It becomes the starting point for evaluation. An explanation becomes material to examine rather than authority to accept. Claims are evaluated in relation to context, evidence, and alternative interpretations, not solely by the coherence of the language in which they are expressed. This approach does not require constant suspicion or rejection of technological assistance. Predictive systems can still contribute meaningfully to intellectual work. They can organize information, suggest possibilities, and help articulate ideas that might otherwise remain unformed. What changes is the way their outputs are approached. Fluent explanations no longer signal that the work of reasoning has already been completed. They signal that reasoning must now begin. The illusion remains visible, but it no longer determines the outcome of the interaction. Instead, it becomes one feature of an environment in which judgment operates with a clearer understanding of how knowledge claims are produced.

Clarity, in this sense, is not a single achievement. It is a continuing practice: the steady effort to interpret persuasive language without confusing fluency with understanding.

18.7 The Reader Who Closes This Book

What They Carry Forward and What They Have Accepted

Reaching the end of this book does not equip the reader with a new technology to master or a set of techniques that guarantees correct answers. The central lesson is simpler and more demanding. The reader leaves with a clearer understanding of the environment in which modern reasoning now takes place. Predictive systems can produce explanations that resemble the language of knowledge. They can organize information, summarize arguments, and generate persuasive accounts of complex questions. These capabilities will continue to develop, and their outputs will likely become even more difficult to distinguish from the language of human expertise. At the same time, the reader understands the limits that accompany those capabilities. The explanations generated by predictive systems arise from statistical patterns in language rather than from comprehension of the world they describe. Such systems can produce plausible statements without possessing the understanding that would normally justify confidence in those statements. The appearance of knowledge can therefore exceed the reliability of the process that generates it.

Recognizing this condition changes the relationship between the reader and the machine. Fluent explanations no longer appear as final authorities. Instead, they become material for interpretation: useful contributions that require evaluation rather than conclusions that settle questions on their own. Persuasive language does not remove the responsibility to consider context, examine evidence, and reflect on what has been said. What readers carry forward is not certainty but orientation. They learn to distinguish between language that appears knowledgeable and reasoning that remains accountable for its conclusions. They develop the discipline to treat generated explanations as provisional rather than definitive. They preserve independent judgment, even in an environment where answers appear effortlessly. None of these habits guarantees correct conclusions in every case. Human judgment remains fallible, and the complexity of the world ensures that uncertainty will persist. Together, these habits preserve the conditions under which careful reasoning remains possible.

When the book closes, predictive systems will continue to generate language with impressive fluency. The illusion of intelligence will continue to arise whenever persuasive explanations are produced by mechanisms that do not truly understand what they generate. What changes is the reader's ability to recognize that illusion without surrendering judgment to it. That recognition marks the beginning of living responsibly in the presence of machines that can speak with the appearance of understanding.

CONCLUSION
Intelligence and Its Imitations

The illusion examined throughout this book will not disappear. It does not arise from a temporary flaw in current systems or from an early stage of technological development that future progress will simply outgrow. It arises from a structural interaction: machines generate fluent language without understanding, while human minds are naturally inclined to treat fluent language as evidence of understanding. As long as those two conditions remain, the illusion will remain as well.

The systems will continue to improve. Their language will become smoother, their explanations more detailed, and their responses more sensitive to context and nuance. The resemblance between generated language and human reasoning will continue to grow. In many domains, the distinction may become difficult to detect in ordinary conversation. Greater fluency, however, does not change the foundation on which these systems operate. Predictive models generate sequences of words by extending statistical patterns learned from a vast corpora of text. They can reproduce the forms through which human knowledge is expressed, including arguments, explanations, summaries, and interpretations, without possessing the underlying comprehension that normally grounds those forms. The difference between pattern continuation and understanding does not disappear as the patterns become more sophisticated. It becomes easier to overlook. For that reason, the illusion of intelligence deepens as technology advances. The more effectively these systems produce language that resembles the products of reasoning, the more readily people interpret that language as evidence of reasoning itself.

The distinction developed throughout this book therefore remains philosophically important. Understanding is not the same as the ability to produce convincing explanations. It includes the capacity to grasp the meaning of a claim, recognize when changing circumstances affect its relevance, revise beliefs in response to new evidence, and take responsibility for the judgments that follow from those beliefs. These capacities belong to a form of agency that predictive systems do not possess. Machines can imitate the linguistic surface of that agency. They cannot assume the responsibility that gives it significance. The presence of fluent machines therefore does not reduce the need for human judgment. If anything, it makes that judgment more important. When language that resembles knowledge becomes widely available at minimal cost, distinguishing appearance from understanding becomes a central intellectual responsibility. Fulfilling that responsibility does not require rejecting these tools. Predictive systems can support research, organize information, and expand access to knowledge in genuinely valuable ways. The challenge is not to avoid using them, but to recognize what they are and what they are not. They are powerful instruments for generating language. They are not minds that understand the world they describe.

Living with that distinction is part of thinking clearly in the age of fluent machines. The imitation will become more convincing. The responsibility to see through it will remain human.

Sources and Suggested Readings

The following works span cognitive psychology, linguistics, philosophy of mind, and artificial intelligence, and provide background for readers who wish to explore the ideas in this book more deeply.

Emily M. Bender and Alexander Koller — Climbing Towards NLU: On Meaning, Form, and Understanding in the Age of Data (2020)

Emily M. Bender et al. — On the Dangers of Stochastic Parrots: Can Language Models Be Too Big? (2021)

Ruha Benjamin — Race After Technology: Abolitionist Tools for the New Jim Code (2019)

Sissela Bok — Lying: Moral Choice in Public and Private Life (1978)

Tom B. Brown et al. — Language Models are Few-Shot Learners (2020)

Nicholas Carr — The Shallows: What the Internet Is Doing to Our Brains (2010)

Thomas L. Carson — Lying and Deception: Theory and Practice (2010)

Noam Chomsky — Aspects of the Theory of Syntax (1965)

Noam Chomsky — Language and Mind (1968)

Brian Christian — The Alignment Problem: Machine Learning and Human Values (2020)

Andy Clark — Being There: Putting Brain, Body, and World Together Again (1997)

Andy Clark — Supersizing the Mind: Embodiment, Action, and Cognitive Extension (2008)

Robert Cialdini — Influence: The Psychology of Persuasion (1984)

Kate Crawford — Atlas of AI: Power, Politics, and the Planetary Costs of Artificial Intelligence (2021)

John Dewey — How We Think (1910)

Daniel C. Dennett — Consciousness Explained (1991)

Daniel C. Dennett — Intuition Pumps and Other Tools for Thinking (2013)

David Dunning — Self-Insight: Roadblocks and Detours on the Path to Knowing Thyself (2005)

Virginia Eubanks — Automating Inequality: How High-Tech Tools Profile,

Police, and Punish the Poor (2018)

Lisa Fazio et al. — Knowledge Does Not Protect Against Illusory Truth (2015)

Luciano Floridi — The Ethics of Information (2013)

Luciano Floridi — The Philosophy of Information (2011)

Harry G. Frankfurt — On Bullshit (2005)

Karl Friston — The Free-Energy Principle: A Unified Brain Theory? (2010)

Shane Frederick — Cognitive Reflection and Decision Making (2005)

Daniel T. Gilbert — How Mental Systems Believe (1991)

Alvin I. Goldman — Knowledge in a Social World (1999)

Gerd Gigerenzer — Gut Feelings: The Intelligence of the Unconscious (2007)

Gerd Gigerenzer — Risk Savvy: How to Make Good Decisions (2014)

John Hammond, Ralph Keeney, and Howard Raiffa — Smart Choices: A Practical Guide to Making Better Decisions (1999)

Edwin Hutchins — Cognition in the Wild (1995)

IEEE — Ethically Aligned Design: A Vision for Prioritizing Human Well-Being with Autonomous and Intelligent Systems (2019)

Daniel Kahneman — Thinking, Fast and Slow (2011)

Immanuel Kant — On a Supposed Right to Lie from Philanthropy (1797)

Jared Kaplan et al. — Scaling Laws for Neural Language Models (2020)

Thomas S. Kuhn — The Structure of Scientific Revolutions (1962)

Brenden M. Lake et al. — Building Machines That Learn and Think Like People (2017)

Gary Marcus and Ernest Davis — Rebooting AI: Building Artificial Intelligence We Can Trust (2019)

Lee McIntyre — Post-Truth (2018)

Hugo Mercier and Dan Sperber — The Enigma of Reason (2017)

Melanie Mitchell — Artificial Intelligence: A Guide for Thinking Humans (2019)

Sendhil Mullainathan and Eldar Shafir — Scarcity: Why Having Too Little Means So Much (2013)

Thomas Nagel — What Is It Like to Be a Bat? (1974)

Cathy O'Neil — Weapons of Math Destruction: How Big Data Increases

Inequality and Threatens Democracy (2016)

OECD — Artificial Intelligence in Society (2019)

Michael Polanyi — Personal Knowledge: Towards a Post-Critical Philosophy (1958)

Michael Polanyi — The Tacit Dimension (1966)

Karl Popper — Conjectures and Refutations: The Growth of Scientific Knowledge (1963)

Karl Popper — The Logic of Scientific Discovery (1959)

Neil Postman — Technopoly: The Surrender of Culture to Technology (1992)

Steven Pinker — The Language Instinct: How the Mind Creates Language (1994)

Hilary Putnam — Reason, Truth and History (1981)

Alec Radford et al. — Improving Language Understanding by Generative Pre-Training (2018)

Rolf Reber, Norbert Schwarz, and Piotr Winkielman — Processing Fluency and Aesthetic Pleasure: Is Beauty in the Perceiver's Processing Experience? (2004)

Stuart Russell — Human Compatible: Artificial Intelligence and the Problem of Control (2019)

Gilbert Ryle — The Concept of Mind (1949)

Norbert Schwarz — Metacognitive Experiences in Judgment and Decision Making (2004)

John R. Searle — Minds, Brains, and Programs (1980)

Claude E. Shannon — A Mathematical Theory of Communication (1948)

Steven Sloman and Philip Fernbach — The Knowledge Illusion: Why We Never Think Alone (2017)

Miriam Solomon — Social Empiricism (2001)

Betsy Sparrow et al. — Google Effects on Memory: Cognitive Consequences of Having Information at Our Fingertips (2011)

Cass R. Sunstein — On Rumors: How Falsehoods Spread, Why We Believe Them, and What Can Be Done (2009)

Philip Tetlock and Dan Gardner — Superforecasting: The Art and Science of Prediction (2015)

Amos Tversky and Daniel Kahneman — Judgment under Uncertainty: Heuristics and Biases (1974)

Sherry Turkle — Alone Together: Why We Expect More from Technology and

Less from Each Other (2011)

Ashish Vaswani et al. — Attention Is All You Need (2017)

Shannon Vallor — The AI Mirror: How to Reclaim Our Humanity in an Age of Machine Thinking (2024)

Tim Wu — The Attention Merchants: The Epic Scramble to Get Inside Our Heads (2016)

Ludwig Wittgenstein — Philosophical Investigations (1953)

Stephen Wolfram — What Is ChatGPT Doing... and Why Does It Work? (2023)

Shoshana Zuboff — The Age of Surveillance Capitalism: The Fight for a Human Future at the New Frontier of Power (2019)

Every effort has been made to acknowledge relevant sources. Given the synthetic nature of the work, some ideas draw on broader intellectual traditions and may not be individually cited. Any omissions are unintentional.

www.ingramcontent.com/pod-product-compliance
Lightning Source LLC
Chambersburg PA
CBHW071429230926
51846CB00001B/164